The Great Parade

Also by Peter Filichia

Strippers, Showgirls, and Sharks:
A *Very* Opinionated History of the Broadway
Musicals That **Did Not** Win the Tony Award

Peter Filichia

THE GREAT PARADE

*

BROADWAY'S ASTONISHING,
NEVER-TO-BE-FORGOTTEN
1963-64 SEASON

ST. MARTIN'S PRESS ≈ NEW YORK

THE GREAT PARADE. Copyright © 2015 by Peter Filichia All rights reserved. Printed in the United States of America. For information, address St. Martin's Press, 175 Fifth Avenue, New York, N.Y. 10010.

www.stmartins.com

Library of Congress Cataloging-in-Publication Data

Filichia, Peter
   The great parade : Broadway's astonishing, never-to-be-forgotten 1963–1964 season / Peter Filichia.—First edition.
        pages   cm
   Includes bibliographical references.
   ISBN 978-1-250-05135-6 (hardcover)
   ISBN 978-1-4668-6712-3 (e-book)
  1. Musicals—New York (State)—New York—History and criticism.
2. Popular music—New York (State)—New York—1961–1970—History and criticism.   3. Broadway (New York, N.Y.)—History.   I. Title.
   ML1711.8.N3F56 2015
   792.09747'109046—dc23

                                                              2014040746

St. Martin's Press books may be purchased for educational, business, or promotional use. For information on bulk purchases, please contact the Macmillan Corporate and Premium Sales Department at 1-800-221-7945, extension 5442, or write to special markets@macmillan.com.

First Edition: April 2015

10   9   8   7   6   5   4   3   2   1

To John Harrison,
the first person I ever met
who truly understood me.
Luckily, I met him before
the 1963–64 season.

CONTENTS

*

Contents

ACKNOWLEDGMENTS

*

Thanks to my agent, Linda Konner, who's also the love of my life.

Thanks to Michael Flamini and Vicki Lame at St. Martin's—who prove time and time again that Martin isn't the only saint in the office.

Thanks to Al "Skip" Koenig and Bryan Brooks, who were overly generous with information and functions as the best informal editor anyone could ever have.

Thanks to Ken Bloom for providing so many facts and to Val Addams for making available so many figures. What they had on hand about the 1963–64 season proved invaluable.

Thanks, too, to Dale Badway, Harry M. Bagdasian, Aubrey Berg, Mary K. Botosan, Wayne Bryan, Jay Clark, Jason Cocovinis, Drew Cohen, Joshua Ellis, Scott Farthing, Ron Fassler, Larry Fineberg, Freddie Gershon, Alan Gomberg, Marc Grossberg, Kenneth Kantor, Laura Kszan, Lionel Larner, Susan Lee, Robert LoBiondo, Tom Laskey, Jon Maas, Mark Madama, Kevin McAnarney, Richard C. Norton, Erin Oestreich, John Prignano, Paul Roberts, Justin "Squigs" Robertson, Howard Rogut, David Schmittou, Jim Seabrough, Bob Sixsmith, Ron Spivak, Tom Stretton, Robert Viagas, Walter Willison, and the late, great David Wolf.

The Great Parade

CHAPTER ONE

*

The Great Parade of 1963–64

From 1946–47 to 1976–77, every volume of *Theatre World* had the same cover design.

The annual that chronicled the previous theatrical season from June 1 to May 31 displayed on its dust jacket the headshots of six of the semester's most illustrious performers.

In 1963–64, editor Daniel Blum opted for:

- Carol Channing *(Hello, Dolly!)*
- Richard Burton *(Hamlet)*
- Albert Finney *(Luther)*
- Carol Burnett *(Fade Out—Fade In)*
- Beatrice Lillie *(High Spirits)*
- Alec Guinness *(Dylan)*

They were all fine choices. But no Barbra Streisand, who officially became a bona fide star thanks to *Funny Girl*? On April 10, Streisand made the cover of *Time;* a mere forty-two days later, on May 22, she was on the cover of *Life*.

And she wasn't good enough for Blum's dust jacket?

(Maybe Blum had a crystal ball that told him Streisand would never-ever-ever come back to Broadway—and that made him decide not to make a big deal of her.)

Two of the performers Blum did choose also made the cover of *Life* that season. Burton was seen in the middle of Hamlet's "To be, or not to be" soliloquy. Channing, who was shown snuggling up to Horace Vandergelder's cash register, wound up there before making the cover of *Look*, too.

The other Broadway *Life* cover girl was also overlooked by Blum: Elizabeth Ashley, who played the irrepressible newlywed in *Barefoot in the Park*. (The editors at *Life* were apparently more impressed with Ashley than with her co-star: Robert Redford.)

Did Blum choose Finney solely for his Tony-nominated stint as the title character in *Luther*? One could suspect that the *Theatre World* editor was influenced by Finney's suddenly hot Hollywood profile, thanks to his Oscar nomination for playing the title character of *Tom Jones*.

On the other hand, Blum had six previous Oscar *winners* from which to choose: Claudette Colbert, José Ferrer, Alec Guinness, Helen Hayes, Van Heflin, and Joanne Woodward. Aside from Guinness, the rest had to be satisfied with seeing their pictures inside the book.

That season, Woodward co-starred in a comedy with her husband, who didn't have an Oscar—not yet—but was arguably more famous: Paul Newman. He was already Hollywood royalty, along with three other movie stars who could have been blessed by Blum: Kirk Douglas, Charles Boyer, and Lee Remick.

Today we have plenty of movie stars who visit Broadway, but almost always in limited engagements. Some film luminaries think, "Hey, I'll give up three months of Hollywood millions for a mere hundred thousand or so a week on Broadway, where I'll win a Tony that will look nice next to my other awards." (That worked out well for Geoffrey Rush and Denzel Washington. Not as successful was Tom Hanks, who at least received a nomination, unlike Julia Roberts, who didn't.)

But in 1963–64, Burton, Newman, and Woodward were the only ones who'd demanded limited engagements; the others signed for the long haul, ranging from a year's commitment to a run-of-the-play contract. Even Streisand honored her two-year pact.

Besides, no one expected that even Burton would do enough business to run more than four months; none of *Hamlet*'s fifty-nine Broadway productions dating back to 1761 had ever run longer.

Blum might have eliminated Douglas, Boyer, and Remick because each had appeared in a flop—as had Mary Martin. She'd become the First Lady of the American Musical Theater now that Ethel Merman had officially retired from Broadway (again). Despite Martin's three Tony wins (and a special one for taking *Annie Get Your Gun* on the road), she couldn't keep *Jennie* running.

Julie Harris of *Marathon '33* and Helen Hayes of *The White House* had each already won two Tonys, but 1963–64 did not give them their greatest vehicles. Hayes would have a bigger beef with T. E. Kalem of *Time* magazine than with Blum. In A. E. Hotchner's historical pageant, she portrayed the wives of eleven presidents from Abigail Adams to Edith Wilson as well as nineteenth-century gossip columnist Leonora Clayton. Kalem didn't like the play ("Presidential *snip*shots," he called it), but he didn't even mention Hayes by name. What a slap in the face for the star whose forty Broadway appearances had made her the First Lady of the *entire* American Theater.

We can forgive Blum for omitting such luminaries as Tallulah Bankhead, Tom Bosley, Colleen Dewhurst, Peter Falk, Angela Lansbury, Christopher Plummer, Robert Preston, and Cyril Ritchard, all of whom saw their shows prematurely close. So did Bert Lahr, despite winning the Best Actor in a Musical Tony for *Foxy*. But what about Jason Robards Jr. or Barbara Loden in Arthur Miller's *After the Fall*? He was already a star, and she became the Tony-winning toast of the town for her homage to Miller's second wife, Marilyn Monroe. That even got her the cover of the *Saturday Evening Post*.

While we're talking Tonys, Hume Cronyn, who wasn't even halfway through his sixty-two-year Broadway career, won for his Polonius in *Hamlet*. What's more, Cronyn was the first actor honored for a Shakespearean role in the thirty-seven revivals of the Bard's works since the Tonys had begun in 1946–47. And what of Cronyn's castmate Alfred Drake, already the recipient of a brace of Tonys? Both men were *Theatre World* cover-worthy .

Blum may have chosen Carol Burnett just to entice book buyers; she was, after all, well known to the nation from her prolific appearances on the highly rated *Garry Moore Show*. By the time Blum's book went to press, however, the dire handwriting was on the wall for Burnett's *Fade Out—Fade In:* handwriting that was distinctively in her penmanship. (More on that later.)

By the time Blum had submitted his manuscript, Lillie's *High Spirits* must have closed, too. But wasn't Tammy Grimes at least as valuable to the show, given that she appeared in seven songs (in a substantially larger role) to Lillie's four? Certainly *The Saturday Evening Post* thought so; she, not Lillie, got the cover when *High Spirits* was featured.

We *could* go on. Blum might have chosen Sandy Dennis, who was given the Best Actress in a Play Tony for *Any Wednesday*; pop star Steve Lawrence, who'd surprised everyone with his strong acting in *What Makes Sammy Run?*; Emlyn Williams, who dared to play the much-accused Pope Pius XII in *The Deputy*, the season's most controversial play; international star Josephine Baker, who brought in her revue for a couple of weeks in February and did so well that she did three more in April. Blum's awarding Baker the cover would have been a nice type of Lifetime Achievement Award.

Let's face it. No matter which six performers Blum chose, he would have endured criticism for the ones he'd left out. It was *that* strong a season for performers. To paraphrase one of the lines Burton said as Hamlet for his then-record 137 performances, we shall not look upon its like again.

The Tony Awards reveal how impressive a season it was. Let's look at the stats: As the 1963–64 season began, the Tonys had in their seventeen years of existence dispensed a total of 135 performance awards. Actors and actresses representing thirty-six of those wins opened shows in 1963–64—meaning that a theatergoer could have seen more than a quarter of all Tony-winning performers (26.66 percent) in new productions this one season. This doesn't even count Special Tony winner John Gielgud, who was heard but not seen as the Ghost in his own staging of *Hamlet*.

In fact, if one adds in shows from other seasons still playing in 1963–64, a theatergoer could have seen fourteen more Tony-winning performers. That ups the percentage to 37.03 percent. Make that 37.77 percent if you count Jack Cassidy, who two days before opening in *Fade Out—Fade In* won a Tony for his featured role in the previous season's *She Loves Me*. And had Stanley Holloway's musical *Cool Off!* come to Broadway instead of coming off after playing all of five days in Philadelphia, the percentage would have been 38.52 percent—close to two out of every five Tony winners—in just one season.

While *Hello, Dolly!* dominated the final 1963–64 tally with ten Tony Awards, a closer look proves what a solid year it was, for the eight performance winners came from eight different shows: *Foxy*, *Dolly*, *She Loves Me*, and *The Girl Who Came to Supper* were the musicals that sported Tony winners, while *Dylan*, *Any Wednesday*, *Hamlet*, and *After the Fall* were the plays.

Truth to tell, however, the Tony Awards weren't then what they are now, for they were only broadcast in New York. Kinescopes of the early ceremonies show them to be sedate affairs that were unconcerned with glitz or appealing to a more youthful market. Hosting the 1963–64 Tonys was Sidney Blackmer, only seven weeks away from his sixty-fifth birthday. By 2009, Neil Patrick Harris got the job partly because he was a youth-appealing thirty-five.

The issue of youth brings us to a question:

Q: What Broadway producer had the most plastic surgery?

A: Leonard Sillman. He had seven new faces.

All right, it's a joke. To get it, you'd have to know that Sillman periodically (but hardly annually) presented revues called *New Faces of…* that were linked to the year of the opening.

Sillman mounted neither a *New Faces of 1963* nor a *New Faces of 1964*. Had he done so, he would have had hundreds of rookies from which to choose. In addition to Finney, Loden, and O'Shea, newcomers who landed solid roles included Susan Browning, John Davidson, Dom DeLuise, Micki Grant, David Hartman, Tina Louise, Peter Masterson, Martin Sheen, Lesley (Ann) Warren, Sam Waterston, and Gene Wilder. Meanwhile, in the everyone-has-to-start-somewhere department, walk-ons or ensemble members included Gretchen Cryer, Graciela Daniele, Olympia Dukakis, and Ralph Waite, not to mention James Rado and Gerome Ragni, the future auteurs of *Hair,* in two different shows.

And then there was that cast member of *Luther* who played one of four backup singers to a church soloist. None of us has access to Albert Finney's bankbook, but this performer may well have wound up the wealthiest of anyone in the cast, for twenty-two years later, Dan Goggin moved his attention from male members of the clergy to female ones when he wrote *Nunsense* and started a veritable franchise.

If Blum's practice had been to put playwrights on his cover, he would have easily found six blue-chippers: Edward Albee, Paddy Chayefsky, Arthur Miller, John Osborne, Terence Rattigan, and Tennessee Williams. Then theater lovers would have complained that he'd omitted Jean Anouilh, James Baldwin, Enid Bagnold, Bertolt Brecht, and that rising star Neil Simon.

Should Blum have opted for the creators of musicals, his sextet might have been Noël Coward, Betty Comden, Adolph Green, Johnny Mercer, Meredith Willson, and Jule Styne. Styne had had a particularly busy season: He composed both *Funny Girl* and *Fade Out—Fade In*, as well as the incidental music for *Arturo Ui*—and had invested in *Anyone Can Whistle*, a musical by Stephen Sondheim.

No question that Sondheim would never have been a Blum choice, for his satirical musical had been a spectacular flop. George S. Kaufman's famous statement "Satire is what closes on Saturday night" turned out to be true, for *Anyone Can Whistle* closed on the first Saturday night after opening.

Today, of course, satire is what closes on Sunday afternoon. In 1963–64, Broadway was still observing what Christians called the Lord's Day. Today the lucrative Sunday matinee has replaced the lightly attended Monday performance. Only shows that have been running for years if not decades—*Phantom*, *Chicago*—play on Monday to avoid the heavy competition from the new productions that routinely take off that night.

The 1963–64 season also had Al Hirschfeld to caricature it. Shortly after the 1946 birth of his daughter, Nina, Hirschfeld began putting her name into each of his drawings. Lucky for him that he and his wife chose a name that could be drawn with Zorro-like single strokes.

For decades, Hirschfeld allowed theater fans to have the fun of finding a "Nina" or two (or many more) in each drawing. This season, a "Nina" could be found on Colleen Dewhurst's sleeve, Christopher Plummer's coat, Alec Guinness's trousers, Barbra Streisand's pettipants, Tammy Grimes's hair, Josephine Baker's headdress, Mary Martin's bodice, Julie Harris's skirt, Janis Paige's dress, and Florence Henderson's gown.

Little did Hirschfeld know that the Martin Beck Theatre, where he went to caricature Dewhurst in *The Ballad of the Sad Café*, would one day be renamed for him. And he would not be the only representative from 1963–64 who would eventually find his name on a Broadway theater. Joining Helen Hayes, who already had one, would be Neil Simon, Stephen Sondheim, and Samuel J. Friedman.

The first two names are familiar to you; the third probably isn't. Friedman was a press agent who in 1963–64 represented *Fair Game for Lovers*—a comedy about a father's insisting that his teenage daughter live with her boyfriend under his roof—for eight poorly attended performances.

Such a credit doesn't get your name on a theater; Friedman's family paid to have the house renamed in his honor. But in 1963–64, no one remotely saw "naming rights" on the horizon. Today, theater owners are so desperate (or greedy) for money that we may one day be seeing plays in the Kaopectate Theatre.

In this survey, we'll encounter six people who would never have made Blum's cover although their names will come up more often than any of the other luminaries: Howard Taubman, Walter Kerr, John Chapman, Richard Watts Jr., John McClain, and Norman Nadel.

These were the daily critics who served the entire 1963–64 season. Taubman wrote for *The New York Times,* while Kerr worked in that capacity for the *New York Herald Tribune.* By virtue of his newspaper's circulation and prestige, Taubman was the more powerful. Kerr, however, was considered to have theatrical savvy and was the most respected of the half dozen (which is why *he* eventually had a theater named after him, too).

Kerr was a master of the "lede," which is journalism-speak for "lead," a writer's opening line(s). Among Kerr's 1963–64 ledes were "A memorial service for *Café Crown* was held at the Martin Beck last night" and *"Tambourines to Glory* is almost a musical and almost a straight play—and 'almost' is the worst word I know." For *Double Dublin,* it was "Wit has been the principal export of Ireland since the dawn of time, and I am deeply distressed to report that twilight approaches." What's more, Kerr wasn't above using a one-word paragraph to succinctly express his feelings. For *Jennie:* "Drat." For *Baby Want a Kiss:* "Stop." If Kerr sounds insensitive, he could also write a lede that would turn theatergoers into sprinters so that they could be first in line at the box office. All the critics raved for *Hello, Dolly!,* but Kerr expressed it best with "Don't bother holding on to your hats, because you won't be needing them. You'll only be throwing them into the air anyway."

As for Chapman (New York *Daily News)* and Watts *(New York Post),* they spoke to occasional theatergoers who could only afford to sit in the first balcony (as the mezzanine was then called) or the second (which is now simply called "the balcony," so that it seems less far away). McClain *(New York Journal-American)* and Nadel *(New York World-Telegram & Sun)* brought up the rear. A good notice from them was at best useful and at worst better than nothing.

Actually, when the season officially started on June 1, there were seven daily critics. Little did Robert Coleman of the *New York Daily Mirror* know that he had only fourteen more Broadway reviews in his future; his paper would fold on October 16, the day before the opening of *Jennie*. (At least he was spared seeing that.) As a result, Coleman's name won't show up here nearly as often as his brother wizards.

Still, six different voices offering appraisals sounds very good to us now. If these half-dozen reviewers didn't provide great literature, they clearly did their best when attending opening nights that began circa 6:30 P.M., seeing the show, taking their notes, rushing up the aisles during curtain calls, returning to their offices, writing what they could think of then and there—on typewriters, yet—while overhearing editors mutter "Where is it?" so that the review could make the morning edition.

No wonder that they made mistakes. McClain in his review of *Have I Got a Girl for You!* mentioned that one character reminded him of "Duke Masterson in *Guys and Dolls*" and that a Jewish mother summoned up memories of "Molly Bergen."

Taubman admitted in his pan of *Café Crown* that "I chose to attend a preview for a change of pace—and to see a new work apart from the tension of a first night." Yes, and it gave him an extra day to write his review.

Today, reviewing a preview is standard practice. Not only does a critic have far more time to collect his thoughts, he winds up writing better prose because he has more time thanks to having a computer rather than a Smith-Corona.

Producers' concern for the critics is not the reason that the front-line press is now invited to previews instead of opening nights. Today a show has so many producers and backers who want to attend the gala premiere that seats are needed for them. The dozens of critics are relegated to less glamorous performances.

That's just one of the differences between then and now. By investigating 1963–64, we're returning to a time when the sign over the Winter Garden Theatre extended all the way to Fiftieth Street; that it's since been truncated to accommodate an Applebee's restaurant is an apt metaphor for how Broadway has shrunk. The 1963–64 season offered seventy-five attractions, including Martha Graham and her Dance Company, making their ninth visit in twenty years.

Fifty years later, the 2013–14 semester could boast only forty-three attractions.

In 1963–64, a couple who wanted to see a musical would go up to the box office and hand over a $20 bill in exchange for two orchestra seats as well as two dimes in change. But that steep-sounding $9.90 was only germane to musicals; a play's top ticket price was more than 30 percent lower at $6.90.

$6.90 for Burton's Hamlet.

$9.90 for Streisand's Fanny Brice.

A sold-out week would mean $58,000 for *110 in the Shade*. $71,200 for *Here's Love*. $73,300 for *Hello, Dolly!* $81,600 for *Funny Girl*. $82,600 for *Rugantino*. $84,900 for *Fade Out—Fade In*. $91,700 for *Jennie*. $97,000 for *The Girl Who Came to Supper* and *Foxy*.

Today, producers who see their musicals gross $97,000 for one performance would soon be reluctantly making plans for a closing-night party.

Inflation charts say that yesterday's $6.90 has ballooned to today's $51.11 and $9.90 to $73.33; still, that's less than half of what tickets now cost for a Broadway entertainment.

Back then, performances on New Year's Eve cost a few bucks extra. Today all eight performances during Christmas *week* have inflated prices.

Not that producers in 1963–64 were unaware that this was the busiest week of the year. During Christmas week 1963, *Oliver!* doubled its gross. Hell, even the China Institute of America, which planned to do eight performances of the Foo Hsing Theatre's opera *The Beautiful Bait,* knew enough to come to town between December 24 and January 5.

Tickets to plays might have even cost less if their producers hadn't had to pay musicians at each performance. Plays, mind you—not musicals, and not even plays that used incidental music. Plays that didn't offer theatergoers a note of music had four musicians on the payroll getting a nice check every week. The union's rationale was that if a play was playing at a theater, a musical couldn't play there, and that penalized as many as twenty-five musicians.

One 1963–64 play, S. N. Behrman's *But for Whom Charlie,* actually addressed the issue. The title character said to one such musician, "You sit below the stage in a theatre, not playing, not performing any service, pure parasitism, and you have no embarrassment, evidently, at taking pay for doing nothing."

A novelist in the play noted, "Now why can't writers have a union like that?"

Why couldn't theatergoers? Had this practice not been in place, they might have paid $6.50 or even $6 for the best seats.

At whatever price, if you wanted to buy a ticket you had a few options. You could write a check or money order, lick five-cent stamps for two envelopes—one addressed to the theater, one self-addressed—and pray that the second envelope would soon return with tickets. But a few days might pass before the missive arrived, and even more time might go by until a box office treasurer got around to opening and processing it. Avid theatergoers feared that in the meantime, thousands of tickets would have been sold at the window.

Going to ticket brokers was another option. These ranged from Golden/Leblang, the most famous, to desks and counters devoted to ticket selling in hotels. The former got the far better seats, although every agency charged the same $1.50 extra.

And finally, there were scalpers. Some 1963–64 theatergoers were still grumbling about the $50 they'd paid seven years earlier for a pair to see Rex Harrison and Julie Andrews in *My Fair Lady*. Today, of course, it sounds like a steal.

Most theatergoers chose the most obvious option: going to the box office at a time when "buying tickets on line" meant something very different from what it does now.

For smash hits, that meant patrons had to wait and wait and wait for tickets that could be any color of the sixty-four found in the deluxe Crayola box. Today your ticket to Broadway will always be cream and white if you're patronizing a Nederlander theater and pink and red if you're seeing a show at a Jujamcyn house. Most likely, however, your ticket will be blue and gold, for the Shubert Organization owns more theaters—seventeen—than both Nederlander (nine) and Jujamcyn (five) put together. (The other nine Broadway theaters operate under different ownerships.)

No ticket today will be for the Morosco, Bijou, or Helen Hayes on Forty-sixth Street; the playhouse emblazoned with her name on Forty-fourth Street is the second theater to commemorate her. Her previous house and the other two were razed in 1982 in favor of the Marriott Hotel and the Marquis Theatre. The ANTA Washington Square, 54th Street, and Ziegfeld no longer exist. The Hudson is a hotel ballroom. The Mark Hellinger is now a church where you can go and pray that it someday returns to use as a legitimate theater.

Back then, even if you went to a musical comparatively early in its run, you might not see the absolute "original cast." This was still the era of the gypsy—the nickname given an ensemble member who became bored rather quickly and moved to another show and then another. From *110 in the Shade*, Carolyn Kemp left to join *Fade Out—Fade In;* Paula Lloyd and Loren Hightower bolted to be in *Anyone Can Whistle* (weren't they sorry!), and Jerry Dodge moved over to *Hello, Dolly!* To be sure, Dodge was bookwriter Michael Stewart's boyfriend, but the others were just searching for new adventures.

Today, ensemble members keep their jobs as long as they can, for choruses are smaller and competition is keener. There were then no conservatories or universities that offered degrees in musical theater; today, there are more than five dozen.

Theatergoers who wanted liquor during intermission had to leave the theater and find a nearby bar. Not until October 1, 1964—four months after this season concluded—did theaters get the right and the licenses to serve something other than the carefully named "orange drink."

Back in 1963–64, if you couldn't get to Broadway, it would vicariously come to you, either from *Life* or the reviews that *Time* and *Newsweek* printed most every week. From this season alone, sixteen new plays and five new musicals would be published in hardcover (or cloth, to use the then-preferred description). Of them, only *Barefoot in the Park, Dylan, Funny Girl, The Subject Was Roses, Any Wednesday, Luther,* and *Hello, Dolly!* were hits; two-thirds of them were not—and yet still publishers brought them out. The last three even became mass-market paperbacks, along with the money-losing *After the Fall, Blues for Mister Charlie,* and *The Deputy.*

Most playwrights were grateful that the page devoted to a show's cast list mentioned the opening but not the closing date. Paddy Chayefsky was mighty happy that the statement "*The Passion of Josef D.* opened on February 11, 1964" wasn't followed by "and closed eleven days later on February 22, 1964."

Each month, the Fireside Theatre Book Club would offer a hardcover copy of a play or musical to its members. As much as it and other publishers kept theater in the public eye, television was now helping more. Johnny Carson, just starting the second year of what would be thirty years of late-night TV dominance, was still broadcasting from New York. Thus, he could bring on Iggie Wolfington, who was then appearing in *Marathon '33,* June Havoc's play about marathon dancers. Here's a guarantee that anyone who's on *The Tonight Show* tonight will have a higher Q Score than Wolfington.

Better still was *The Ed Sullivan Show,* whose host wasn't good to Broadway simply because *Bye Bye Birdie* had honored him in song. (Frankly, he was a little embarrassed that it had.) Among Sullivan's guests on his first broadcast in 1948 were Rodgers and Hammerstein. Very few weeks went by without Sullivan's showing either a scene from a current Broadway show or a personality who was appearing in one.

Yes, much has changed in fifty years.

And *Spoon River Anthology* is Exhibit A as proof.

Edgar Lee Masters's 1915 collection of 244 poems had people speaking from their graves in a cemetery in a fictitious midwestern town.

Charles Aidman, who had recently co-founded a Los Angeles group called Theatre West with Joyce Van Patten, adapted it. He, Van Patten, and Robert Elston were joined by what had to be their biggest name: Betty Garrett, who'd starred in the musical films of *On the Town* and *My Sister Eileen.*

Most nights, the forty-two seats at Theatre West were filled. Playgoers met Lucius Atherton (Elston), who recalled when he was once young, handsome, and "a knave of hearts who took every trick." Then he aged and was mocked by young girls who saw him as nothing more than a dirty old man.

Many a play and musical uses mistaken identity as a plot device, and Masters even used it in one of his poems. Aidman, using a thick Jewish accent, played Barney Hainsfeather, who was burned beyond recognition in a train wreck. So was John Allen, who was taken for Hainsfeather and was buried in a Jewish cemetery, while Hainsfeather was unhappily buried among a bunch of WASPs.

Spoon River suggested that a small town can breed small-mindedness. It also had quite a bit to say about marriage. Margaret Fuller Slack (Van Patten) wanted to be a writer and was promised by the town's wealthy druggist that if she married him she'd have all the time in the world to write. Instead, she spent her life tending to their eight children. Ollie McGee (Garrett) told of how her husband and marriage "robbed me of my youth and my beauty." Mrs. Charles Bliss (Van Patten) talked about the "preachers and judges" who encouraged her and Charles to stay married "for the children," resulting in two kids siding with her, the two others with him, and no one being happy at all.

Music leavened the proceedings, although musical comedy star Garrett didn't sing any of it. Naomi Caryl Hirshhorn and Hal Lynch sang twelve folk standards ("He's Gone Away"; "Skip to My Lou") and wrote four, including a lovely little waltz, "Spoon River."

If it sounds a little too scholarly, it was right at home at UCLA, where it moved for a six-week run. Perhaps many audience members related to the husbands and wives who spoke about all the disappointments delivered by wedlock (with an accent on the second syllable). Have you ever witnessed an antimarriage remark in any theater getting anything less than a knowing laugh or a resigned grunt?

Producer Joseph Cates saw it at UCLA and decided to bring it to Broadway with a little help from his brother, Gilbert, who would later be greatly associated with Hollywood's Academy Awards.

Cherry-picking shows from the hinterlands is now standard procedure, but back then most producers operated differently. If they were to import a play, it would be from London; otherwise, they found their shows the hard way by actually sitting down and reading scripts. Dropping into a theater on a college campus would seem to be a waste of time.

Not for Cates, who decided to bring *Spoon River Anthology* to Broadway. It wouldn't be a costly enterprise. Some of the budget of $35,000 (!) was spent on four benches, two chairs, a lectern, and six actors. Whoever suggested that approach has been lost to the ages; no set designer was ever credited. There was a lighting designer, however, but he was a rank beginner: Jules Fisher, long before he'd win nine Tonys.

Cates booked the Booth from the Shubert Organization, but the landlords were already looking for another tenant; how long could a show called *Spoon River Anthology* last, anyway? They were certain that it would easily endure two losing weeks in a row—which was enough to allow landlords the right to invoke the stop clause and evict their current tenant in favor of a new one.

Taubman called the show "A glowing theater experience." Kerr: "Excellent." Chapman: "Quite an inspiration." Watts: "Moving and beautiful."

McClain: "Enormously warm and compelling." Nadel: "A powerful evocation of life." Coleman: "Absorbing theater."

With quotations that were more respectful than exciting, business wasn't hot. *River* wasn't drowning, but, yes, there were soon two weeks in a row that the show didn't meet expenses, and the Shuberts took advantage of the lapse in business. They signed a contract with the producers of *Once for the Asking*, which would come to town on November 20—a few scant weeks away.

Like *Spoon River*—as the show was soon officially renamed to make it sound less literary and more entertaining—*Once for the Asking* was written by a first-time Broadway playwright and mounted by two first-time producers. But at least it was a comedy, and while it didn't have box office stars either, its leads were all solid pros: Russell (*Call Me Madam*) Nype, Jan Sterling, and Scott McKay. *Spoon River* would have to leave or close by November 16 after a mere forty-nine days to make room for *Asking*'s November 20 opening.

To everyone's surprise, Cates decided to move, despite the fact that the best theater he could get was the Belasco. What a comedown to relocate from Forty-fifth Street between Broadway and Eighth—the block with the most legitimate theaters (eight) and the best walk-in business—to a section of Forty-fourth Street on the "wrong" side of Broadway, where no other theater resided. Theatrical foot traffic seldom ventured that far east, so walk-in business and impulse buying simply wouldn't happen.

And wouldn't you know that *Once for the Asking* lasted all of one night? How irked Cates and company must have been that they had to endure a costly move to accommodate a comedy that had already received unanimously negative reviews from the five Boston critics during the tryout. Couldn't it have just closed there?

Cates kept *Spoon River* alive at the Belasco for forty-seven days for a total of 111 performances. That may not be a long run, but in 1963–64 it outdistanced Mary Martin's musical, Terence Rattigan's drama, and Kirk Douglas's vehicle.

One reason was that Hugh Downs, then host of *The Today Show*, came to see it, loved it, and offered to put it on his morning broadcast. Not only that, he arranged for the cast to do a half-hour cutting.

A half-hour! Could *that* happen today? For that matter, would Sony now make an original cast album, as its forebear Columbia Records, then the most prestigious label for Broadway, did?

The result? *Spoon River* was a hit—which on Broadway is solely defined by a producer's returning an investment and delivering a profit. Only eleven of the season's productions would eventually be able to brag that they made money, but *Spoon River* was one of them.

A low-tech evening of people reciting doleful poetry in a production that endured a money-sucking move nevertheless made a profit? Perhaps even more miraculous was that in 1963–64, a troupe known as the Obratzov Russian Puppet Theatre could bring to town a double bill featuring *Aladdin and His Wonderful Lamp,* book what was then Broadway's biggest theater—the one called the Broadway— and stay for seventy-six performances, longer than forty-three other 1963–64 entries.

Does anybody see this happening today?

We'll visit a season when it could.

CHAPTER TWO

*

The Musicals

What a fitting metaphor: a season that had a great parade of stars also had "parade" mentioned in four of the season's most anticipated musicals.

That's about all they had in common. Each of the four experienced a different fate.

One was a smash hit that in 1970 became the longest-running musical in Broadway history (at least for a few months): *Hello, Dolly!* The first act ended with Carol Channing's Dolly Gallagher Levi vowing to rejoin the human race in "Before the Parade Passes By."

One was a solid hit: *Funny Girl.* Its Act One concluded with Barbra Streisand's Fanny Brice demanding "Don't Rain on My Parade" and insisting that nothing would keep her from the man she loved.

One was a long-running flop: Meredith (*The Music Man*) Willson's *Here's Love.* It began with two dozen singers and dancers replicating the Macy's Thanksgiving Parade.

And one was a financial disaster, but a musical whose assets and liabilities are still being debated lo these fifty years later: *Anyone Can Whistle.* The second of its *three* acts featured Broadway musical newcomer Angela Lansbury singing about "A Parade in Town."

Dolly first. Here was the musical version of Thornton Wilder's *The Matchmaker,* the slight rewrite of his 1938 flop *The Merchant of Yonkers.* Matchmaker Dolly Gallagher Levi (Carol Channing) allegedly was out to find a mate for the wealthy Horace Vandergelder (David Burns), but we knew long before he did that she planned to match him with herself (even if he, like a previous customer, did have a countenance a little bit like Scrooge).

Mrs. Levi made her plans again perfectly clear at the end of the first act, when she was determined to put her widowhood behind her "Before the Parade Passes By." And yet when the musical left for its pre-Broadway tryout in Detroit, that song wasn't even in the show.

It certainly wasn't one of the songs that composer-lyricist Jerry Herman feverishly wrote over a weekend in 1962 to prove to producer David Merrick that he could do the job.

Merrick had first asked Bob Merrill to write the score. Merrill might well have done it had the producer not already asked Gower Champion to direct and choreograph. The songwriter wasn't entirely happy with the way Champion had handled his *Carnival* in 1961, so he refused the offer.

Apparently Michael Stewart, who wrote the book to *Carnival*, either had a better experience with Champion or was willing to let bygones be bygones; he agreed to provide *Dolly*'s libretto. Stewart wanted Herman, and surreptitiously gave him a script so that the songwriter could be better informed of what songs were needed.

Herman often tells the story of composing the music and lyrics to four songs in a three-day span, but he's shortchanging himself. There were actually five, if you count "Call on Dolly," which started the show, as a separate entity from "I Put My Hand In." Herman has said, "They're perfect counterpoint to each other, although we never did them that way."

The scene in which Dolly would get Vandergelder's impoverished employees Cornelius Hackl and Barnaby Tucker "Dancing" was next. Herman also had an idea that Champion used: The song would spill out into the street and have everyone pair off, but would leave Dolly all alone at song's end.

Then Herman tackled a song for Irene Molloy, the widow whom Dolly is supposedly matchmaking with Vandergelder. "Ribbons Down My Back" has often been criticized for bringing down the full-speed-ahead pace of the show. But imagine how we'd feel if Herman's first effort had stayed in the spot. Doesn't "I Still Love the Love I Loved When First in Love I Fell" sound awfully arch? That Irish-tinged ballad also indicated that Mrs. Malloy wasn't ready to move on; "Ribbons Down My Back" told us she was.

And that fifth song? As Herman's old friend (and eventual Cornelius Hackl)

Charles Nelson Reilly later divulged, it was set to a melody that Herman had written some years earlier. "The spirit of the chase is what it's all about," was its first line, replaced by "Put on your Sunday clothes when you feel down and out."

Herman didn't even get all three days to write. He had to finish before Sunday morning, for he needed that entire day to teach the songs to his friend Alice Borden, who was then appearing in *Stop the World—I Want to Get Off* but had Sunday off. If this were happening today, she would have to beg off to do her 3 P.M. matinee.

Borden apparently did her part, for Herman got the job. He then specifically started writing for Ethel Merman, who Merrick was sure would do the show: "World, Take Me Back" and "Love, Look in My Window" both expressed Dolly's need to rejoin the human race. But when Merman refused the offer, out went the two songs meant to showcase her voice.

No one noticed that both songs served an important lyrical purpose—expressing feelings that would eventually permeate "Before the Parade Passes By." That song was still months away.

Champion, in mulling over potential Dollys, thought of Nanette Fabray. She, however, was insulted when Champion asked her to do "some exploratory work" with him. This was akin to auditioning, and a star of her magnitude wasn't having that.

Fabray may have been vulnerable because she'd just closed *Mr. President*, the Irving Berlin can't-miss smash that missed by quite a bit—and the musical that was supposed to make her a bona fide Broadway star. When that didn't happen, Fabray, despite getting the show's only Tony nomination in the performance categories, may have felt that Broadway regarded her as damaged goods. She would *not* audition. After all, hadn't she been choreographed by Champion in *Make a Wish* in 1951? He'd known for years what she could do.

Norma Desmond had a point when she said that "great stars have great pride," but was Fabray a great star? We've all seen a performer be brilliant in one role and stink in another; there's good reason why the English language includes the word "miscast." So Champion was well within his rights to take a let's-see attitude.

"No, no," Nanette said to Champion, thus short-circuiting her career. She never did another Broadway musical; the closest she came was appearing ten years later in a comedy that played three weeks of previews and one official performance. It was called *No Hard Feelings,* and one must wonder if she harbored any toward Champion for not simply giving her Dolly Levi.

Compare this to Channing's story. Herman, Champion, and Merrick went to Long Island to see her do Shaw's *The Millionairess.* Herman was impressed, but he had virtually no sway compared to Champion and Merrick, who came away with the opinion that Channing wasn't right.

Channing thought otherwise. The lady had once recorded Marc Blitzstein's *No for an Answer,* but that didn't mean that she was about to take it. She invited Champion to her apartment, and when he didn't show up until midnight, she nevertheless worked with him for hours. By the dawn's early light, she'd convinced him that she'd work out just fine as the matchmaker who loved to meddle in what was then titled *Dolly: A Damned Exasperating Woman.*

Even by the time *Hello, Dolly!* arrived in New York, its opening-night tickets still sported that previous title. Dumping that moniker was an inordinately smart move. Although most every musical today offers a colon (*Matilda: The Musical; Motown: The Musical; Newsies: The Musical*), there's something decidedly *un*musical in seeing a colon in the middle of an actual title—as opposed to an exclamation point at title's end. The creators were wise to remove the colon and name the show after its biggest production number and its song that was destined for greatness.

But had *Dolly: A Damned Exasperating Woman* been retained, it would have almost been the show's title song, thanks to Vandergelder's complaint to Dolly, "You're a Damned Exasperating Woman." It would be only one of two big numbers that David Burns would have and then lose.

In a move that now sounds extraordinarily foolish, Champion had promised Burns that Vandergelder would have the first-act finale. Why make such a guarantee? Gone were the archaic days of the '20s when Cliff Edwards could demand a contract—and get one—that specified that he'd come onstage at 10 P.M., play his ukulele and sing a song *of his own choosing,* and be done for the night. Since then, musicals had become much more integrated, and such practices had been dumped (and none too soon).

But a promise is a promise. Herman devised a clever song for Vandergelder in which he told how Yonkers's most promising citizen—a "half a millionaire"—made his money although he'd only started with "A Penny in My Pocket."

The biggest surprise was Vandergelder's stating in the song that he was capable of a charitable act. "I gave my nickel to a blind man," he sang, which inadvertently reaped benefits when "the blind man left me all his meager savings in his will." That allowed Vandergelder the capital to buy ice and deliver it to homes. Then he had the bright idea to chop the large blocks into cubes, thus maximizing his profits. Or so he thought; actually, by crushing the ice into chips, he made even more money.

His industriousness motivated a bigwig to hire him and allow him to marry his daughter. Alas, she died suddenly but left Vandergelder with enough money to buy "an acre, a silo and a steed. All Yonkers started buying grain and hay and feed. And now I've made half a million." But lest Vandergelder forget his skyrocketing rise to success, he still had and cherished that first penny to remind him of how far he'd come.

Nice idea, good lyrics, and a perky melody, too. And what a *coup de théâtre* Champion could deliver by bringing onto the stage more than a hundred items, one by one, to show the vast extent of Vandergelder's wealth. Wouldn't *that* be the ultimate showstopper?

In fact, no. Too bad that Herman and Champion didn't notice early on that Wilder's *The Merchant of Yonkers*, which centered on Vandergelder, was a thirty-nine-performance failure, while *The Matchmaker*, which celebrated Dolly, ran more than twelve times longer. This musical was called *Hello, Dolly!* and not *Hello, Horace!* Audiences didn't want to know more about him as Act One closed; they craved more of her.

Herman claims that he's the one who suggested that Dolly get the first-act closer. Luckily for Champion and Merrick, Burns's contract had not included any clause about it. It simply became one of those promises that wasn't worth the paper it *hadn't* been printed on.

Burns was gracious enough to let the number go, but Champion still faced a bigger problem. How could he tell his producer, famed for his Vandergelder-like miserliness, that the number for which he'd paid thousands upon thousands for props would have to be cut? (Merrick, of course, found a way to sell each and every item for a handsome profit—and without benefit of eBay.) The new parade would also mean an extra $40,000 in costumes. Even the intrepid Champion must have feared for his life when telling Merrick that one expensive production number would need to be replaced by another.

Merrick indeed balked, so Champion called his bluff and offered to buy him out. As we'll soon see, Merrick was about to bail out of another 1963–64 musical that looked promising. If both were to succeed and he wasn't part of either, he'd look pretty foolish. Broadway, for the first time in nearly a decade, would start questioning his supposed wisdom.

Or was Merrick influenced by the line that he heard Dolly say each night: "Money, pardon the expression, is like manure. It's not worth a thing unless it's spread around encouraging young things to grow."

(Has any economist ever disagreed?)

Whatever the case, Merrick okayed Champion's impulse. The final scene of Act One had always been set for the annual Fourteenth Street Parade, so why not celebrate it in song?

The story has been told many times that after Herman auditioned for Merrick he was told on the spot, "Kid, the show is yours." That turned out to be only partly true. The show was always Merrick's for if it had been solely Herman's, the young composer-lyricist would have prevented Charles Strouse, Lee Adams, and Bob Merrill from coming in and giving advice (and probably more than that).

Merrick obviously feared that Herman might not have an exciting Act One closer in him, so, as Strouse has often said, the producer summoned him and Adams to Detroit. Before they committed themselves to going, Strouse asked if Herman had been told, and Merrick assured him that he had. However, once they arrived at the hotel and ran into Herman, who "turned ashen white," Strouse realized that Merrick had told one of his many lies.

Strouse has often implied that he and Adams wrote the scene leading to "Before the Parade Passes By," the song itself, and the scene that led to the reprise and intermission. In exchange, they'd get 1 percent of the show, which turned out to be substantially more than they could have imagined. That was the price for their keeping mum. Author Steven Suskin, then working in the Merrick office, says that he mailed out checks to Strouse and Adams each week. Those checks weren't exactly installments on the option for their upcoming *Golden Boy*.

At a book signing in 2010, Strouse broke his silence. He recalled being at the filming of a PBS special in which Herman said that he wrote "Before the Parade Passes By." Said Strouse, "I wanted to kill him." But he was mollified when Herman at least admitted that the two songwriters had written their own "Before the Parade Passes By," whose title he appropriated and went off on his own to write. Strouse also acknowledged his 1 percent, shall we say, commission for what he'd contributed.

There is an irony here: Herman had already written an entire off-Broadway musical called *Parade,* yet others had to point out the value of the word for his first-act finale. After all, if Irene Molloy got an introspective moment to tell us she was getting over her deceased husband, shouldn't Dolly? "Before the Parade Passes By" didn't go into the show until December 29, during the Washington tryout—a mere eighteen days before the Broadway opening—but it scored from its first performance.

On to the second-act opening, in which Cornelius and Barnaby take Irene and her assistant, Minnie Fay, to dinner at the lofty Harmonia Gardens: The men have convinced the women that they have money enough to treat them, but every penny counts, so they inform the ladies that walking is the way to go if you truly have "Elegance."

Was this a Herman song? Suskin says that during his employment with Merrick he mailed weekly checks to Bob Merrill, too. Aside from that, some circumstantial evidence suggests that Merrill was involved, namely, the lyric "All the guests of Mr. Hackl are feeling great and look spectac-alar."

Is it possible? Let's look at the way Merrill gleefully tortured lyrics in other shows and see if a pattern emerges.

Exhibit A: In his next show, *Funny Girl,* he had Eddie Ryan (Danny Meehan), Fanny Brice's best friend, tell the lass, "Kid, my heart ain't made of marble, but your rhythm's really har'ble."

Exhibit B: In his *next* show, the ill-fated *Breakfast at Tiffany's,* he had Holly Golightly's would-be beau shake off the idea of marriage by singing, "The lucky bachelor; gee, to me, no set-up could be nat'chuler."

Exhibit C: A year after that, Merrill's two teens who love a pianist in *Henry, Sweet Henry* sang, "Your crazy music truly tickles us, although your whole technique's ree-dick-el-uss."

They're all perfect rhymes, yes, but only because Merrill mangled the words in the style of "Hackl are" and "spectac-alar." None of this would ever hold up in court as evidence that Merrill wrote "Elegance," so infer what you will.

Was Merrill, who'd turned down *Hello, Dolly!* in the first place, always destined to wind up working on it?

After the Harmonia Gardens set rolled in and the maître d' supervised the "Waiters' Gallop," the big moment came. At the top of the staircase the demure curtains parted to show Mrs. Dolly Gallagher Levi looking the best she had in years.

Freddy Wittop devised an elaborate gown, not to mention a matching headdress. Champion certainly gave Channing enough time to get into it, for in addition to the fifteen-minute intermission, he kept Dolly offstage for another fifteen minutes, whetting his audience's appetite for her big entrance.

Dolly's outfit was red for a reason. In a more benign custom than Alfred Hitchcock's inserting himself in his own movies, Merrick enjoyed seeing his favorite color—red, by now already known on Broadway as "David Merrick red"—on some woman in each of his musicals. That concept would reach its apotheosis here.

So why did this "Welcome home" number become a legendary showstopper? Perhaps for a reason that the TV series *Cheers* would later stress: the value of being at a place "where everybody knows your name." Wouldn't we all want to be appreciated—nay, loved—by the staff of a restaurant we visit?

A big help was the passerelle—the little walkway that encircles the orchestra pit—that Champion had devised. Why don't more musicals use this inviting device? It brings the action that much closer to the audience and gives them at least the feeling that they're so close to the performers that they can touch them. Or did *Dolly* use it so effectively and memorably that few have ever dared to replicate the concept? (The recent *Rocky*, with its pull-out boxing ring, showed there was plenty of excitement to be had by bringing the action closer.)

Dolly opened on January 16—coincidentally enough, the date that Ethel Merman was born in 1906, 1907, 1908, 1911, or 1912, depending on whom you believe.

Chapman: "The most exciting numbers I have seen since Jerome Robbins staged *West Side Story*." McClain: "A pot-walloping hit." Nadel: "A glorious jewel to top this or any season." Watts: "One of the season's musical smashes."

We already know that Kerr advocated hats in the air. Taubman wasn't as eloquent, but no producer ever finds mundane "The best musical of the season."

The reviews were as stellar as the fictional raves that Merrick had had his press agent dream up two years earlier for the notorious and hilarious *Subways Are for Sleeping* ad. Broadway's twenty-five-month drought of smash hits—extending back to *How to Succeed*'s opening on October 14, 1961—was over.

Soon the rest of the nation would be apprised, too, through Louis Armstrong's surprise smash single of the title song. His gravelly rendition of "Hello, Dolly!" allowed him to have his first No. 1 hit since 1932. On May 9, Armstrong, nearly sixty-three years old, became the oldest artist to reach the top of the singles chart.

When the Tony committee met to dispense nominations, it acknowledged the musical, Stewart, Herman, Channing, Reilly, Merrick, Wittop, set designer Oliver Smith, musical director Shepard Coleman, and Champion (twice).

Notably absent from the nominees was David Burns. Perhaps the committee felt that Burns had all the Tonys he needed. He'd already won two, most recently for playing Senex in *A Funny Thing Happened on the Way to the Forum* and previously in *The Music Man* as Mayor Shinn, one of the few Tony-winning musical roles that didn't require a note's worth of singing. Perhaps Burns was neglected because he almost didn't sing in *Dolly*. After he warbled "It Takes a Woman" early on, he wasn't heard again until the final moments of the show, when he got a thirty-three-word reprise of the title song.

All the above-named Tony nominees won, save Reilly, who lost to aforementioned lame duck Jack Cassidy of *She Loves Me*. Coleman's win would be the last time that a musical director would be celebrated, as the category was dropped. As for Coleman himself, he was the first Tony winner to be fired, when Peter Howard replaced him as conductor. (Oh, that Merrick!)

Many had assumed that Barbra Streisand would cop Best Actress in a Musical; that would give *Funny Girl* at least *something*. It wound up winning nothing. Channing emerged triumphant, and oh, how she relished her unexpected renaissance. She'd been saying for years she rued walking into a restaurant or ballroom where there was a live orchestra, because the bandleader would inevitably play "Diamonds Are a Girl's Best Friend" from her 1949 triumph in *Gentlemen Prefer Blondes*. Hearing the same song for fourteen straight years was just too pathetic. Now she'd finally been able to surpass that achievement.

Little did Channing know that for the next fifty years whenever she walked into a restaurant or ballroom that featured a live orchestra, she'd hear the band play "Hello, Dolly!"

But she enjoyed each and every photo opportunity—and thereby hangs a tale. Whenever Channing joined a group of celebrities who were about to be photographed, her then-husband, Charles Lowe, would ensure that she was on the far left. That way, when the picture was published, the caption would have to start with the words "Carol Channing" before all the other stars were listed. In later years, after his death, Channing didn't speak well of Lowe, but he was devoted to her, had her best professional interests at heart, and rarely if ever missed one of her thousands of performances as Dolly.

Champion received the most credit for the show's success. Harold Clurman called him "the Tyrone Guthrie of musicals." Certainly Tyrone Guthrie wasn't "the Tyrone Guthrie of musicals," not after the laborious production he'd given *Candide* in 1956. But credit where it's due, Guthrie did have a big Broadway hit with a play that would become a musical: *The Matchmaker.*

Champion was a champion in another respect: He wouldn't settle for a smash hit that he knew could be even better. For most of 1964 and much of 1965, he found himself displeased with "Come and Be My Butterfly." The production number came after the title song, when Vandergelder thought that he saw Cornelius and Barnaby in the restaurant. Why weren't they in Yonkers working? He tried pursuing them, but the floor show got in his way. A bunch of "nymphs" fluttered around singing, "Won't you come and be my butterfly and fly away with me on a pink petunia pillow? We will dream away the day while the naughty pussy willow and the sly calla lily tickle us silly."

Most directors enjoying a smash would invoke the "If it ain't broke" clause, but Champion believed that a wonderful show could be made more wonderful. As if David Burns hadn't lost enough material! But more than a year and a half after opening, Champion put in "The Polka Contest" (of which Jerry Herman wasn't enamored).

Champion had waited to make the change until he had to put in a new Dolly, just before Channing would embark on a national tour. An irony: Ginger Rogers, who'd co-starred with Channing in a not-so-hot 1956 film called *The First Traveling Saleslady,* would replace her.

Alas, without Channing, the show stopped selling out. Later, Martha Raye and Betty Grable weren't able to bring it back to SRO status. But Pearl Bailey and her all-black company did. Frankly, if Merrick hadn't had the idea of an African American production, *Hello, Dolly!* would have probably closed after the 1967 holiday week, winding up with around 1,600 performances and a respectable fourth-place finish on the long-run list (behind *My Fair Lady, Oklahoma!,* and *South Pacific).* With Bailey's rejuvenation (with a *lot* of help from the frequently appearing Thelma Carpenter), the show became a new must-see.

Phyllis Diller followed and was highly acclaimed for playing the character and not her persona of an utterly jaded housewife. Then Merman finally took over in the role that was originally earmarked for her. In came "World, Take Me Back" and "Love, Look in My Window," making the show top-heavy and overlong. Merman fans didn't mind at all.

Forty-fourth Street had long been known as "Hit Street," because a parade of great shows had played there. It's certainly where Rodgers and Hammerstein always wanted to be; they chose theaters on that street for the first eight of their nine shows. *Hello, Dolly!* at the St. James staunchly upheld the reputation for the next seven years. Yes, 2,844 performances was quite a number in those days. As of this writing, *Dolly* is the seventeenth-longest-running musical in Broadway history—but it can still boast that it returned 1,048 percent on each investment, which many longer-running shows cannot.

After it finally played its last performance, the December 28, 1970, *New York Times* reported that "the First Fiduciary Trust of West 44th Street, otherwise known as *Hello, Dolly!,* closed yesterday."

Yes, but only on Broadway, and only for a while. Although by then, post-*Hair,* some considered *Hello, Dolly!* as quaint as *Blossom Time,* but *Dolly* has never really gone away again. In June 1967, when Channing closed in Houston, she said in her curtain speech, "Maybe David Merrick will have a grand *Hello, Dolly!* revival in the year 2000, and we'll all come back."

Although Merrick was never actively involved in any of the three subsequent Broadway revivals of *Dolly,* Channing was only four years off in her wish. Her final performance as Dolly took place on January 28, 1996, at the Lunt-Fontanne Theatre.

By then, Jerry Herman had learned that when he wrote the title tune, he had written Carol Channing's future life story. Just as Dolly was welcomed back to the Harmonia Gardens with open arms (and high kicks), Channing was cherished by audiences when she brought the show back to Broadway in both 1978 and 1995—and in between to many a theater from sea to shining sea.

Of course, her doing the show approximately 5,000 times invited when-will-she-stop criticism. Female impersonator Michael West did a video called "Door-to-Door Dolly," in which he portrayed Channing so desperate to perform her signature role that she made cold calls to houses in every neighborhood, knocking on doors and performing the show for any housewife who answered. Even a dog's chasing her round and round in circles in a backyard wouldn't stop her rainbow tour.

Merrick and Champion probably never envisioned that they'd have a longer-running success, but they did. In 1980, *42nd Street* started a run that would last 600-plus performances more than *Dolly*'s. Champion didn't live to see it, for he famously died on *42nd Street*'s opening night. Merrick wasn't able to fully enjoy its success, for he suffered a profoundly debilitating stroke in 1983.

But their legacy with *Hello, Dolly!* lives on. Not counting his show-doctoring, Gower Champion was officially associated in one way or another with eighteen Broadway musicals. That means his biographer, John Anthony Gilvey, had hundreds upon hundreds of song titles as the possible title of his book.

What he chose was *Before the Parade Passes By*.

When Rick McKay crafted the opening of his 111-minute documentary *Broadway: The Golden Age,* he had thousands of film and TV clips to choose from.

What he chose was "Before the Parade Passes By."

'Nuff said?

Although *Hello, Dolly!* didn't have a parade song at first, *Funny Girl* almost didn't wind up with a parade song at all.

When composer Jule Styne and lyricist Bob Merrill wrote "Don't Rain on My Parade," they earmarked it as one of the show's first numbers. A young Fanny Brice would rail against her dubious mother and wary neighbors who were discouraging her show business ambitions.

After bookwriter Isobel Lennart couldn't write a solid enough scene to support the song, "Don't Rain on My Parade" was dropped.

It was just another setback for producer Ray Stark, who'd decided in the early '50s that he'd make a film about the star who became his mother-in-law when he married Frances Arnstein in 1939. By the time the '50s were ending, no one in Hollywood had shown enough interest, so Stark started thinking about a stage musical.

He must have felt that he needed some help, for he agreed to co-produce with David Merrick (and would take a "produced in association" credit for Merrick's upcoming production of *One Flew over the Cuckoo's Nest,* too.)

Merrick in turn brought in Broadway's most valuable director-choreographer, Jerome Robbins, who'd given him *Gypsy.* That mastermind had some good ideas—such as moving "Don't Rain on My Parade" to the end of the first act.

Fanny had experienced a lovely night with gamester Nick Arnstein in a posh Baltimore restaurant. Now, however, it was the morning after; both were at the train station, he on his way to New York en route to Europe, and she off to Chicago for her next stop with *The Ziegfeld Follies.*

Just before the reluctant Fanny was to board the train (and soon after she had to deliver the clunky line of dialogue "You can't take an audience home with you"), she abruptly decided that she'd instead follow Nick. When her loyal friend Eddie Ryan urged "Don't," she answered with the stirring song that matched the drama of bringing down a curtain. Broadway once again had one of its favorite themes: love vs. career.

If "Parade" had been dropped, Styne wouldn't have been out too many man-hours of composing. Some of the melody—the part that starts "I'm gonna live and live now" and ends with "Hey, Mr. Arnstein, here I am!"—was originally in his 1961 musical *Subways Are for Sleeping*—at least until rehearsals. There, "A Man with a Plan" had Charlie Smith singing about his new girlfriend, Martha Vail. "Buy her a floor and a door!" went Betty Comden and Adolph Green's lyric. "Buy her a rose, twelve of those!"

Barbra Streisand would receive plenty more than twelve roses for *Funny Girl.* She wasn't quite twenty-two when she opened the show on March 26, 1964; no wonder that hundreds of Broadway observers had doubted that someone so young could pull it off.

Most agreed that two years earlier Streisand had been brilliant when portraying overworked and underloved Yetta Tessye Marmelstein in *I Can Get It for You Wholesale*. At that point, she wasn't even twenty. But there the new-comer had had all of one solo and was heard in three other numbers. What Styne and Merrill had in mind was a tour de force with many more songs, a musical that only a true star could carry.

Well, the show was to be called *Funny Girl*, and what Streisand was singing in her increasingly popular nightclub appearances reiterated what *Wholesale* had proved: The girl was funny.

Actor Barry Dennen saw that early on. Today we remember Dennen for his long tenure as Pontius Pilate in *Jesus Christ Superstar*. Before Streisand washed her hands of him, he suggested that she do a freewheeling and campy version of "Who's Afraid of the Big Bad Wolf?" Expert arranger Peter Matz obliged.

Both men also conceived of a driving, up-tempo rendition of the previously elegant and syrupy "Lover, Come Back to Me" (from the operetta *The New Moon*, yet). The way Streisand giggled after she sang, "When I remember all the little things you used to do," she made clear that she was thinking of sex-ual matters that had never occurred to Nelson and Jeanette.

This was 1962. When singers did Cole Porter, their ballad of choice was either "Night and Day" or "Begin the Beguine"; for an up-tempo number, they opted for "Just One of Those Things" or "You Do Something to Me." Den-nen instead told Streisand to do "Come to the Supermarket in Old Peking" from Porter's dull 1958 TV musical *Aladdin*. The song had made little impres-sion when Cyril Ritchard had sung it, but once again, Streisand with Matz made it sound brand-new and funky.

Those who'd heard about Streisand's act at the Bon Soir and Blue Angel—and Jule Styne was certainly one of them—were often startled once she came onstage. In an era where singers were expected to have faces as pretty as their voices, Streisand was lacking. As Pete Hamill would later famously write in a *Saturday Evening Post* feature, "What there is would hardly launch a thousand ships. Her blowzy, reddish-brown hair slops over a pair of blue eyes that appear crossed, and her nose would fit just as comfortably on Basil Rath-bone."

Ah, but that description could also apply to Fanny Brice.

Still, Stark, Merrick, and Robbins had their doubts about Streisand. *Funny Girl* had to tell the story of Brice's disappointing and tempestuous marriage to Julius W. Arnstein, better known as Nick when he wasn't using six other aliases—including John Adams.

The trio wasn't impressed that Streisand's professional dramatic experience was little more than Millie in *Picnic* at the Malden Bridge Playhouse near Albany and the Butterfly in Karl Capek's *The Insect Comedy* off-off-Broadway.

Styne and plenty of others disagreed. They said that Streisand's nightclub appearances alone indicated that she could handle drama. They pointed anyone who doubted to her signature song—and, yes, at the age of twenty, she already had one: "Happy Days Are Here Again," a three-decades-old barnburner that Streisand sang in a startlingly different way. While it had always been straightforward and celebratory, Streisand's slow and deliberate rendition revealed a survivor who'd worked long and hard to defeat adversity and win happiness. Finally, after a struggle that was touch-and-go for far too long, she had at last emerged exhausted but victorious. And wasn't she also implying that such a setback would never dare to happen to her again?

Equally dramatic was "Cry Me a River." It had always involved a wronged woman who had no intention of forgiving the man who'd cheated on her. However, the contempt that Streisand gave the line "Now you say you *love* me"—virtually spitting out the word "love"—made clear that he had no chance of a second chance.

Compare Streisand's approach to ones taken by such '50s female singers as Patti Page, Gogi Grant, and Kitty Kallen. They relied on their pretty voices to make the words pretty, too. Streisand searched for meaning in the lyrics and then acted accordingly. Wasn't that a strong indication she could do the same with Merrill's lyrics and even Lennart's book?

No matter what bigger star was mentioned for Fanny Brice—and several were—Streisand always stayed in the running. Robbins wanted Anne Bancroft, who said she'd star if *Funny Girl* were a musical *à clef* loosely based on Brice's life and unconstrained by facts. She didn't even want the name Fanny Brice to be used.

Frances Arnstein Stark nipped Bancroft's idea before it could bud. This show was meant to keep her mother's name alive, as indeed it would. How many today would know Fanny Brice had it not been for *Funny Girl*—or, perhaps more accurately, Barbra Streisand?

Ray Stark said he didn't want Bancroft because she had "a lack of humor and warmth." Streisand had those qualities—then, although she would eventually discard them as her career escalated. But Mr. Stark's coolness toward Bancroft may have been another case of a husband yes-dearing his wife. Who'd want to listen to the missus complain each morning, noon, *after*noon, and night that he'd hired the wrong actress?

Not that Ray Stark was nothing in the entertainment world; he'd been a successful agent who counted Richard Burton and Marilyn Monroe among his clients. He was also a co-producer of a Merrick show—*The World of Suzie Wong*—through his Seven Arts Productions. Of course, Merrick had been in charge for that production; who'd be the man in charge here?

Another wrinkle: Bancroft and Merrill had once been an item. Lovers may well be very special people, but these two certainly weren't the luckiest people in the world in the way that the relationship had *not* worked out. Who knows how much sticky romantic residue was left from those days? How often would it impact their professional relationship?

By September 1962, Bancroft was no longer an option—which made Robbins quit. Streisand was still mentioned, but Mary Martin had always been Frances Arnstein Stark's choice. Others around Broadway were saying of Martin, "Funny, she doesn't look Jewish," while noting that Streisand did (and for good reason).

But Martin was leaning toward a musical about another early twentieth-century star: Laurette (*The Glass Menagerie*) Taylor. Interestingly enough, Arnold Schulman, its bookwriter, was taking the path that Bancroft had suggested with *Funny Girl:* change the heroine's name and not be hemmed in by facts. Hence, the musical that might have been *Laurette* became *Jennie*—and Martin's next vehicle.

To be sure, Martin would have sold tickets to *Funny Girl,* but that wouldn't have made her right for it. Stephen Sondheim knew it, too; he'd been courted to write lyrics at the early stages when Martin was mentioned, but couldn't see her doing it, and thus couldn't see himself doing it.

True enough. Consider Fanny Brice as Miss Marmelstein. No problem. Now try Mary Martin in the role. Problem. (Not that Brice or Streisand would have done as well by Nellie Forbush, Peter Pan, or Maria von Trapp.)

No, Martin was not their funny girl, and not because she was approaching fifty. Nevertheless, Frances Arnstein Stark would have taken her, for hagiography and box office seemed to be her first and second orders of business. She was disappointed when *Jennie* jettisoned the possibility.

Interesting: In 1985, Martin performed a one-woman retrospective in which she sang her signature songs and also mused on the hit musicals she'd turned down. She mentioned *Oklahoma!* as well as *Mame, My Fair Lady,* and *Kiss Me, Kate,* but she didn't mention *Funny Girl.* Is that because she assumed the audience wouldn't have been able to picture her as Fanny Brice, while they could have envisioned her in the other roles?

Martin's turndown also impacted her son, Larry Hagman. He was seen and not cast as Fanny's friend Dave (eventually renamed Eddie)—and this at a time when he desperately needed a job. (That would change.)

So Streisand was *still* in the running when another shiksa was approached: Carol Burnett. She was smart enough to state that a Gentile should automatically be disqualified. By now Merrick was even considering moving Georgia Brown from his production of *Oliver!* to *Funny Girl.* At least Brown was Jewish— and if she could handle a musical that serious, she certainly could conquer *Funny Girl*'s Act Two.

Eydie Gormé would have signed on if her husband, Steve Lawrence, had been cast as Nick. We have reason to believe that they and the show would have ultimately succeeded; if Steve-and-Eydie could run the inferior musical *Golden Rainbow* for virtually all of 1968, they undoubtedly could have taken *Funny Girl* to a two- or three-year run.

In February 1963, Streisand suddenly gained ground by releasing a collection of her nightclub hits on *The Barbra Streisand Album.* Her personal life was going well, too; she married her *Wholesale* leading man, Elliott Gould, on March 21, 1963. They moved into Lorenz Hart's old apartment at 320 Central Park West, which she paid for partly from having sung Hart's "I'll Tell the Man in the Street" on her album.

Gould signed to play Gabey in a London production of *On the Town.* Its director-choreographer, Joe Layton, wanted Streisand, too, to play the man-hungry Hildy. Streisand thought she'd better stay close to home in case she needed to prove her mettle on a moment's notice to the *Funny Girl* staff. She would be called back seven times to reaudition. In between, in May, she was asked to the White House to perform "Happy Days Are Here Again"—the

Democratic anthem since Franklin D. Roosevelt's 1932 election—for President John F. Kennedy.

What good publicity. By the time the 1963–64 season officially began on June 1, only thirteen long-playing records in the entire country were selling better than *The Barbra Streisand Album*. A month later, the album cracked the Top Ten.

But would new director Bob Fosse want to work with her? The issue soon became moot, for Fosse suddenly quit—apparently because he heard that Ray Stark was going around town asking people if he'd be the right director for *Funny Girl*. Hey, how many hits had Stark had compared to Fosse's five?

Fosse's quitting enabled one of his previous success stories to get a job: Carol Haney, whom he'd made a semistar in *The Pajama Game* via "Steam Heat" and "Hernando's Hideaway," was hired as choreographer. (Of course one has to ask if Fosse's signature slithering sexual style would have been right for a Ziegfeld-era musical.)

So who could and would direct? Merrick suggested Garson Kanin, who'd staged his near-hit *Do Re Mi* reasonably well. Kanin had actually known Brice, too.

He had one commonality with Robbins and Fosse: All three didn't like that song called "People." Robbins might have been inclined to keep it if Dave and Nick joined in singing with Fanny, but...

The faith that Styne and Merrill had in "People" could be proved by two of their working titles for the show: *A Very Special Person* and *The Luckiest People*. To this day, it's the song most associated with Streisand, who finally got the part on July 25, 1963—just as Gould was closing his eight-week flop *On the Town*.

Streisand started working on her bio. Until she'd opened in *Wholesale*, bios were boilerplate affairs: *I did this show, followed by that show, which was followed by that show.* These laundry lists were so matter-of-fact that few theatergoers bothered to read them.

Perhaps Streisand realized that after she performed "Miss Marmelstein" theatergoers would dive into their *Playbills* to discover who this funny girl was. Thus, Streisand would entertain on the page as well as the stage.

"Not a member of the Actors' Studio," the *Wholesale* bio had begun, which was odd enough. But "Born in Madagascar and reared in Rangoon, she attended

Erasmus Hall High School in Brooklyn" must have made many an eyebrow shoot up.

Some may have smelled a put-on, but Streisand seemed so exotically strange that her attending high school in Brooklyn may have seemed the most difficult part of that sentence to believe. So when *Funny Girl* was being readied, *Theatre Arts* magazine in, alas, what would be one of its final issues (it ceased publication in January 1964 after a forty-eight-year run), published a quick story on Streisand's whimsical approach to bios. It was headlined "Playbull."

Meanwhile, now that Styne and Merrill knew who they were writing for, they could get more specific. "Stiff upper nose, Brice," Streisand sang, referencing her most-talked-about feature. (And don't audiences love when a performer has guts enough to acknowledge a flaw?) This occurred in a reprise of "Don't Rain on My Parade" at the final curtain. It had replaced a song called "I Tried." And while we can't judge a song by its title on a sheet music cover, which title sounds more inherently interesting? There aren't many musicals where the same song closes each act, but *Funny Girl* would be one of them. That's a pretty great accomplishment for a song that had almost been discarded.

While many works deal with career vs. love, this one dealt with career *and* love. Thus, *Funny Girl* needed a dynamic leading man. First choice Christopher Plummer said he'd opt for a different Jule Styne property: *The Ghost Goes West*, which Styne was writing to lyrics by his son Stanley. In actuality, Plummer had his eye on a very different musical, albeit on film. It would turn out to be more successful than *Funny Girl*. Its name was *The Sound of Music*.

Styne wasn't discouraged. He may have qualified as the world's biggest Sydney Chaplin fan, and he got his wish when his star from *Bells Are Ringing* and *Subways Are for Sleeping* decided to do his third Styne musical in fewer than eight years.

It would, however, turn out to be Chaplin's last appearance on Broadway. And on December 12, six days after rehearsals began, Merrick decided that he'd seen the last of his participating in *Funny Girl*. He'd been becoming increasingly aware that he wasn't quite co-producing with Stark, but that Stark felt that he'd taken him on as *his* co-producer. Stark, not Merrick, had hired Merrill and Styne—even though the former had done two shows with Merrick and the latter had done three.

Even in-law blood is thicker than water, so Merrick could never get more than 12½ percent of the show from Stark. He couldn't bear to be second-in-command to a producer who without him had done one show, a flop (*Everybody Loves Opal*). He'd sell his share back to Stark—who was so certain of success that he didn't object to Merrick's steep $150,000 buyout fee.

Rehearsals saw the loss of Fanny's "I Did It on Roller Skates (and I Can't Wait to Do It on Skis)"—which had inspired the show's logo, a roller-skater turned upside down. The drawing turned out to be an apt metaphor, for *Funny Girl* would be turned upside down during its tryout engagements in Boston and Philadelphia.

There'd also be another loss in rehearsals: Allyn Ann McLerie, a veteran of seven Broadway musicals during the past twenty years. Her character of Nora, a Ziegfeld beauty who was there to provide contrast and conflict with the less-than-lovely Fanny, was written out.

Would that have happened had Jerome Robbins still been in charge? He'd cast McLerie in *On the Town* and *Miss Liberty* and had made her his Anita in the 1960 *West Side Story* revival.

"Barbra belts a smash!" ran the headline on the *front-page* review that Alta Maloney of the *Boston Traveler* gave the show on January 13, 1964. Not everyone agreed, including Styne. During his fifty-plus-year career, he was fond of quoting the bromide "Musicals aren't written, but rewritten." He certainly proved it with *Funny Girl,* given that he would later count fifty-six different melodies that he'd written for this score.

Theatergoers filing into Boston's Shubert Theatre three days later found a slip in their *Playbills* with a "Corrected running order of scenes and musical numbers." Comparing the two, they saw that four songs had already been dropped.

Act One saw one excision: "A Temporary Arrangement," in which theatergoers met Nick before Fanny did. As he settled into his new hotel, he sang that his in-flux existence was "a permanent way of life."

Act Two had more deletions: "It's Home," set in the Arnsteins' new Long Island manse; "Took Me a Little Time," where Fanny expressed how she came to see her marriage for what it was; and "Sleep Now, Baby Bunting," in which Nick held little Frances in a basket while Mommy was off performing.

Was the last-named eliminated simply because of what had happened during the Saturday opening? While Chaplin sang "Mommy is a big star!" he'd

35

dropped the basket he was holding, which revealed that nothing was in it. Rather than tax Chaplin, a new song had a male chorus of gamblers come on and sing how Nick had "Larceny in His Heart." After Fanny learned of his chicanery, she'd sing a new song, "What a Helluva Day," to her mother (Kay Medford) back on Henry Street.

Speaking of Henry Street, the song by that name wouldn't be written until Philadelphia; "A Helluva Group" was the original song, replaced by "Block Party," which was in turn replaced by "Downtown Rag," and only then "Henry Street." That Ray Stark had broken his leg and was in a cast for both out-of-town runs was a good metaphor for the state of *Funny Girl*.

One song that surprised many by not staying in was "Something About Me," made to mirror Brice's famous "Baby Snooks," a mischievous but not mean moppet. In the production number, the male chorus members were stethoscope-wearing doctors, and the chorus girls were dressed in pink baby clothes. Out came Brice dressed in blue baby clothes, which made her wonder "Why did the stork in his shipment provide me with extra equipment?"

As the show packed up to leave Boston for the Forrest in Philadelphia, many observers felt that *Funny Girl* still had a painfully long way to go. Sports coaches are fond of telling their players "There's no *i* in 'team' " to stress the group dynamic. Ah, but there is an *i* in "musical," and Streisand decided to become it. She stopped believing in Lennart and Kanin and in effect began supervising—nay, took over—script and direction. Singing "I'm the Greatest Star" day after day after day after day apparently made her believe it.

Kanin wasn't happy that he was forced out, but Streisand wanted Robbins to return, and what Barbra wanted, Barbra got. The deposed director would get a type of revenge sixteen years later when he wrote *Smash*, a novel about a troubled musical, demanding star, and naive producer.

Once Robbins came to Philadelphia and saw that Streisand had done quite well with the role, he decided to show-doctor. Hell, if he had been willing to help the four-alarm disaster *Ankles Aweigh*—which he did—he certainly could do the same for a Styne-Merrill musical with an exciting new personality.

One also had to wonder how Allyn Ann McLerie took the news that Robbins was returning. Did she sit by the phone waiting for his "Please come back" call?

Robbins's presence also meant that Haney's choreographic services were no longer required. And to think that he'd helped make her the toast of the town eight years earlier when co-directing *The Pajama Game.* (Haney died only fifty-four days after *Funny Girl* opened. The official cause of death was not a broken heart but bronchial problems.)

Robbins obviously needed time, but the Forrest had already booked the tryout of *Anyone Can Whistle* that would start on March 2. So Stark made a decision that very few producers have ever made with an out-of-town tryout: He'd move his show to another theater in the same city.

That meant everyone's last choice in Philadelphia: the Erlanger Theatre at Twenty-first and Market Streets. It was an ornate house, but it was out of the way, more than a mile away from the official theater district where the Forrest, Locust, Shubert, and Walnut Street Theatres were all clustered near each other.

Give Stark credit. Many a comparative neophyte would have brought his show right to Broadway to save the cost of a move that had never been part of the budget. Stark, however, wanted to get it right. Coming prematurely to New York might start a word-of-mouth blizzard that *Funny Girl* wasn't that good.

Besides, by that point, Stark knew he'd get a profit from those extra weeks in Philly, what with Streisand's rapturous greeting by the critics, who'd given her plenty of the city's brotherly love. Indeed, the Erlanger run sold out in hours—even on a weekday when people had to trudge to the box office, get in line, and wait their turns.

What's interesting is that Robbins didn't take official credit on the window cards or cast album. One might expect he would, for when *Dylan* wanted to include the song "New York, New York" from Robbins's *On the Town*, he saw to it that the *Playbill* stated it was "used by kind permission of Jerome Robbins."

On March 26, 1964—neither the originally announced February 14 date nor the delayed February 27 debut—*Funny Girl* finally opened at the Winter Garden. Critics couldn't help noticing that this "original" musical was unoriginal: funny girl gets boy, funny girl loses boy, funny girl gets brave about it.

And yet, isn't there a good deal of inherent drama in a wife's wondering, fearing, and dreading what her husband would be like now that he's getting out of prison? That could have made a most compelling song. Lennart instead flashed back to Fanny's show business beginnings, success, and stardom.

How much stronger and gutsier the musical would have been, too, if near the end Fanny had had an introspective song in which she acknowledged her mistake in settling for skin-deep beauty. Eleven years later, Roxie Hart in *Chicago* would recall that she once dated "this well-to-do ugly bootlegger. He used to like to take me out and show me off. Ugly guys like to do that."

Many ugly women feel similarly. *Funny Girl* would have profited from a scene and song in which Fanny acknowledged that Eddie Ryan was the true love of her life, because he believed in her when she was nothing and was drawn to her despite her unattractiveness. Fanny could have broken our hearts when admitting that her constantly being told that she wasn't pretty when she was young skewed her value system at an early age. Her way of becoming attractive was grabbing a groom who "was prettier than the bride"—and look what happened.

McClain didn't mind: "It should be a smash." The others let their reservations fly. Watts: "A disappointing entertainment." Nadel: "It has fallen short of its own potential." Taubman: "It oozes with a thick helping of sticky sentimentality." Chapman: "A solid bio, no doubt." Kerr: "Suppose we settle for a TKO." (That, for those who don't know boxing terms, is the next best thing to a knockout.)

At least they liked it more than Harold Clurman, who said that none of the songs were "any good" and the music was "hogwash." We can't attribute this opinion to senility; Clurman was a mere sixty-two years old. But to paraphrase Susan Johnson in *Donnybrook!*: "Where are your ears?" It's a question to ask of Nadel, too, who said of Styne's work, "It would be nice if one of his melodies could grab you."

Yet everyone immediately appreciated—nay, cherished—Streisand's performance. First and foremost was Kerr's lede: "Everyone knew that Barbra Streisand would be a star, and so she is." Nadel: "Hail to thee, Barbra Streisand." (Funny that he didn't add an exclamation point.) McClain called her "this remarkable young lady" in paragraph two and upped it to "this fabulous young lady" by paragraph nine.

Those who had worried about Streisand's acting ability saw that issue put to rest. Watts said she "sings brilliantly and acts sympathetically." Taubman felt that "she conveys a note of honest emotion underneath the clowning." Styne must have felt particularly validated when reading Chapman—"She handles any kind of song and she is an excellent actress"—for that's what he'd been saying since his trips to the Blue Angel.

During the 1961–62 Tony Awards dinner, Merrick had told Phyllis Newman, featured in his own production of *Subways Are for Sleeping,* that he hadn't voted for her, but for Streisand in his *Wholesale.* We can easily infer that Merrick didn't vote for Streisand in 1963–64, what with his withdrawing from *Funny Girl* and having Carol Channing as her competition. Charity, even for smash hits, begins at home.

And Carol Channing's home is where the Best Actress in a Musical Tony Award went to live.

In his opening-night review of *Funny Girl,* Kerr said of Streisand, "Long may she wave." What Streisand waved was bye-bye to Broadway in favor of roles in nineteen feature films, starting with re-creating Fanny Brice. On her first try, she received an Academy Award, albeit in a tie with Katharine Hepburn for *The Lion in Winter.*

Worth noting: In the early '60s, Streisand lived in an apartment with a rat— yes, a genuine *Rattus norvegicus,* as the scientists say—whom she named Oscar in "honor" of her horrible landlord.

By the *late* '60s, Streisand had a very different Oscar living with her.

And by the late '70s, Barbra Streisand had again played Brice—not on stage, of course, but on film in *Funny Lady,* conceived and co-written by *Jennie*'s Arnold Schulman. John Kander and Fred Ebb wrote a song that perfectly summed up Streisand's experience with *Funny Girl:* "How Lucky Can You Get?" If in the late '50s Stark had gotten financing for his planned movie about Fanny Brice, what would have happened to Streisand?

Something. Something good. Something spectacular. Although she would never again deign to do Broadway, we will see Barbra Streisand's name in this book again and again.

The overture to *Here's Love* didn't start off with a bang.

In fact, when the houselights dimmed, if a theatergoer was still reading Bernice Peck's *Playbill* fashion column "On a Personal Bias"—or if he was talking to the person he'd brought with him—he might not have even noticed that music was already playing.

But when it increased in volume and the house lights went completely dark, many longtime theatergoers must have relaxed and assumed they were in for an excellent show. They were hearing an approaching great parade through the show's exhilarating title song, "Here's Love."

Strangely enough, there was no exclamation point after the show's title. That's odder still given that artist Talivaldis Stubis had created a logo that showed slimmed-down hearts with big red circles underneath—making each look like an exclamation point.

Actually, no exclamation point after the title turned out to be fair warning that *Here's Love* was nothing to get excited about.

Matters didn't seem that way at the outset. *Here's Love* was the musical version of the beloved 1947 movie *Miracle on 34th Street.* Most Americans knew it; even those who hadn't seen the film during its first run had caught up with it, thanks to television's routinely broadcasting it each December. Few didn't know the story of the jolly, bearded, heavyset man who insisted that his name was Kris Kringle, and that he indeed was really Santa Claus.

There he was onstage at the Shubert, courtesy of Laurence Naismith, who'd inherited the part that had won Edmund Gwenn an Oscar. Providing him and all the other characters with dialogue, music, and lyrics was the beloved Meredith Willson. He'd done all these tasks for the Tony-winning smash *The Music Man* in 1957–58, although he'd "only" provided the score to the hit *The Unsinkable Molly Brown* in 1960–61.

All right, the second show wasn't as memorable as the first, but here Willson had a musical that would start with one of the world's great extravaganzas: the Macy's Thanksgiving Day Parade backed by a marching band. And had there ever been a marching band that Meredith Willson didn't like?

But first, as in the film, Kris pointed out a flaw. Here he told a Central Park toy vendor that the reindeer weren't in the order in which they always flew. Soon after, Fred Gaily (Craig Stevens), a young lawyer, walked up the stoop of the building in which he'd just rented an apartment. There he saw a little girl reading: eight-year-old Susan Walker (Valerie Lee), who was waiting for her mother Doris (Janis Paige) to finish supervising the about-to-start Macy's Thanksgiving Day Parade.

Alas, the man hired as Santa had shown up drunk. Kris was even more outraged than Doris. Given that he bore more than a passing resemblance to Santa, she quickly hired him.

Now the Great Parade and the musical could start in earnest. And how could it not be a Great Parade with Michael Kidd choreographing it? He'd already won five Tonys for choreography, which is even more impressive when one realizes that he received those in the first thirteen years of the awards.

Kidd didn't disappoint. He brought on rows and rows of dancers, banjo players, and trumpeters, as well as children who danced on xylophones rolling across the stage. Willson came up with a terrific song in which everyone celebrated "The Big Calown Balloons."

That isn't a typo. Willson enjoyed playing around with words; witness "waddayatalk," "pick-a-little," "shipoopi," and "yazzihampers" in his two previous shows. For whatever reason, he'd decided that these balloons would represent not clowns but *calowns*.

No matter. The song sung by the parade watchers was tuneful, expansive, and rhythmic. As it morphed into dance music, it maintained that excitement, thanks to arranger Peter Howard (who would soon do equally magnificent work on *Hello, Dolly!*).

Howard may have erred, however, by adding a bit of "O Come, All Ye Faithful," "Deck the Halls," and even that 1915 piano novelty hit "Nola." More than one critic would later remark that these old songs were the best in the score.

Still, when the fifteen-minute sequence ended, many longtime theatergoers sat back in satisfaction. The Great Parade had gotten the show off to a terrific start.

But as it turned out, Willson squandered most of the opportunities *Miracle on 34th Street* had given him. Out of the next eleven songs he wrote—not enough to make up a score, really—only two were good, three were adequate, and five were so unmelodic that one wonders how the performers could even learn them. Worse, two of them were irrelevant to the story.

This was truly lamentable, for *Miracle on 34th Street* offered so many possibilities for songs that it could have become a through-sung musical if the genre had existed then. Doris's second-in-command could have sung with glee after he'd discovered someone who greatly resembled Santa Claus in the (Saint) nick of time to replace the drunk. Doris could have had a patter song in which she micromanaged everyone.

Because Doris grew up naively believing that life meant living happily ever after, she wants to protect her daughter, Susan, from making the same assumptions and mistakes. Her single-mindedness extends to ensuring that Susan not embrace fairy tales—especially the one that bilks children into believing in Santa Claus.

Instead of a tender waltz in which Doris cautions Susan not to expect Prince Charming, Willson wrote "Arm in Arm," a mother-daughter bonding song in which both decide that the dirty dishes from dinner can wait until morning to be washed.

The film had already musicalized the scene in which a non-English-speaking Dutch girl was in line at Macy's to see Santa; Kris joined her in a song in her native language. This sequence must have convinced Willson that he was preordained to do this musical. On his radio show that ran from the '30s to the '50s, one of his regulars was folk singer Miranda Marais; she hailed from Amsterdam, so she could provide him with the Dutch lyric to "The Bugle," citing the toy that the little girl wanted.

It turned out to be one of the score's standouts. But it was all of sixty-one seconds long.

When Macy's began telling customers where they could buy products it didn't stock, everyone could have sung "The Store with a Heart." Once the policy proved good for business, store managers could have warbled "You Can't Argue with Success." Kris's statement "Christmas isn't just a day. It's a state of mind" cried out for song, too.

In a way, Willson wrote that one through his title song. "Here's Love" matched a jaunty melody with a laundry list, stating how at least during the Christmas season, rivals and enemies should forget their differences and dispense peace and good will: "Miami to Los Angeles, and Dallas to Fort Worth . . . CBS to NBC." Kris offered the olive branch to Michelob and Blatz, and the army and the navy, as well as Rosh Hashanah and Easter.

If Willson's title song for *Here's Love* made him seem too good to be true, he did sneak in one dour critical comment: "And the devil to Fidel." Of course, he had no way of knowing that more than fifty years later, Castro would still be around, or that many Americans would feel the same way their forebears did in 1963.

And because Hollywood's then-biggest star was soon to embark on her fifth marriage in fewer than fourteen years, Willson sent love from "Elizabeth Taylor to husbands in review." The cast album doesn't reveal that in the theater the orchestra played an extra measure of music to give the audience enough time to laugh at the lyric without having to miss the next line.

The song was generic, but it worked because Kris was singing to a store full of customers he didn't know personally. When he tried to get Susan into the Christmas spirit, Willson should have been more specific—along the lines of Kris's dialogue in the film when he suggested that Susan "travel" to a land called "Imagi-*nation*." With a twinkle in his eye, he said, "How would you like to be able to make snowballs in the summertime? Or drive a bus down Fifth Avenue?" He also cited the joys of being "the Statue of Liberty in the morning and in the afternoon fly[ing] south with a flock of geese. You've got to learn to pretend!"

There's your title. And when Kris teaches Susan to drop her inhibitions enough to pretend to be a monkey—both scratching and making apish sounds for nothing more than the fun of it—there's your dance break.

What Willson wrote instead was a song that began "Expect things to happen like the people in the fairy tales do." The sixteen-syllable phrase got the song off to an awkward start, and the melody that followed did nothing to help.

Musicals are famous for "want" songs, and Susan should have had one. In the film, Kris asked her, "What do you want for Christmas?" and when she responded that she would like "a house with a backyard with a big tree and a swing," Alfred Newman's background score kicked in. When Hollywood composers bring in their music, that's almost a certain hint that there can be a song for that spot. Newman did the advance work, but Willson didn't pick up on it.

Instead, Willson gave Fred a want song *for* Susan. "My Wish," Fred sang, with a dull melody set to many a platitude: "May a star be as bright, as bright as your smile...May your place in the sun bring you peace"—and so on.

The fact that Stevens had a substandard voice didn't help the ballad. Accomplished singers are said to have "money notes." Stevens could have been said to have "bounced check notes."

Meanwhile, fate seemed to be conspiring against Kris, for the authorities wanted to commit him for insisting that he was St. Nick. Fred wanted to represent him in court, but even Santa Claus can get discouraged. "You can't quit!"

the screenplay had Fred say. "You can't let everyone down!" Not only should this have been turned into a song, but it also should have been one that moved the action forward when Kris realized that Fred was right and then made the decision to be stronger than before.

Doris still needed convincing. Perhaps she, too, would have come around at least a little if Fred had been able to sing a song based on his line "Faith is believing in things when common sense tells you not to." Later in the show, when she came to see his way of thinking, she could have reprised it.

Yes, there would be the danger that such a song would have come across as too climb-ev'ry-mountain sentimental or too much of a cheer-upper. But an inspired professional songwriter should have been able to rise to the challenge. Willson instead tried to make us believe that Kris could win over Doris by singing about "Pine Cones and Holly Berries" and other symbols of Christmas. And damn if Doris didn't join him in counterpoint with "It's Beginning to Look a Lot like Christmas."

Oh, *that* comes from this show, you're thinking? That's a *wonderful* song! Indeed it is—as it was in 1951 when Willson wrote it simply for the pop market. Unlike today, when yesterday's pop song is now considered de rigueur in any new score, back then interpolations into Broadway shows were considered bad form. Willson attempted to ameliorate the violation by counterpointing it with a new song.

But a few mentions of holiday garnishes wouldn't crack as tough a nut as Doris and turn her around. That was clear by the next Willson song, in which Fred expressed his frustration with her in a song condescendingly titled "Look, Little Girl." There aren't many ballads that could be said to have a genuinely ugly melody, but this is one of them. And if hearing the doleful melody once wasn't bad enough, Willson had Doris introspectively reprise it.

Now came one of the most embarrassing songs ever to invade a major musical. Fred was in his apartment with his friends while he waited for Doris to arrive. She was already late, and Fred told his "jarhead" buddies why: "She Hadda Go Back," he sang, because "she forgot her gloves." As the song continued, he envisioned Doris always getting sidetracked for some stereotypically feminine reason: putting on perfume, checking her appearance in the mirror, etc.

The result was an insult to women, music, and lyrics. Even a 1963 audience couldn't like Fred when he reduced the woman with whom he was supposedly falling in love to the lowest form of cliché. More to the point, this wasn't a worthy appraisal of a woman who'd risen to executive status in a company that was dominated by men.

Fred also said that his unerring knowledge of the female species would allow him to forecast the precise second Doris would finally arrive. Damn if his doorbell didn't ring at the moment he'd predicted. He opened the door—to a Girl Scout selling cookies.

All that for *that*? And how was this relevant to *Miracle on 34th Street*? Here was a prime example of a show killing time—and killing its story in the process. Frankly, "She Hadda Go Back" seemed to be a song that Willson had in his trunk and used to entertain at parties in his native Iowa.

Just before the Detroit tryout, Willson did come up with a solid winner for the courtroom trial: R. H. Macy took the stand and sang that he'd staunchly come to believe that "That Man Over There" was Santa Claus. But Willson followed it with the *second* most ludicrous song of the season, "My State." For when Fred saw that he was getting nowhere with the judge, he managed to praise Kansas—the state from which the judge hailed. Suddenly everyone was singing a spirited march in honor of the Sunflower State, where "it rains on the wheat" so "the whole world could eat."

An eleven o'clock number that had nothing to do with the plot?

And where was the song when Kris actually delivered to Susan her "house with a backyard with a big tree and a swing"? The girl should have had the chance to show unmitigated joy, but Willson instead pulled his punches and didn't provide the scene where Susan got her wish. The way he chose to end the musical showed that he didn't even buy the anything-can-happen, have-faith message of *Miracle on 34th Street*—for the house in which he put Doris and Fred was merely a display in Macy's window.

Four reviews were not the kind you'd put in Macy's window. Taubman said it "does not soar and does not enchant." McClain just happened to use a homonym for "soar" when he wrote that he was "sorely disappointed." Watts: "Its concentration on benevolence could bring out the beast in you." Kerr: "The evening's comedy is primitive … a careless, coarse, slap-sticky tone in the book is what makes a now-and-then shambles."

Here's good indication that the other critics didn't carry as much influence.

Nadel's "a joyous and bountiful gift of entertainment," Chapman's "all the cogs mesh smoothly," and the *Mirror*'s Coleman's "Don't miss it!" couldn't make the show into a hit.

Producer Stuart Ostrow came to the conclusion that he'd made a mistake by signing an untested Hollywood director, Norman Jewison. He fired him between the Detroit and Washington tryouts and before Philadelphia. As his replacement, Ostrow simply hired himself. Odd that he didn't promote his choreographer to do the job, given that Michael Kidd had already directed four musicals (although *Li'l Abner* was the only hit among them).

Jewison's first attempt at directing for Broadway would be his last. He went to Hollywood, where he was better appreciated, as his seven Oscar nominations and Irving G. Thalberg Memorial Award proved.

The Band Wagon is a fun-filled movie musical, but it does tell one great lie to a naive public. The screenplay has pretentious director Jeffrey Cordova revamp his writers' standard musical comedy into a new version of *Faust*. Out of town it went, and out of town it bombed. So Cordova turned over the reins to another director—but stayed around to see how things would work out.

In the real world, a director who resigns leaves faster than the speed of summer lightning—and a fired director, such as Jewison, leaves even faster. Why stay around and see some of the people you hired avoid looking at you out of pity? Worse, others would look you straight in the eye and bestow doleful or condescending looks.

Here's Love limped through the fall and spring, cherishing every sale it made. It received not a single Tony nomination; only three other musicals that season were shut out, and those ran a total of 113 performances. By spring, Stevens and Paige had bolted and left Richard Kiley and Lisa Kirk to do the dirty work.

Besides, what kind of Christmas musical can't get even one Christmas standard out of an entire score? In three years, Jerry Herman would give birth to one when he wasn't even trying, just writing for the moment in *Mame* when his heroine told her discouraged nephew and employees "We Need a Little Christmas."

Here's Love was able to offer Broadway Christmas in July—at least for the first twenty-five days of the month. But then the Great Macy's Thanksgiving Day Parade came to an end. It was a miracle on Forty-fourth Street that such an awful musical could last 334 performances.

Too bad that *Here's Love* didn't practice what it preached and send people who came to its box office next door to the Broadhurst, where the far more estimable *110 in the Shade* was playing.

Could it have sent them two doors down to the Majestic, where *Anyone Can Whistle* was playing?

Yes—but not for very long.

Did *Whistle* producer Kermit Bloomgarden break a mirror soon after his smash-hit *The Music Man* opened in 1957? By the 1963–64 season, the esteemed Bloomgarden had had almost seven years of solid bad Broadway luck.

Aside from sponsoring a thirteen-month run of Lillian Hellman's *Toys in the Attic* in 1960–61, Bloomgarden had produced six flops. His last musical, *Nowhere to Go but Up* in 1962–63, had the poorest run of all: It had opened on a Saturday night and then closed the next Saturday after nine performances.

Bloomgarden's next musical—*Anyone Can Whistle*—would do the same.

Well, bookwriter Arthur Laurents and composer-lyricist Stephen Sondheim *had* created a most atypical show. Says Lawrence W. Fineberg, an investor in the original production, "Laurents and Sondheim had little choice but Bloomgarden. Merrick said that the show should be modestly produced at a theater like the Booth [the second-smallest on Broadway]. Laurents and Sondheim wanted a bigger show than that, but they might have gone along with him had he not made a bigger demand: Merrick didn't want Laurents to direct.

"They turned to Feuer and Martin, who, after reading the book, said that they didn't even want to hear the score. Saint Subber said the same and produced *Barefoot in the Park* instead. That left Bloomgarden, who had a murderously hard time raising the needed $350,000. It didn't allow for much to promote *Anyone Can Whistle* during its Philadelphia tryout and Broadway run."

How awful for the producer of the already legendary *Death of a Salesman* and *The Diary of Anne Frank*, such respected hits as *The Most Happy Fella* and *Look Homeward, Angel*, and such succès d'estime as *The Crucible* and *A View from the Bridge*. Did Bloomgarden's stable of investors no longer have confidence in him? Or had too many died?

Those who'd survived must have looked forward to examining the prospectus. Laurents and Sondheim had previously worked together on two household-name musical classics: *West Side Story* and *Gypsy*. After those, Sondheim had provided the entire score for the Tony-winning musical *A Funny Thing Happened on the Way to the Forum*.

Ah, but Sondheim had only written lyrics to the first two hits, whose music was respectively written by the more highly regarded Leonard Bernstein and Jule Styne. Sondheim's music for *Forum* had not been particularly well received (although that consensus would change over time). And now he'd again try to write music?

West Side Story and *Gypsy* could each boast direction by the already legendary Jerome Robbins. Merrick wasn't the only one who was wary about Laurents directing. Conventional wisdom insists that those who stage their own works often become myopic about problems in their beloved scripts.

Merrick had already hired Laurents as director in 1962 for *I Can Get It for You Wholesale* (which Laurents had not written). Credit where it's due, Laurents did a solid job of staging the dark musical. It didn't turn out to be a moneymaker, but few on Broadway thought that anyone could have done a better job of directing it.

Laurents's biggest contribution to *Wholesale* was his sharp eye in casting that aforementioned newcomer Barbra Streisand. If Laurents could have his way, he'd work with her again and make her his quirky lead character.

Robbins had also choreographed *West Side Story* and *Gypsy*, but *Whistle* would rely on Herbert Ross for its dances. Ross certainly had Broadway experience, for he'd choreographed eight Broadway musicals—but all had failed. Ross might have been more depressed if he'd been told then that his next show after *Whistle* would be *Kelly*, which would run one-ninth as long.

Ross was also somewhat responsible for another early problem. Ming Cho Lee, an up-and-coming set designer, was hired, but when he showed Ross a model, the choreographer said the set wouldn't allow him room enough for dances. After Lee took his model and went home, Laurents hastily recruited the highly regarded William and Jean Eckart to take over.

A similar setback occurred with musical direction. Sondheim wanted Lehman Engel to conduct, but Bloomgarden preferred Herbert Greene. Bloomgarden relented and hired Engel, but was haunted by his disloyalty to Greene, who'd been his musical director since *The Music Man* (which Greene had not-so-incidentally also co-produced).

Engel eventually felt the ill will and left, but Bloomgarden didn't have an easy time getting the man he wanted. Greene didn't mind overseeing an orchestra that contained a second fiddle, but he hated being cast in that role by Sondheim. Still, he signed on.

Stumbling blocks such as these so early in the process usually point to a show that won't succeed or even get on. Bloomgarden barely avoided the latter fate by taking on newcomer Diana Krasny as co-producer. She would later become more famous for hooking up professionally and romantically with the thirty-years-older Herman Shumlin, who was at the time busy producing and directing *The Deputy*, a play that would become even more controversial than *Whistle*.

Krasny, too, had trouble selling the show to her backers. Laurents and Sondheim had established on their script's title page that this would not be standard commercial fare. In an era where the usual under-the-title sobriquets were "a new musical" (*Funny Girl; Here's Love*), "a new musical comedy" (*Foxy; Café Crown; Hello, Dolly!*), or even "a new musical play" (*110 in the Shade*), *Anyone Can Whistle* rejected all these boilerplate descriptions and proudly proclaimed that it was "a wild musical."

Yes, but an experimental show gives everyone license to experiment. This can mean that few will be on the same page, but it also suggests that there will be much trial (and tribulations) and error.

Like Feuer, Martin, and Subber, many money men and women turned down the show after reading the script (or, more likely, *some* of the script). But backers always have a tougher time with original musicals. Investors considering *Hello, Dolly!* might well have remembered seeing *The Matchmaker* on Broadway during its 1955–57 run or the 1958 film version; each provided a frame of reference. Similarly, those who pondered putting money into *Here's Love* could recall the warmth they felt when seeing *Miracle on 34th Street*. Although Laurents's story involved both a romantic match and a miracle, it wasn't a business-as-usual musical—and that type of musical doesn't always do business.

Case in point: *Anyone Can Whistle* started out with the Narrator intoning, "This town manufactured a product that never wore out. This is what happened." The stage direction then stated, "Immediately, a building falls down; a crack appears in the façade of City Hall; the Hotel Superbe's sign teeters at an angle; and signs fly in reading 'Closed,' 'Vacancy' and 'Help!' "

A musical about the need for planned obsolescence? That would be a first. (And a last.)

Backers' auditions—nearly three dozen of them—saw would-be angels fly away once they heard Sondheim's atypical score. A musical that contained a song called "Simple" was anything but. "Song" is quite the understatement, for "Simple" lasted a quarter hour—literally unheard of then in Broadway musicals. This piece alone must have made potential financiers who watched and listened in the various apartments and ballrooms display when-will-this-end glazed smiles on their faces.

Goddard Lieberson, president of Columbia Records, had done quite nicely by the *Gypsy* and *West Side Story* cast albums (not to mention the latter's soundtrack, which had stayed on the charts for three years—and *fifty-four weeks* at No. 1). Nevertheless, even Lieberson would put only an undisclosed "token investment" in *Whistle*.

Eventually, however, the needed monies were scraped together. Exhibit A that the production had little to spare: If producers want a picture of their show on a *Playbill* cover, they pay extra. For the Philadelphia tryout, Bloomgarden and Krasny saved by opting for a no-extra-cost generic shot of an audience watching a show.

That picture showed a fuller audience than the Forrest Theatre would see during the March 2–21, 1964, break-in. Not that grossing $46,000 and change out of a potential gross of $65,000 is so bad. But even then, musicals were expected to do better than 70 percent capacity while out of town.

A frequent observation made about *Whistle* is "It was ahead of its time." It certainly was in that it called attention to itself that it was a musical. In recent years, we've see this routinely happen in *Monty Python's Spamalot* ("Whatever happened to my part?"), *Urinetown* ("I don't think too many people are going to come see this musical"), and *The Producers* (Ulla's observation that Bloom moves "so far downstage right").

For better or worse, *Anyone Can Whistle* got there first. After Mayoress Cora Hooper Hoover did her opening number with her four-man chorus (patterned after Kay Thompson's famous act with the Williams Brothers), Laurents's stage direction said that "Cora gives the last boy a playful little shove so that she can take the bow for the number alone." Later, "Cora, who's been struggling to get a glove on, holds up her hand for everything to stop. And it does, both music and scenery." At another moment, a child named Baby Joan ostensibly delivered a miracle—a rock suddenly started spouting water—before the stage direction had the kid "return to the footlights" where she'd "curtsey modestly."

Today such shenanigans are more widely accepted, because many ignorant attendees believe that musicals are silly anyway, so why not make them as ridiculous as possible? In those days, musicals were considered loftier entertainment, so some Philadelphians thought that Laurents and Sondheim were lowering the bar, while the creators in turn liked that they were giving musical theater a hotfoot.

The miracle brought Nurse Fay Apple into town. This was the role that Laurents wanted for Streisand, but, as we've seen, she opted for a different 1963–64 musical.

In her place was Lee Remick, now an Oscar-nominated Hollywood star. Fine, but Remick's total Broadway experience was a five-performance appearance eleven years earlier in a poorly received comedy.

So could she sing?

The audience wouldn't immediately know. As the Narrator blatantly explained at the top of the show, "Our girl won't be along for eleven minutes." And when she did come on, in her first song she stated, "The play isn't over by a long shot."

Already some Philadelphians were regretting that.

Fay was the local asylum's nurse, who brought her charges into town on the off-chance that the rock's water would have curative powers. The influx of tourists and pilgrims were wary of these "Cookies," as they were condescendingly called. Cora wanted them all returned to the asylum that she disparagingly termed "the Cookie Jar."

Speaking of Cookies, Angela Lansbury had made a name for herself by portraying tough ones throughout her twenty-plus-year career. Lansbury had received her first Oscar nomination in 1944 for playing a supercilious maid in *Gaslight;* her most recent Academy Award nod was in 1962 for her evil clandestine Communist mother in *The Manchurian Candidate.*

And while Laurents and Sondheim may have missed Lansbury's unfeeling mother in the latest Elvis Presley vehicle, *Blue Hawaii,* they knew that she was Hollywood's go-to bitch. Wouldn't she be ideal for Cora, who occasionally referred to herself in the third person or said to an underling, "You are at my disposal—like garbage"? Comptroller Schub said that he was "the most important man in town—next to the mayoress." In essence, Cora agreed with him: "No wonder you have a lady mayor, you male impersonators," she snarled.

Laurents tried to leaven this by making Cora bubble-headed as well. She called her chief of police "a nymphomaniac," and while her point may have been that he was womanish, nothing in the script indicated that he possessed a voracious sexual appetite; that flaw was given to Schub.

Sondheim wrote, "Laugh at the kings or they'll make you cry," and Cora was worth laughing at. Even if a new idea was inscrutable, she'd brand it "Brilliant!" simply because it was new.

"Brilliant" is what Laurents and Sondheim thought Lansbury could be. Their cold-call letter to her resulted in her accepting the role.

But could *she* sing?

Lansbury would eventually win four Best Actress in a Musical Tonys. But a listen to *Whistle*'s cast album and then her next one—*Mame*—shows a marked difference. With each new musical, Lansbury became more confident in her singing, but her voice in *Whistle* wasn't yet at full potential.

Still, before rehearsals began, Lansbury was miffed that Fay had five songs and Cora a mere four. She demanded another, and Sondheim went to work and came up with "A Parade in Town." We have Lansbury to thank for it.

(And to think that *Dolly* and *Whistle* got their iconic parade songs on the road, and *Funny Girl* almost lost its second-most-recognizable song before it hit the road.)

Back to the plot. Fay expressed some doubts about the miracle—which Schub didn't want to hear. He'd already been planning to manufacture statuettes of Baby Joan in "small, medium and life-sized," so he wasn't going to give up his possible prosperity that easily.

So Schub went into attack mode. "You're in love with science," he accused Fay. "You can't believe in anything that can't be proved in a laboratory." Schub knew that such an approach would work with the "sane" people around him: Many an average person believes that people who have faith are automatically good and people who don't have it are inevitably bad; the more faith a person has, the better a person he's perceived to be.

Laurents and Sondheim knew better.

In fact, audiences learned soon after Baby Joan's curtsey that Schub was the one who believed more in science. He'd gone into a cave and placed in it a surreptitious pump from which the water would flow. Some "miracle."

Fay responded to Schub with a harangue that contained more than two dozen phrases and sentences— even more than King Arthur shouted at the end of the first act of *Camelot*. Remick then followed it with "There Won't Be Trumpets," a song that sounded shrill to 1964 ears.

Don't blame Remick; her voice, while small, was decent. It would have been better still had she not been battling a bout of tonsillitis.

What *else* could go wrong?

And while "tonsillitis" might seem to be an excuse given to the media by *Whistle*'s press agent, Remick proved she was genuinely afflicted, for soon after the run she had her tonsils removed.

After the long speech and song, Cora & Co. realized that the so-called insane (mere nonconformists, really) were mixing unobtrusively with the so-called sane pilgrims. Alas, no one could tell who should be allowed to walk the streets and who should be committed. (Laurents and Sondheim had been around show business long enough to have met many supposedly sane people about whom they had their doubts.)

Then J. Bowden Hapgood arrived. Management and creators wanted Keith Michell for the role, but Bloomgarden and Krasny—no surprise—couldn't meet his price. They had to settle for Harry Guardino, who'd recently been nominated for his second Golden Globe Award for *The Pigeon Who Took Rome*.

But could *he* sing?

Absolutely not.

Still, Guardino had the swagger, confidence, and authority needed for the role of an eminent psychiatrist who'd be welcomed by the townspeople. (The town's resident psychiatrist fully admitted that he couldn't recognize his patients' faces because he only saw them "when they are lying down." Well, there goes the good word-of-mouth from the actual psychiatrists who'd see the show....)

Hapgood ostensibly weeded the sane from the insane in the aforementioned "Simple," filtering mumbo-jumbo wordplay through his savoir faire. That approach intimidated most everyone, so few questioned that much of what he said was meaningless: "The opposite of safe is out. The opposite of out is in. So anyone who's safe is in."

Even ardent *Whistle* fans may not be acquainted with those three lines, for they don't appear on the cast album. As impossible as it may seem, "Simple" was even longer in the theater than it is on the thirteen-minute album cut. Sondheim apparently felt that he needed that much time to make comments on the way Americans perceived race, color, creed, religion, and life in general.

So "Simple" was purposely filled with many a cliché: "Beauty is skin deep." "Ours is not to reason why; ours is but to do or die." "I am the master of my fate and the captain of my soul." Sondheim didn't call each a cliché but used the synonym "watchcry." That may have been another mistake; "watchcry" was a word with which much of the audience was unfamiliar.

The one watchcry that Sondheim didn't use, however, was one that expressed how many in the audience felt after Hapgood judged some people sane, then he changed his mind: "Fool me once, shame on you; fool me twice, shame on me." By now, many theatergoers were more interested in when the strange song would end and less concerned with what it had to say.

Did Laurents and Sondheim realize the cruel irony that one of their working titles for the show—*The Natives Are Restless*—was now referring to the audience?

Finally, "Simple" and Act One concluded with Hapgood's deciding "You are all mad"—and he didn't just mean pilgrims and Cookies. With a finger-point, he included the audience in his diagnosis.

Actually, if one defines "mad" in the colloquial sense—meaning *angry*—then, yes, Hapgood had a point; many in the audience had become genuinely incensed at what they'd seen.

Some wondered why no love story had emerged. Wasn't every musical supposed to have one? Ah, but Act Two quickly got to it. Hapgood was visited by Fay—but only in a manner of speaking. She had donned a wig and a French accent, both of which suddenly made her feel freer. Sondheim wrote a nice pastiche here, "Come Play Wiz Me," with a fun lyric twist at the end: *"Mais oui*—we may!"

Even words as mundane as "Bonjour" had English translations amusingly projected onto the back wall by a subtitle machine. Laurents complained that the device didn't work efficiently because it was cheaply made. Eventually he and Bloomgarden came to blows—literally—over this and other issues.

What *else* could go wrong?

Laurents rewrote to make clearer that people who adopt a new identity often allow themselves to become in effect different people when encountering those who don't know them. Workaday Fay became the exotic "Lady in Red from Lourdes."

Fay still wasn't quite who she wanted to be, though, for shedding all inhibitions is never a simple task. Fay wanted to whistle—the perfect metaphor for being happy-go-lucky and free 'n' easy—but she couldn't. "You can't take lessons in whistling," Fay mourned (which is *almost* correct).

Sondheim's title song was one of the most beautiful of the season and would remain a highlight of his entire career. In it, he strangely had Fay sing "I can dance a tango"—an odd image, given that that dance suggests a greater uninhibited freedom than whistling.

Fay bedded Hapgood. Theatergoers who'd seen plenty of onstage beds had never witnessed one like this; its headboard, as the stage direction said, could "light up like a pinball machine when the activity warrants." And it did—although it sometimes said "Tilt." (Yeah, sex is sometimes like that—especially with people who can't whistle.)

Soon Laurents was again commenting on average citizens who lead lives of all-too-quiet desperation. "If he weren't a psychiatrist, I'd swear he knew what he was doing." "Machines are getting to be as bad as people." "I was a practicing idealist. Now *that's* mad." Hapgood said the only real miracle was "being alive" (a sentiment that Sondheim would stress the next time he wrote a full score).

Not that Laurents wasn't above making room for a little shtick:

Cora: Don't panic.
Schub: Don't *you* panic.
Cora: But we must do something.
Schub: Of course we must do something.
Cora: I am doing something.
Schub: What?
Cora: I'm panicking.

This formulaic joke got one of the biggest laughs of the night.
The real business at hand was expressed in Sondheim's countercultural

"Everybody Says Don't." Hapgood commented on Fay's inability to be completely herself because she felt constrained by society's many rules. He urged her to "make a noise" and rebel: "I say *don't*—don't be afraid."

Many Philadelphians had endured the Depression, World War II, the atom bomb, Korea, McCarthyism, and the Cold War; all those experiences were enough to make them toe the line so that they could keep the necessities and luxuries they felt they'd painfully earned. So when both the sane and the insane sang, "We like questions," that was the difference between them and the audience. "The Greatest Generation" would leave any revolution to its successors—the baby boomers who'd been indulged from birth and eventually dared to question authority.

Here's where *Whistle* was most ahead of its time. Trouble is, baby boomers hadn't yet aged themselves into theatergoers.

Philadelphia had a hard time understanding why a character called Telegraph Boy sported a long white beard. (He was, incidentally, played by Alan Johnson, who in four years would choreograph "Springtime for Hitler" for *The Producers*.) Putting an old woman into a straitjacket was bad enough, but then to shunt her into a cage? Even a charming remark such as Hapgood's saying, "Usually, I walk, but when I don't want to get anywhere, I dance," didn't land.

Actually, dancing would be the only department in which *Anyone Can Whistle* did land and would be uniformly lauded. The show's one Tony nomination would go to Ross for his choreography, thanks to two important ballets, both of which were composed by Sondheim—which was another departure. Usually a Broadway composer leaves dance music to someone else, but Sondheim was so committed to the project and inspired by it that he opted to do that job, too.

The first ballet occurred after Hapgood had encouraged Fay to destroy her patients' records. "That's tearing up people," she complained. "Most people would like to be torn up and set free," he insisted. Fay started ripping, and the Cookies started dancing freely, for they could finally, as the stage direction dictated, "be what they want." So too did Fay "dance freely and happily" before she walked toward Hapgood as the Act Two curtain fell.

Some theatergoers must have accepted this as a happy ending and wondered why no curtain calls followed.

Because Act Three was coming.

Not for everyone. Many in the Forrest who indulgently stayed for Act Two now took the second chance to unobtrusively leave.

But some who stayed may have later told those who'd bolted that they'd missed an even greater ballet. Although "The Cookie Chase" has at least survived through Sondheim's music on the cast album, that's scant consolation. The dance in which the so-called sane were captured and the so-called insane escaped has been irretrievably lost.

Cora and Fay then sang "There's Always a Woman." Each damned a member of her own sex as "a run in the stocking, the snag in the zipper ... it's Jacqueline the Ripper" before deciding "There's nothing as low as a woman."

Such misogyny! And while Cora and Fay each invited the other to lunch, both revealed their real feelings in asides. Cora surreptitiously called Fay a "sneak, cheat, frump, bore, leech," and "witch," while Fay deemed Cora a "thief, crook, fake, bag, crone," and "ghoul." All this was set to a melody that seemed to be a demented waltz version of "Once in a Lifetime" from the previous season's *Stop the World—I Want to Get Off.*

Stop the show—the Philadelphians who'd remained in their seats wanted to get out. All right, every show must have a villain, and Cora, especially with Lansbury in the role, fit the bill. Even in one of her happiest numbers she joyfully made the statement "There isn't a murder I couldn't commit." And when she discovered that Fay had destroyed the town's medical records, she pointed to the nurse's eiderdown coat and told her subordinates, "Get the tar. You can use her own feathers."

So Cora's duplicitousness in "There's Always a Woman" felt right. But *et tu,* Fay? Until this moment, theatergoers could at least try to root for Fay, for she seemed to be nice and was the closest person with whom they could identify. Now she was drawn to be as deceptive as Cora. That was too much. So was Hapgood's criticism of average people when he said of the miracle, "They need it! You could lead them by the hand into this cave, show them that electric pump and they would still say it's a miracle."

As Act Three was still offering a bit of back-and-forth on who was crazy and who wasn't, Laurents and Sondheim metaphorically made their audiences crazy when they had Hapgood admit to Fay that he was no doctor. He'd simply been taken for one and let the label take hold without correcting it. He was actually—yes!—a Cookie.

That possibility had never dawned on Cora and her cohorts. They had a shrewder plan, anyway: to smear Hapgood as an "Enemy of God" and an "Enemy of the Church." Soon the town was using such colorful terms as "Communist! Fascist! Red!" and going all the way to "Egghead!"

Laurents was remembering when he was blacklisted during the McCarthy witch hunts. When he had Fay grimly say, "And after the way they worshipped you," he may have been recalling 1950 through 1954, when he wasn't asked to write the screenplay for a single film.

And after the way they worshipped you. Laurents and Sondheim, once the recipients of raves, would now know how Hapgood felt. The Philadelphia reviews were, as Sondheim recalls to this day, "humiliating." Said one critic, "It hasn't got a clear idea of what it wants to do or even what direction it means to take."

Sondheim and Laurents didn't give up. They decided that Fay's opening speech and song were overkill and one had to go. In a move one wouldn't expect in a musical, "There Won't Be Trumpets" walked the plank while the speech stayed. "There's Always a Woman" was also excised.

Meanwhile, Lansbury knew full well that there had been some discussion of her being replaced by Nancy Walker. That was more than mere talk, she discovered, when she saw Walker seated in front of her at one performance.

Ironically, Lansbury would profit from a cast member's becoming deathly ill and being forced to leave. Sondheim insists that's what happened after Henry Lascoe, playing Schub, had a heart attack. "Lascoe, an old pro if there ever was one," wrote Sondheim in his lyric collection *Finishing the Hat,* "had made [Lansbury] feel like an amateur. The minute his much less confident understudy [Gabriel Dell] took over, she felt free to blossom, which she spectacularly did."

No such happy fate awaited the musician who was crushed by a dancer who stumbled into the pit. While Lascoe took nearly six months to die, the musician lasted only a week.

What *else* could go wrong?

After twenty-four performances, the show left Philadelphia. As Bloomgarden and Krasny were again faced with the extra expense of putting a photo of the production on the *Playbill,* they continued to pinch pennies. At least the program had a different look; New York generic *Playbills* preferred an out-of-focus photograph of traffic on a busy street.

Forty-fourth and Eighth Avenue was not a busy corner during *Anyone Can Whistle*'s previews, so Laurents and Sondheim begged Bloomgarden and Krasny for a postponement. By now, both producers had seen the show and its audiences enough times to know that no amount of work would turn it into a hit. Besides, it wasn't even a case of spending good money after bad; there was simply no money at all.

If daring subject matter wasn't enough, *Whistle* was profane—in a manner of speaking. No Broadway musical to this point had ever dared to use the word "shit." Even the notorious Mr. Glick in *What Makes Sammy Run?* would only tell an enemy "Go spit in your hat." But now, *Whistle* would come the closest by having Hapgood say "merde" in the scene where he and Fay spoke in pidgin French.

Four years later, the English translation of "merde" would be introduced in *Hair*; the profanity soon became so ho-hum that it was even included in a Richard Rodgers musical, *Two by Two,* in 1970. But then would be then, and now was now.

The fake miracle was pinned on Hapgood. Fay was furious with him for pulling her this much out of her shell without easing her out all the way. And there was a "Here we go again" ending, thanks to a nearby town that got its own miracle. The message was that people have short attention spans and easily abandon what had so recently fascinated them, just to move on to the new hot thing and the latest stupidity.

Fay sang that she admired Hapgood's "imperturbable perspicacity," and Laurents and Sondheim exhibited precisely that. Hapgood told Fay, "And if you fail, you fail," and to many audiences and critics, Laurents and Sondheim had. In "A Parade in Town," Cora asked, "While I was getting ready, did a parade go by?" It did for Taubman, Kerr, and Watts. When they encountered Cora and her lackeys, townspeople, and pilgrims in *Anyone Can Whistle,* they did not parade but panned.

Taubman: "There is no law against saying something in a musical, but it's unconstitutional to omit imagination and wit." Kerr: "An exasperating musical... Forget it." Watts: "Ponderously heavy-handed and clumsily vague... meandering, devious and not very enlivening in its humor... an unfortunate letdown."

One can only imagine the looks on Sondheim's and Laurents's faces when they read Chapman. "An unusual, far-out musical with a briskly syncopated score, educated lyrics, original and frisky dances, waltzing scenery and an imaginative story" put smiles on their faces until they read "which the cast and I had to cope with rather strenuously."

Their smiles, however, stayed put when they read all twelve paragraphs that Nadel and McClain each wrote. Sondheim's lyric saying that "any parade in town without me must be a second-class parade" was felt by Nadel and Mc-Clain, who believed that Broadway would be second-class without this show. Wrote the former, "You have no idea how many breath-taking surprises are in store for you," while the latter raved, "It is fey and fantastic and I believe it will give you a happy escapist evening" and predicted it would provide "the sweet smell of money."

Not at all. The twenty-four-performance Philadelphia run would surpass the run in New York—even if one counts the twelve previews. *Whistle,* in fact, would be one of the first Broadway shows to play more previews than actual performances.

More to the point, the gross for the one full week was $35,675. Suddenly that $46,683 in the last week at the Forrest looked very good—and that was achieved at lower ticket prices than Broadway's. No other 1963–64 musical that tried out in Philadelphia grossed more there than in New York.

Bloomgarden and Krasny saw no wisdom in spending more money on ads that trumpeted quotations from less influential critics. Without endorsements from the almighty Taubman and Kerr, some people—ironically, the type that *Whistle* was indicting—would assume that the show couldn't possibly be any good. Laurents and Sondheim paid for an ad in the *Times;* as a result, the show cost them even more.

And Sondheim's score? Taubman: "Several pleasing songs, but not enough of them to give the musical wings." Kerr: "The lyrics worked long and assiduously to drive the social lessons home." Watts: "The score suffered from the composer's determination to escape any accusation of giving the audience a good, lively tune."

In other words, there's not a tune that makes you go bum-bum-bum-di-dum.

But Chapman liked this "briskly syncopated score with educated lyrics." Even McClain, who loved the show, admitted that "the score may not be immediately ingratiating, but the lyrics were bright and original." Nadel wrote that "Sondheim's music and lyrics deserve an entire review in themselves"—and meant it as a compliment.

The most prescient critic of all turned out to be *Billboard*'s Mike Gross. He said that *Anyone Can Whistle* "strays from the Broadway formula with an imaginative flair that will take time to catch on."

It did—but what an afterlife *Anyone Can Whistle* has had in the last half century. Much credit goes to Goddard Lieberson, who was under no contractual obligation to record a show that ran so short a time—but he did. His admiration for the score had to be immense, for he even had Remick do "There Won't Be Trumpets." How many producers of cast albums bother to record the cut songs?

Alas, in those days when a vinyl record was lucky to reach an hour in length, time constraints forced Lieberson to remove "There Won't Be Trumpets" from the album as well. Remick's recording had to wait until May 1988, when the compact disc's greater time allowance could restore the song to its original spot.

Yes, twenty-five years later, the original cast album of *Anyone Can Whistle* was still being manufactured. No other musical that failed to hit double figures in performances has ever been released as an LP, cassette, both four- and eight-track tape, CD, and download.

The recording certainly kept the show alive, but Random House published the text in hardback, too. Not long after it went out of print, a small publisher reissued it. Music Theatre International secured the license for the amateur market, and still leases it.

Janet Hayes, who appeared as part of "Simple," years later started the York Theatre Company and made *Whistle* one of her first Sondheim revivals. A concert version played Carnegie Hall in 1995 with Bernadette Peters (Fay), Scott Bakula (Hapgood), and Madeline Kahn (Cora). Not only was "There Won't Be Trumpets" included, but "There's Always a Woman" was, too.

Lansbury was on hand to emcee. "Welcome to a town that's so broke that only a miracle could save it," she started out, conveying the subtext that she was speaking about New York City, too. After the audience realized the joke and laughed, she added, "Thirty-one years ago, I myself was the mayoress of such a town—for a very short term."

Having a much longer life is a Kingston, New York, firm that deals in whistles and calls itself—yes—Anyone Can Whistle. Granted, after all these years, there's still a Manhattan eatery called Hello, Deli! But how many musical flops become famous enough to get a non-show-biz concern named after them?

David Merrick saw his musical production of *The Matchmaker* do substantially better than his musical production of *The Rainmaker*.

Dolly, as we've seen, stayed around Broadway for nearly seven years; *110 in the Shade* could run only a little more than nine months. And while it did pay back after a modest national tour, it should have done better than a 34 percent return. Composer Harvey Schmidt and lyricist Tom Jones wrote an excellent score to N. Richard Nash's adaptation of his own play.

The title may have impacted business. Hits usually have titles that celebrate their characters (*The Phantom of the Opera; Cats; The Lion King*) or where they take place (*Chicago; 42nd Street; La Cage aux Folles*).

Aside from the 1939 flop *Very Warm for May*, how many musicals have given a weather report in their titles? (And *Very Warm for May* was actually about a girl named May whose misadventures got her into hot water. Matters got very warm for May.)

"We wanted to call it *Rainbow*," says Schmidt. "The Rodgers and Hammerstein office told us that Oscar had written a show by that name."

Yes, thirty-five years earlier, and it ran for all of twenty-nine performances. No one would have remembered.

But did people remember *The Rainmaker* to the point where it had been overexposed? Plenty had seen the original 1952 TV production, and some more had attended the subsequent Broadway play during its modest 125-performance run in 1954–55. Then at the end of 1956 came the very successful film version.

Katharine Hepburn received an Oscar nomination for her Lizzie Currie, the most prominent potential "old maid" in a '30s midwestern town. She was taken with Deputy File (Wendell Corey), who'd been divorced and was afraid of another commitment.

These two wouldn't be pushed together until Starbuck, "the Rainmaker" (Burt Lancaster) showed up. Because the citizens had been enduring a terribly long drought, Starbuck knew that they were desperate for any solution to the problem—including his claim that he could bring rain.

Lizzie's younger (and not-too-bright) brother, Jimmie, believed him. Her father H. C. (Will Geer) had his doubts but was willing to take a chance and pay Starbuck's $100 fee. Lizzie's older brother, Noah, was disgusted by their father's decision, but Lizzie was the most infuriated of all.

Starbuck was smart enough to exploit his enemy's weakness. He hit Lizzie where she *didn't* want to live—in her father's home, unmarried, childless, and a glorified housekeeper. He did come to be quite fond of her, however, so when File and the law came bearing down on him for his previous cons, he begged Lizzie to leave with him. That spurred File into action, and Lizzie, who all her life couldn't get one man, suddenly had two vying for her.

Mentioned for the musical was—here we go again—Barbra Streisand. Considering the way her looks were regarded in 1963, she would seem to have been right for a potential old maid. But would a prairie take a Jewish girl?

Instead, Inga Swenson, late of *New Faces of 1956,* would finally get a chance to establish herself. She'd most recently been standing by for Julie Andrews in *Camelot.*

Merrick signed Hal Holbrook for Starbuck and was happy with his choice—until he heard that Richard Rodgers had ceased collaborating on *I Picked a Daisy* with all-too-slow lyricist Alan Jay Lerner (who morphed it into *On a Clear Day You Can See Forever*). Now Robert Horton, then a TV star on the top-rated *Wagon Train* and earmarked as *Daisy*'s leading man, was suddenly available.

Two weeks before *110* rehearsals began, Merrick grabbed Horton. Said Holbrook, "Under the rules of Equity at that time, Merrick could hire as many actors as he wanted for a certain role, but then could give one the part, and have the others stand by—which I certainly wasn't interested in doing in that point of my career. Back then, Equity didn't have a law against that, but thanks to my wonderful lawyer, they now do. I got a settlement—but I'd much rather have got the show."

Merrick's dirty trick did leave Holbrook free to join the new Repertory Theater of Lincoln Center; there, he got two solid seasons of work, which was one more than *110* would have given him.

Perhaps the property *was* overexposed. But on the other hand, wasn't *The Matchmaker* equally as overly familiar? It had opened more than a year after *The Rainmaker* on Broadway, and, with 486 performances under its belt, had run nearly four times as long as Nash's play. It had a film version, too, in 1958, although it didn't do the business that *The Rainmaker* did.

Still, while *110* had opened fewer than seven years after *The Rainmaker*'s movie, *Dolly* had debuted fewer than six. Each property would seem to have had the same danger of having audiences say, "Oh, we just saw that."

But the difference is that *110* had N. Richard Nash writing the book and Joseph Anthony directing, while *Dolly* had Michael Stewart on book and Gower Champion running the show.

This isn't just a case of the Nash-Anthony team not being as talented or accomplished as Stewart-Champion, although a case could certainly be made for that, too. And if one questions Anthony's abilities with musicals—he was then most famous for his still-running comedy smash *Mary, Mary*—remember that he'd directed *The Most Happy Fella,* too.

But *The Rainmaker* on stage and on film were both Nash-Anthony collaborations, too. Their since-day-one experience with the property might have meant an in-place template that prevented them from reimagining the show. Yes, they brought on Snookie, Jimmie's would-be girlfriend, who had merely been mentioned in the original play. But she had appeared in the film version.

Conversely, Stewart and Champion were new to *The Matchmaker,* so both men greeted the play with fresh eyes, from which any musical adaptation can profit. Granted, one decision had been already made for them by *Matchmaker*'s screenwriter, John Michael Hayes: drop Wilder's final act, which, truth to tell, always seemed superfluous. The director of the *Matchmaker* film was Joseph Anthony, whose fresh eye on *that* property may have made him more inclined to drop Act Three.

In *The Matchmaker,* Dolly simply walks into Horace's private dining room in the Harmonia Gardens and starts conversing with him. We know what happens in the musical: a showstopper that follows a frenzied "Waiters' Gallop." And whether you preferred "Come and Be My Butterfly" or "The Polka Contest," each was a new idea.

Where were the surprises in *110?* Even those who didn't know the play or movie would infer that there was a big rain a-coming, for why else had the stage been fitted with a grate from wing to wing?

So *Dolly*'s putting new wine in old bottles made a difference, while *110*'s recycled approach didn't. For that matter, Wilder had let his imagination soar, too, when he first wrote the play. He was adapting Johann Nestroy's 1842 farce, *Einen Jux Will Er Sich* (*He Wants to Have a Lark*), to which he added a most important ingredient: Dolly Levi.

110 did get some fresh blood from Broadway newcomers Schmidt and Jones, who were oh-so-proud that their *The Fantasticks* had recently played its 1,000th off-Broadway performance—and was still running! Both writers were Texas natives, so Schmidt could infuse his music with that wide-open-spaces sound, and Jones could provide convincing lingo for tough Texas men. In contrast, they had Lizzie use her soprano to almost exclusively sing lofty-sounding songs. The title of their closing number—"Wonderful Music"—turned out to be genuine truth-in-advertising.

Jones has said, "In our eagerness to do it right—and in our terror of doing it wrong—before the show went into rehearsal, we had written 114 songs. We felt that whenever we got in trouble out of town, we could just go to our hotel room, lock the door, order a drink from room service, turn on the television set, and the next day come out looking very tired and say, 'Well, we got one for you.' "

Here's a question we have for them: Did those other songs vary greatly from the Nash-Anthony template? Did they experiment only to find that their bookwriter and director didn't want them to go out on an imaginative limb? An inordinate number of lyrics are taken directly from the play's dialogue; indeed, the start of Starbuck's first boastful speech was musicalized almost word-for-word.

Taubman: "*The Rainmaker* had a touch of magic," but "it has disappeared in this adaptation" and "not even a lightning bolt could ignite it." Kerr accused Nash of not "sharpening the lines that are left to any sort of cutting edge." Chapman found the show "top-notch," but his opinion that "the director knew exactly what he wanted and he got it" wasn't one that would be emblazoned on window cards and three-sheets.

Watts said that it was "a little short of festivity" and that "the narrative lacks the glow of excitement and brilliance that could have transformed a pleasant musical play into a sparkling and resounding delight."

On the other hand, Nadel took an if-it-ain't-broke stance and praised Nash for "a blessed minimum of line alterations." McClain called it "our first top-flight musical of the season," but warned that the original play "never did the business it deserved."

Perhaps *110* didn't because it wasn't a natural property for a musical. Lizzie is passive in getting what she wants, while Dolly Levi won't let anybody or anything get in her way. Lizzie had one song ("Raunchy") where she promised to take action (which she didn't.) She also had half of one duet ("You're Not Foolin' Me," with Starbuck) where she showed gumption—but only after Starbuck had goaded her. Otherwise, Lizzie had *five* introspective songs, four of which were tender ballads.

Inga Swenson's Lizzie didn't overly impress Taubman ("attractive and talented"), but the others were far more appreciative. Nadel: "Swenson strikes the evening's heartiest humor." Chapman: "A dazzling new musical comedy star took over the stage for keeps." McClain: "Swenson is responsible in just measure for enough heart to make this callous observer blub openly." Watts: "The most beautiful ugly duckling." Kerr said, "I urge you to see her just to watch her explode."

Unfortunately, the audience on April 22 watched Swenson slip on the wet stage. She was out for three solid months. Given that she had the best reviews and was the only over-the-title star to be Tony nominated, her absence certainly didn't help the box office.

But neither did the tame adaptation.

"I really do believe that the music and the lyrics are among the best that I have ever done," Noël Coward wrote of his score for *The Girl Who Came to Supper.*

Perhaps Christopher Plummer didn't. Just as he'd promised Jule Styne he'd do his new musical *The Ghost Goes West* to extricate himself from playing the dull role of Nick Arnstein, Plummer gave that same explanation/excuse to Coward when he was asked to portray Grand Duke Charles, overseeing the mythical Carpathia in 1911.

Laurence Olivier thought enough of the role to play it on stage (with Vivien Leigh) and screen (with Marilyn Monroe)—but that was respectively for the

1953 play *The Sleeping Prince* and the 1957 film that was retitled *The Prince and the Showgirl*. Both were the work of the still-esteemed Terence Rattigan, who in 1963–64 was more interested in his new play, *Man and Boy*, than his old one; hence, he chose not to be the musical's bookwriter.

Did Plummer feel what many Broadway observers felt once they heard to whom Coward had entrusted the book? Why did Coward, purveyor of elegance extraordinaire, choose Harry Kurnitz, whose last Broadway effort was *A Shot in the Dark*? To be fair, Kurnitz's script was loftier than the knockabout farcical screenplay used in the 1964 Peter Sellers film. Still, Kurnitz's style of boulevard comedy was located in a far less sophisticated neighborhood than Coward's.

The show's title seemed more like Kurnitz's idea than Coward's, for it clearly referenced Kaufman and Hart's *The Man Who Came to Dinner*. But at least it was clearer than Rattigan's two titles, which should have been *The Sleeping Prince Regent* and *The Prince Regent and the Showgirl*. Audiences could be pardoned for assuming that Charles (José Ferrer) would be next in line to rule Carpathia; isn't that the usual fate of a prince? A few scenes had to pass before they realized that Charles had been married to the Carpathian queen, who'd since died; thus their son, Nicolas, now a teenager, was too young to claim the throne that was rightfully his. That Charles treated his son as a kid and not a future king provided some of the show's comedy and tension.

But what of the Girl? She was Mary Morgan (Florence Henderson), a chorus girl in that new American musical *The Coconut Girl* now playing in London's West End. Charles and Nicolas were in town for the coronation of England's new king, George V, and Charles slipped away to catch the show, after which he went backstage and invited Mary to his royal suite.

That spurred Mary to sing in delight "I've Been Invited to a Party"—not realizing that the "party" was for all of two people. In the film, when Marilyn Monroe learned the truth, she dryly stated, "I know all about these harmless little 'tête-à-tête suppers *a deux*.' I've fought my way out of quite a few. 'Champagne, and I hope you like caviar and something cold to follow. But we really don't want the servants around, do we? It's so much more fun serving ourselves, don't you think?' And then after the supper—'You must be tired after the show, Miss Morgan. Why don't you put your feet up on the sofa?' I know every line in the script: feed lines, punch lines, laugh lines, and the funny business in between."

Isn't that a song you want to hear? But Coward didn't write it —also missing the opportunity for a funny reprise when Mary turned out to be accurate and Charles would sing those statements down to the last syllable.

Instead, Coward gave Mary a swirling waltz in which she envisioned that "the belle of the ball is me," holding the final "is" for four seconds and trilling it before the final "me."

Mary hailed from Milwaukee, but you'd never know it from her syrupy, operetta-like music. Where was her all-American razz-ma-tazz? The story involved a clash between European and American cultures, so the music should have reflected that.

One might rebut that Marilyn Monroe sang in *The Prince and the Showgirl* and that the song she sang sounded as if it came from an operetta. But that could be seen as an effort to have the Prince Regent relate better to her—or to show that she was trying to reach him. Besides, Monroe's song was a presentational one, not an introspective one. In *The Girl*, when Mary sang her inner feelings to us alone, we should have heard music and lyrics that seemed colloquial, not lofty, not necessarily lovely—but *American*.

As Nadel would observe, "She speaks a very common English then sings a refined English"—reiterating that Coward's tone was very different from Kurnitz's.

Coward did well by Charles, who sounded appropriately proper—although audiences may have been alienated when Ferrer rolled his *r*'s mercilessly. If he seemed pretentious, a recording that Coward made of the score showed that the star was simply obeying his composer-lyricist, who apparently influenced director-choreographer Joe Layton, too.

Charles fed Mary vodka, sweet-talked, and tried for sympathy with the "I'm lonely" tactic. Imagine his fury when she fell asleep.

The audience was about to doze off, too. The next scene didn't hold much promise: Nicolas, with no official business to perform, felt the need to get out of the regal residence and go on the town. During his walk, he happened to pass the spot where busker Ada Cockle entertained each night.

And that's when the musical took off.

In *Theatre World, 1963–64, The Girl Who Came to Supper* received a three-page spread—but Tessie O'Shea, who played Ada, was the only cast member to get a full page to herself (not to mention that aforementioned Tony Award as Best Featured Actress in a Musical).

O'Shea was onstage for all of eleven minutes—the least stage time that any Tony winner in that category had had in the fifteen years that the prize had been given. Yet Coward and Layton left no doubt that they had chosen the right woman to perfectly recapture the English music hall sound in a medley of four songs. Their titles alone were evocative: "London Is a Little Bit of All Right," "What Ho, Mrs. Brisket," "Don't Take Our Charlie for the Army," and "Saturday Night at the Rose and Crown," all leading to a reprise of the first one.

Yes, they all sounded as if they came from ideas that Coward had written years earlier on napkins during late-night cocktails and filed away for future reference. The audience certainly didn't mind, for this was the sparkplug that *The Girl* needed. To say that O'Shea stole the show isn't strong enough; her theft could have been called the perfect crime.

Once Ada had finished, Nicolas moved on, and so did O'Shea, to her dressing room. She spent the rest of the performance paying bills, talking on the telephone, eating a batch of her famous frankfurter chutney salad (seriously; she even published the recipe in her own cookbook), and waiting for the moment she could take her curtain call and get the cheers that Ferrer and Henderson would have liked to receive.

Although O'Shea's act was fit for a king, her divertissement did take the audience away from the story. Kerr obviously thought that this was more than a little bit of all right, for his review spent the first six of his twelve paragraphs dealing with no one else. At first glance, Chapman didn't seem as effusive, for he bestowed ninety-five words on O'Shea—but he respectively gave Ferrer and Henderson twenty-two and twenty-seven.

That Henderson was no Marilyn Monroe hurt the show's premise. Although she was still six years away from her sunny mom in *The Brady Bunch*, Henderson had already established herself as sweetness and light as Laurey in a City Center *Oklahoma!* revival and in the title role of *Fanny*. Unlike Monroe, she didn't radiate the sex and savvy that would make a prince regent assume that she'd make herself available for a one-night stand.

Not until the show's twelfth song did Mary get to cut loose, when she did a medley from *The Coconut Girl* for Nicolas. It was funny, especially when she sang her chorus-girl harmony and nothing else. (Although as critic Marc Miller has noted, when she had her solo moment in which she identified herself by her character name, Sally, she shouldn't be singing harmony there. Perhaps no one noticed because it was so late in the show and minds had already wandered.)

Here Henderson purposely overdid the operetta feeling, but there wasn't much difference from the lofty material that Coward had given her. What's more, it wasn't as galvanizing as O'Shea's showpiece.

In the end, the message that a freethinking American woman can conquer a stiff-upper-lipped European man seemed overly familiar. As might have been predicted, the Prince Regent lost a good deal of his stuffiness and warmed to Mary's insouciant ability to be herself. There was one surprise in store: The Prince Regent took Mary's suggestion that Carpathia should embrace democracy. In the original play and film, he did not.

While Nadel may have been right about the discrepancy between the speaking and singing Mary, he was quite wrong when he said that *The Girl* would "stay the season." There's long been a theory that plays and musicals about people in show business are doomed to fail because the average theatergoer can't be expected to care about their difficulties. American audiences might feel even less empathy for the so-called problems of royalty.

Besides, Taubman said the show "refuses to waft us back into the magic land where such fables can charm and even ring true." Kerr damned it with faint praise—"a lot to look at"—before simply damning it: "They should have let *The Sleeping Prince* lie." After Watts called it "a romantic delight," he sounded redundant in calling Coward's score "delightful."

On the other hand, McClain said, "Not since *My Fair Lady*—and there is a slight affinity between the two—have I been so moved by a musical."

Some would question the adjective "slight." That both shows had Oliver Smith replicating London during the second decade of the twentieth century wasn't the only similarity. *Girl* followed the template set by *Lady*: the irascible man speak-singing about a female he considered beneath him, followed by her showing off her beautiful voice. And as dustman Alfred P. Doolittle had done before her, O'Shea spiced up matters with her music hall ditties.

Doolittle differed from Ada, however, in that his character was genuinely integrated. He brought some tension into *My Fair Lady* when he arrived at Henry Higgins's house and demanded some recompense for his daughter. Then one of his chance remarks spurred Higgins to flippantly recommend him to a millionaire, who in turn left in his will an annual grant of four hundred thousand pounds to Doolittle. Seeing the parvenu have mixed feelings about having to turn respectable was part of the fun.

The best musicals seem brand-new when unveiled. Audiences may not have consciously noticed the parallels between *Girl* and *Lady*, but they very well might have felt that the "new" enterprise seemed somehow familiar. Perhaps they couldn't put their finger on it, but they didn't put those fingers together to clap wildly, either.

On March 14, 1964, a day after O'Shea's fifty-first birthday, the show closed after a 112-performance run. Ten weeks later, when she won her Tony, she was the first woman who had ever emerged victorious in the Best Featured Musical Actress category after so short a run.

Although BBC Radio did get around to airing a revised version in 1979, *Girl* is the only one of Noël Coward's eight musicals that has never received a first-class London production. Apparently few agreed with Coward "that the music and the lyrics are among the best that I have ever done."

In Coward's 1941 hit *Blithe Spirit*, the medium known as Madame Arcati was about to hold a séance at Ruth and Charles Condomine's house. The person she used to connect with the spirit world was a child named Daphne. To get her attention, Madame Arcati sang a little nursery rhyme:

> *Little Tommy Tucker*
> *Sings for his supper.*
> *What shall he have*
> *But brown bread and butter?*

The moment Madame Arcati finished, she turned to the Condomines and their guests, the Bradfords, and said, "I despise that because it doesn't rhyme at all. But Daphne loves it. She likes a tune she can hum."

Both Madame Arcati and Daphne would have loved *High Spirits*, then, for the "improbable musical comedy," as it advertised itself, had a mostly marvelous score full of perfectly crafted rhymes. "Music and lyrics by Hugh Martin and Timothy Gray," said the window card, but Martin later acknowledged that he wrote approximately 80 percent of the music, while Gray penned about 80 percent of the lyrics. Considering the strength of the score, it was Broadway's loss that they only collaborated on this one show.

All right, Madame Arcati had a one-joke song, in which she admitted that "I've Never Had a Man" before adding those all-important four syllables, "ifestation." As Sondheim later learned with "Can That Boy Ffff-ox-Trot," the first time around, the joke gets a titanic laugh, but as it gets repeated, it starts sinking quicker than the *Titanic*.

(No wonder, then, that both songs were dropped in Boston.)

But the rest of the *High Spirits* score is, if not 24 karat gold, at least 18 karat. Martin and Gray had no problem finding the sophisticated sound to complement Coward's longest-running Broadway hit.

Remember the plot? Charles (Edward Woodward) was a novelist who wanted to write about the occult, so he'd invited local medium Madame Arcati (Beatrice Lillie) to his home to learn, as he told her, "the tricks of the trade."

That term made for a most unhappy medium, but Ruth (Louise Troy) would soon be far less happy. Arcati and Daphne inadvertently summoned up Elvira (Tammy Grimes), Charles's first wife, back from the great beyond five years after her death. How wicked *and* imaginative Coward was in detailing the cause of death: "She started to laugh helplessly at one of the BBC musical programs and died of a heart attack."

Martin and Gray played fair by giving each of their leading ladies a song that served magnificently as an eleven o'clock number. Lillie went first with "Talking to You," in which she held a conversation and did a dance with her Ouija board. Then Grimes got "Home, Sweet Heaven," in which Elvira decided to return to her own abode and "sit 'round King Arthur's table; Freud and Cain and Abel, Barnum and Bailey, Oscar Wilde and me." Some sneered that it was a mere list song (forty-one luminaries were named in three minutes), but it had some delicious interior rhymes, too. ("And with his good looks, Robin Hood looks fit for ransom.")

The trouble was that after these, two songs were yet to follow, and they were the weakest in the score. Moral of the story: don't do your eleven o'clock numbers at ten o'clock.

Coward admired "Home, Sweet Heaven" so much that he wrote his own lyrics to supplement Martin and Gray's. ("King Charles's spaniel—a golden cocker—jumps up and knocks poor Whistler's mother off her rocker.") They never went into the show, even when it was being readied for London later that year; Coward was content to sing them at parties for the remaining nine years of his life.

He's lucky he lived that long, given that he'd taken on directorial duties, too. Between *High Spirits'* tryouts in Boston and Philadelphia, the sixty-four-year-old Coward was utterly exhausted if not ill, probably after the difficulties and disappointment he'd had with *The Girl Who Came to Supper* only four months earlier. *High Spirits'* co-producer Lester Osterman sought Gower Champion to take over the direction, and, to the surprise of many Broadway observers, the esteemed director-choreographer, who'd not that long ago emerged from his own *Dolly* tryout hell with a smash, agreed.

From most accounts, Champion accelerated the pace and made Grimes, Woodward, and Troy a bit more zany to complement Lillie's madcap performance. Still, it was a show that didn't have a Gower Champion look, which may be why he didn't put his name on it.

Kerr had a point when he said the show was "smoothly arranged, pleasantly intimate, an amiably easygoing improvisation that is long on casual charm and short on ideas." Yes, it was pretty straightforward, although Martin and Gray, providing the book as well, did try to open it up by having Lillie ride a bicycle (a stationary one, alas) along a road. They took us to a hotel, her studio, and then her bedroom.

Yes, none seemed particularly necessary, although the songs in each of these instances—the appealing "The Bicycle Song," the breezy "Faster than Sound" (in which Grimes flew), the pulsating "Go into Your Trance," and the witty "Talking to You"—were all solid songwriting achievements.

Grimes's numbers were more plentiful and better, with a particularly fetching "You'd Better Love Me (while you may)" challenge to Charles, followed by a blue-note-filled "Something Tells Me (that tonight is the night)."

Opening night was certainly a good one for Grimes, for the critics showed their appreciation. Kerr said that she was "a passion of mine," while Watts approved of her "characteristic style." Chapman called her "an oddly seductive spook," Nadel said she was "a swift and sly version of an ectoplasm," not to be confused with Taubman's description of "a gauzy, restless ectoplasm." McClain said that she had "the fine, fey quality of a ghoul."

(Who knew that ghouls were "fine and fey?" Perhaps Arcati had visited his house, too.)

All very well and good, but Lillie got the type of notices known as love letters. Suddenly the raves bestowed on Channing and Streisand seemed as lukewarm as day-old dishwater.

"A cause for celebration," wrote Taubman in his opening paragraph, "because it has brought back Beatrice Lillie."

"I will remember it as the musical comedy in which Beatrice Lillie killed me," stated Kerr.

"Beatrice Lillie's performance reaffirms her place in the recorded history of the 20th century along with the Battle of Jutland," stated Nadel, citing the biggest naval conflict of World War I, before adding "and the Salk vaccine."

"Lillie did overpower me," Chapman admitted, "but it wasn't her fault. All she has to do is give me one innocent leer and I'm a goner."

"It has the inestimable blessing of providing the superb Beatrice Lillie the opportunity for displaying her magic touch," wrote Watts. "She is at the peak of her art in her incidental business and is nothing short of uproarious."

"Everybody concerned with *High Spirits*," wrote McClain, "should be required to kneel several times a day and pray for the perseverance and good health of Beatrice Lillie."

Coward apparently felt differently. He wrote a little poem that ended "Beatrice Lillie is a twat who's driving master mad." And if that four-letter noun sounds a trifle vulgar, what about the one he used in the first line that began with *c?*

But McClain was right. One could credit the show itself for the house record set the week ending June 13: $70,012 (thanks to standing room; capacity was $69,500). However, Grimes's vacation the week ending July 11 caused the gross to slip to $48,042, but Lillie's seven-day holiday during the week ending December 27—some of which involved the lucrative Christmas week—plummeted the gross to $18,448.

Maybe Daniel Blum knew what he was doing after all when he put Beatrice Lillie and not Tammy Grimes on the cover of his *Theatre World*.

* * *

Doesn't the title *The Student Gypsy, or The Prince of Liederkranz* suggest a single character? No, the one who'd apprenticed herself to gypsies was Merry May Glockenspiel, while the Prince of Liederkranz was someone else entirely.

Rick Besoyan had had a three-year off-Broadway hit from spoofing operetta with *Little Mary Sunshine.* Now he decided to send Broadway a new send-up. To use one of those x-meets-y clichés, it was *The Student Prince* meets *Gypsy Lady.*

But this time, they didn't get along.

The original plan was to open in Boston on Christmas Day 1962, then Philadelphia on January 14, 1963, prior to a Broadway opening on January 31. Not only was producer Sandy Farber forced to postpone until September, but money was so tight that he would be compelled to open cold on Broadway without benefit of even one out-of-town tryout—a rarity back then. Although RCA Victor did invest in the show, it would give Farber no more than $10,000.

He was glad to have it.

Here comes Barbra Streisand again, for Earl Wilson said that "she was reading for Merry May." Indeed she was—to get Ray Stark and everyone else connected with *Funny Girl* a little worried that they might lose her. But Besoyan, who directed as well, must have always had Eileen Brennan in mind; she'd been his first Mary Sunshine and helped make the show a hit.

Audiences first met "Papa" Johann Sebastian Glockenspiel (and, yes, "Papa" was always put in quotation marks). Although his country, Singspielia, had just lost the Twenty-Two Year War with Liederkranz, "Papa" was happy that peace had been restored. His fetching daughters Ginger and Edelweiss were looking forward to the returning soldiers. "Look at that cloud of dust ahead!" one cried.

Alas, soldiers on horseback weren't responsible. The dust was raised by their sister, the gawky Merry May, who wasn't "picking up her feet as usual."

Ginger and Edelweiss sang, "You are looking well, my dear—for you." Despite her thick glasses and impossible hair, Merry May would like some "Romance," as she sang before she decided to leave home so that she could "learn to be beautiful, glamorous, and seductive."

Too bad that before she could make these important changes she met Rudolph von Schlump, whom she deemed "the prettiest man I ever saw." The square-jawed hero corrected her—" 'Handsome' is the word"—before expressing his hope that "Somewhere" he'd meet his true love.

"Romance" and "Somewhere" seemed to be genuine operetta and not parody. And yet, after Rudolph finished his song, he stated, "There now! I feel
quite improved after that."

We wouldn't expect an operetta spoof to have something in common with
the forward-looking *Anyone Can Whistle*. But both shows used an "It's only a
muuuusical" rationale to get laughs.

After Rudolph left, Merry May reprised "Somewhere" word for word, save
a few pronouns, and met phony elixir salesman Muffin T. Ragamuffin. Both
were soon accosted by Zampa, the Queen of the Gypsies, and her son, Gryphon, whose girlfriends had a habit of dumping him. "You've got to take better
care of your things," chided Zampa (played by Shannon Bolin, better known
as Joe Boyd's wife in *Damn Yankees*).

Gryphon fell for Merry May, but she wanted Rudolph and pretended to be
a princess to impress him. Secret identities ran rampant. "Papa" was in reality the King of Singspielia. Rudolph was actually a prince. Merry May
dressed to pass as a young man.

If the Singspielia girls' falling in love with the Liederkranz boys wasn't
enough (and apparently Besoyan felt it wasn't), once Merry May took down
her hair and removed her glasses, Prince Rudolph finally was able to sing "My
Love Is Yours," which was followed by her singing it, too.

Their engagement infuriated "Papa" as much as it enraged Rudolph's
father, King Osgood the Good, who'd promised his son at birth to Elsie Umlaut. She gave a piece of cheese to everyone she met as a peace offering as well
as an example of Liederkranz's primary industry. (Had *Student* been a smash,
the Cheese Association just might have signed Linda Segal, who played Ms.
Umlaut, to a long-term contract.)

Merry May wanted Rudolph to honor his father's promise to Elsie. When
Gryphon caught them talking, he assumed she was cheating on him. "Don't
beat me now," Merry May implored him. "Later, after we're married." It was
meant to get a laugh, and if it did, we're all sorry about it now.

In the end, Zampa was revealed as a former lover of both "Papa" and Osgood, so she convinced the two to end the Montague-Capulet feud and let
the kids marry—in a mere twenty-one words. That they both capitulated so
quickly was allegedly part of the fun.

If it sounds rather lame, it wasn't much more convoluted than the average minor comic operetta, and the whole thing was supposed to be a spoof any-way. But Besoyan's music and even his lyrics didn't suggest operetta as much as second-rate '40s musical comedy. He may not have intended to cross over to the newer form, but his score certainly did.

That wasn't the only roadblock. *Little Mary Sunshine* had a sincere appre-ciation for operetta that its successor didn't. *Student* had the Liederkranz Gren-adiers sing to the Glockenspiel Girls, "You'll always be the one adored—until I'm tired or I'm bored." That was far more sardonic than the words Besoyan had given his Forest Rangers—eight of the twelve adjectives found in the Boy Scout Oath: "friendly," "courteous," "kind," "reverent," "brave," "cheerful," "thrifty," "obedient." The innocence of *Little Mary* brought back an even sim-pler era than the '50s, in which it opened.

Student also had anachronisms, while *Little Mary* did not. After Zampa mentioned "Gypsy cards," Muffin assumed that she was about to pull out a deck and tell a fortune or two. No, what Zampa meant was that "if you want to be a vagabond, you have to join the United Gypsy Guild." She later mentioned an upcoming gypsy convention, too.

And those names! *Little Mary* took place in Colorado, not in silly Singspielia, where virtually all citizens had names as unlikely as their country. *Little Mary* instead had the much more grounded Cora, Henrietta, and Mabel respectively in love with Pete, Slim, and Tex, who were under the command of Captain Big Jim Warington, not Colonel Helmut Blunderbuss. The only name in *Little Mary* that was said with a wink was Nancy Twinkle's; *The Student Gypsy* winked so much that it seemed to have a nervous tic.

Besoyan's choosing overly fanciful names suggested that he couldn't think of good ones, was desperate for laughs, and hoped he'd amuse by offering ri-diculous surnames that real people would never have. For the annual Hasty Pudding Show, Harvard University's juniors and seniors could sophomorically name their characters Rhoda Rooter, Mary Wanna, and Roland DeHay; Broad-way audiences expected pros in 1963–64 to be funnier.

Over-the-top humor often makes a show hit rock bottom. During *The Student Gypsy*'s two-week stay, it never received an invitation to RCA Victor's recording studio. At least Brennan wasn't out of work long; she went from one of 1963–64's shortest-running musicals to its longest when she played Irene Molloy in *Hello, Dolly!*

* * *

What Makes Sammy Run? had a blue-chip title, thanks to Budd Schulberg's 1941 classic novel about a young man who would do anything to get ahead. Producer Joseph Cates could be considered courageous or crazy for signing Steve Lawrence to play him. Yes, Lawrence could sing, but could he act?

And then Cates booked the notorious 54th Street Theatre, where *The Student Gypsy* had just been one of the house's many flops, although not its biggest: Said Kerr of one infamous 1958 musical, "Nor will I say that *Portofino is* the worst musical *ever* produced, because I've only been seeing musicals since 1919." At other times, the 54th Street was where long-run hits (*Damn Yankees, The World of Suzie Wong*) went to play out their runs and die.

Nevertheless, *What Makes Sammy Run?* at 540 performances became the longest-running show in the theater's history. How could it happen with antihero Sammy Glick? Brooks Atkinson's famous review of *Pal Joey* stressed, "Can you draw sweet water from a foul well?" Joey was a mere braggart and philanderer; what would Atkinson have said about Sammy, who made shady deals, blamed others, betrayed lovers, and caused a friend to commit suicide—all to get to the top in Hollywood?

Two years before *Sammy* opened, *I Can Get It for You Wholesale* offered us a lesser stinker in Harry Bogen; he lied, romanced a woman he didn't love to get her money, and caused a business associate to go to prison before his business eventually went bust. None of these activities inspired admiration, but they weren't as horrible as Sammy's machinations.

Yet *Wholesale* ran about half as long as *Sammy*. One can't blame the score; although Ervin Drake did some impressive work for *Sammy,* Harold Rome did far better by *Wholesale.*

But Steve Lawrence was far more famous than Elliott Gould. And because audiences weren't familiar with Gould, they might have subconsciously felt that he was really as bad as his character. Lawrence, on the other hand, was well known as the charming husband of the Steve-and-Eydie (Gormé) franchise. He'd recently had a No. 1 hit in which he begged a young miss to "Go Away, Little Girl," creating a persona of someone who wanted to do the right thing. Lawrence was such a natively appealing performer that theatergoers could rationalize that he was just *pretending* to be mean, which would allow them to still like him.

Drake may not be known by the general public, but his name was on two standards: one each from the '40s ("Tico-Tico") and '50s ("I Believe"); before the '60s were over, he'd have another: "It Was a Very Good Year." *Sammy*'s hit song was supposed to be "A Room Without Windows," our antihero's come-on to Kit. The swingin' tune was recorded by dozens of artists, and as late as 1998, when the *Will & Grace* pilot aired, Jack McFarland was heard singing it.

(Credit where it's due, the song did have a Sondheim-worthy rhyme: "If they said, 'Friend, how would you like to spend the long *hereafter*,' I'd tell 'em what *we're after*.")

Schulberg had his brother, Stuart, co-write the book. As in the novel, they started with a flashback in which *New York Record* theater critic Al Manheim (Robert Alda) remembered "little ferret" Sammy Glick, the copy boy who took a story from one desk to another.

"It's a good job this year," said Sammy. "If I still have it next year, it'll stink."

Although Sammy was smart enough to know that jobs grow old, his attitude didn't make him popular with the writers. Only Al urged them to "give him a break." Little did Al know that he'd soon become a Glick victim when Sammy told the editor that Al had made a mistake on a producer's name. Sammy bragged that his squealing got him two free tickets to the new play starring Lunt and Fontanne—which he sold for $5 in order to get a new pair of shoes, his first virgin pair.

Al forgave him, but was less indulgent when Sammy offered the editor his own article on radio that was immediately available for typesetting while Al's column wasn't yet finished. One reason why Sammy's was ready to go: He'd plagiarized it.

So it wasn't much of a leap for Sammy to take co-worker Julian Blumberg's script, put his own name to it, and sell it to Hollywood. Once Sammy arrived, he showed sensitivity for the first time when singing "(This should have been) My Hometown." Drake wrote the right song for the right moment, for audiences needed to see Sammy acting tenderly, even if only toward a city and not a person.

Odd, too, that Sammy Glick never changed his name as many in Hollywood did to mask their Jewish roots. Certainly Sidney Leibowitz did—to Steve Lawrence. Then again, the Schulbergs didn't.

The brothers introduced some wan comic relief by naming an actor Tracy

Clark (who of course brought Spencer and Gable to mind) and an actress Rita Rio (as opposed to the 1927 Broadway hit *Rio Rita;* she was Rita Royce in Schulberg's novel). Both of them starred in *Queen of Sheba,* which caused its director to say, "After this one, I think the Bible has had it."

At least studio head Sidney Fineman liked the picture, even if its writer, Kit Sargent, did not. Sammy was happy to meet this "brisk, bright, long-legged, attractive" woman—a good description of Sally Ann Howes, who played her and had to be convincing in her attraction to this "little ferret." As Drake wrote to a lofty soprano melody, "I've got a tender spot for all the strange ones."

It's an awkward line. And while many women are attracted to stinkers and Kit's "Spare me the saint" fits the profile, the objects of their affection are usually strong, silent butch types. Steve Lawrence wasn't by any means effeminate, but he had to play an inveterate talker who was blatant about his machinations.

The Schulbergs apparently didn't feel the need to make Sammy subtle or to have him keep his cards close to his vest. "What kind of sissy word is 'fair'?" he yelled. "Whatever's good for Sammy Glick is right; whatever is bad is immoral, unethical and unconstitutional and, in other words, stinks."

As David Merrick (who stayed clear of *Sammy*) liked to say, "Are we having fun yet?"

Kit couldn't appreciate Al, who had come to Hollywood because one of his plays had been optioned. She said to him, "Your only problem is you're a nice man," to which he answered, "Give me a fighting chance to clear my name."

Al decided to be a good loser when singing "Maybe Some Other Time" to Kit. It wasn't as beautiful a melody as Leonard Bernstein's "Some Other Time," but it qualifies as one of the prettiest show songs of the '60s—and a few other decades, too.

"Welcome to the land of milk and Sammy," said Glick, who ostensibly taught Al and Kit to write for films in "Lights! Camera! Platitude!" Sammy believed that one cliché could serve any genre: comedy, drama, musical, or horror movie. His one-size-fits-all approach reiterated that he was a provider of product and hardly an artist—unless one considered him a rip-off artist and, shall we say, bullshit artist.

"His" picture *Monsoon* was shown as a dream ballet, one of the last ones seen; after twenty years, the device seemed threadbare. As for *Monsoon,* it of course owed a heavy debt to W. Somerset Maugham's *Rain.* Rita Rio wound up "naked—but pious," which was enough to make it a hit, thanks to Julian Blumberg's ghostwriting, which landed him a cool $50 that Sammy paid him out of his $550 payment.

Sammy's one love song to Hollywood gave way to sex songs to women. Here was a boy who couldn't hear "No" whether it involved business or romance—which, of course, he mixed together. Attention from Kit wasn't enough; Sammy had his sights on Laurette Harrington, but only partly because she was the daughter of the studio's owner, H. L. The Schulbergs enjoyed describing her in stage directions as "a striking, spoiled aristocrat given to daring costumes and behavior" and in dialogue as "that cute little black spider" who "makes trouble faster than her old man makes money."

At the end of Act One of *The King and I,* Hammerstein in his stage direction asked of his title characters, "Who is taming whom?" There, however, Anna and the King were out to make Siam a better country. "Who is taming whom?" could have applied to Sammy and Laurette, but in this case, each had no lofty goal but simply wanted to conquer the other.

So what would it be: Sammy's taming of the shrew or Laurette's taming of the shrewd? She phoned him just as he was about to bed Kit, whom he immediately left low and dry. Ah, but when Sammy arrived at Laurette's, the haughty hottie told him that she'd since had a better offer. What makes Sammy humiliated?

Not his next picture, which was a smash. When interviewed, he sang "I Feel Humble," in the manner that megalomaniacs often adopt. Laurette implied that he should feel humble, for she found the picture "hilarious—especially the serious parts."

How convenient of the Schulbergs to have Sammy hire both Al and Kit so that they could spend enough time together; this way, she could come to love Al instead of Sammy, and both could then leave his employ. Meanwhile, Sammy was busy betraying studio head Sidney Fineman to H. L. Harrington with half-hearted endorsements ("He's doing the best he can"), which, all too conveniently, H. L. revealed verbatim to Sidney.

What was left for Sidney but suicide and the top job for Sammy? He got Laurette to suggest that they do "The Friendliest Thing"—meaning sexual intercourse. With a melody that was revealed as slowly as an anaconda in thick sagebrush and a steadily suggestive lyric, it was a song that Cole Porter would have been proud to have written.

Laurette was friendly on their wedding day, too. After the reception, when Sammy went upstairs, he didn't find her changing into her going-away outfit. She was, however, metaphorically going away from him by cavorting with the studio's newest star as her wedding dress lay on the floor.

What would a serious post-1959 musical be without concluding with a "Rose's Turn"? Sammy admitted that "Some Days Everything Goes Wrong" before giving the impression that he'd bounce back.

During the show's Philadelphia tryout at the Erlanger, some days everything *was* going wrong. Cates was unhappy. (Here's hoping that his five-month-old daughter, Phoebe, wasn't exacerbating the problem by keeping him up nights.) He decided that director Arthur Storch had to go and that Abe Burrows had to come in. Three seasons earlier, hadn't Burrows had a smash with *How to Succeed,* which also had an antihero in J. Pierrepont Finch?

Ah, but Finch was in a cartoon of a show and wasn't as unlikeble as Sammy Glick.

Burrows cut the show's first song, "Two-Cent Encyclopedia"—a journalist's nickname for a newspaper. It was conceived to have multiple Sammys running around the paper's office to show his speed. Choreographer Matt Mattox and the doubles could never quite make it work, but it appears to be a musical scene that would have amused.

Burrows was not, however, responsible for the loss of "Don't Bite the Hand That Feeds You." Sammy's song to Al about the need to play ball with your bosses didn't make the cut because the Schulbergs' mother didn't like it.

When mothers add their two cents to a show, the show usually doesn't even make two cents.

Burrows needed more time, so *Sammy* postponed its January 23, 1964, opening around the same time that *Funny Girl,* also in Philadelphia, decided it couldn't be ready for its new opening date of February 27. So *What Makes Sammy Run?* took it instead, and left the Erlanger just in time for Streisand's show to move there.

Drake has since said, "We were deprived of staging a tougher show by Cates, who felt it would not appeal to the audience of that time. Both the script and the songs were softened, and Steve Lawrence's Sammy was played fetchingly. The audiences loved him, but we felt the novel had been betrayed."

Burrows in his memoir *Honest Abe* saw it differently. He called *Sammy* "a show I doctored and helped to turn into a smash hit."

And if you believe that, here's some soy sauce that will take stains out of a white dress. Abe wasn't being honest. *What Makes Sammy Run?* was far from a "smash hit," for it lost $285,000 of its $400,000 investment.

Burrows could make some believe his statement because of those 540 performances. There was a time when 500 meant champagne, caviar, and perhaps a lifetime of lucrative residual rights. *Milk and Honey* had proved a year earlier with its 543-performance run that a show could now run fifteen months and not pay back its investors.

Taubman: "An uninspired musical." Watts: "Nothing takes place to supersede *Pal Joey*." Kerr didn't know how Drake felt about Burrows, but the songwriter must have nodded in agreement when he read, "It starts out as a hard-headed, mean-minded musical," but "every so often—every too often—it grabs hold of the very things it means to be satirical about and uses them to be cozy and cute." Drake must have come out with another "Yes!" when he saw Chapman's assessment that "Burrows has kept it moving. But moving backwards, maybe."

The quotation that went on window cards was Nadel's: "The most zestfully evil musical of the year." McClain approved, too, while mistakenly predicting "it should prosper."

Lawrence emerged triumphant. Taubman said he "puts over a song expertly and exuding blue-eyed charm." Nadel: "He looks better snarling than ordinary men do smiling." Watts: "Vigorous and courageously realistic." Chapman: "He acts his thankless role admirably and vigorously." McClain: "For a nightclub performer, he has exceptional gifts."

Kerr was the most enthusiastic, calling Lawrence "ferocious, agile, plausible, deft with a dance-step and deft with the knife—in every conceivable way, first-rate."

So Lawrence's star power sold the show—and unsold it. He started missing performances, which helped (to quote a Drake lyric) like a burglar helps Fort Knox. Four and a half months into the run, not long after Lawrence had received his Tony nomination, he took a week's vacation. His replacement was pop star Paul Anka, who later bought the back page of *Variety* to trumpet his triumph. The full-page picture showed all three stars taking their curtain calls—except that Howes and Alda were still bowed at the waist, their faces pointed to the floor and unseen, while Anka was standing straight, looking out and grinning away.

After blowing all that money on the ad, one might assume that Anka was interested in Broadway. He certainly wasn't when asked to succeed Lawrence—which Cates asked him to do when Lawrence started ad-libbing. When the star started dropping "I Feel Humble," Cates complained to Actors' Equity. Did Lawrence enact revenge by missing the entire lucrative Christmas week?

Lord knows what the house record for performances at the 54th Street would have been had Steve Lawrence not treated *What Makes Sammy Run?* the way that Sammy Glick treated everyone.

On October 20, 1985, the Shubert Theatre played host to *Our Hearts Belong to Mary*, a tribute to one of Broadway's most beloved stars: Mary Martin. The title, of course, came from "My Heart Belongs to Daddy," the song that Cole Porter had provided for Martin's breakout hit *Leave It to Me!* in 1938.

To whom do you go for a new lyric for what would be the title song for a female star? Why, Jerry Herman, of course. And on the big night, the packed house of 1,400-plus heard Herman accompany Carol Channing, who sang his new lyric:

"She played a nurse. She played a nun. She played a boy who was a fairy."

The audience gurgled with pleasure as it respectively recognized references to Martin's stints as Nellie Forbush in *South Pacific*, Maria von Trapp in *The Sound of Music*, and the title character of *Peter Pan*.

The second section began, "She packed the house as Preston's spouse"—meaning Martin's final musical hit *I Do! I Do!*, in which she'd portrayed Robert Preston's wife. Later came the lyric "In sailor suit or strumming the lute, our hearts belong to Mary."

The second reference was to *Lute Song*, the play with music that Martin had done in 1946. It had only run four months, but it was such atypical Broadway fare—a semimusical adaptation of an ancient Chinese play—that Martin was lauded for being daring enough to tackle it. Needless to say, Herman also included a reference to *Hello, Dolly!*, his own musical, which Martin had played in London and Vietnam.

Then came a final section that mentioned songwriters whose music and lyrics Martin had introduced. "From Weill to Noël, from Schwartz to Cole..."

Schwartz?

Did Martin do a production of *Godspell* that we didn't know about? Had she been a replacement Berthe in *Pippin*?

Herman meant not Stephen Schwartz but Arthur Schwartz, who, along with longtime lyricist partner Howard Dietz, wrote *Jennie*.

Herman's "Our Hearts Belong to Mary" used 210 words; *Jennie* was given precisely one of them—befitting the shortest-running musical that Martin ever brought to Broadway. It played eighty-two performances, lost $550,000, and closed on December 28—not even bothering to take in all that New Year's Eve money.

That's how much Martin and everyone else just wanted it to end. And yet on paper, the show looked good—meaning the paper on which the prospectus was printed. Those who read the papers that made up the script weren't as impressed.

Still, Mary Martin in a new musical? Sign me up.

Martin was initially high on the project. Laurette Taylor, on whose life bookwriter Arnold Schulman was loosely basing his libretto, had become Martin's friend a few years before the *Glass Menagerie* legend died in 1946.

Noted producer Cheryl Crawford had had a hit with Martin in *One Touch of Venus* and had wanted to work with the star again. Twenty years and two weeks had to pass before it happened. In her memoir, Crawford called *Jennie* "the toughest production I ever tackled"—and this from someone who'd produced or co-produced fifty-eight shows.

That Crawford was co-producing made matters harder, for her partner was Richard Halliday, Martin's husband. The Hallidays insisted on Vincent J. Donehue as director, and, as Dietz would write in his memoir, "he, a TV director, was totally under the Halliday thumb." That they rehearsed at the woeful 54th Street Theatre might have suggested in advance that trouble was on the horizon.

When Martin talked to the press, of course, she made it all seem like chocolate truffle lollipops and blue roses. "The real fun is the preparation. This is the best part of a show, " she said in between her battles with Dietz.

The big issue concerned "Before I Kiss the World Goodbye," a glorious song—albeit a recycled one. Take a look at the first pressing of the original cast album of *Oliver!* and you'll see on the back cover that David Merrick was planning to produce Dietz and Schwartz's musical version of Paul Gallico's bestselling 1958 novel *Mrs. 'Arris Goes to Paris.* There a British charwoman is so taken with her employer's wardrobe that she wants some haute couture for herself before she kisses the world goodbye. Hence the lyric, "And have a fling in Paris, France."

Of course, anyone would welcome a fling in Paris, France, so once the project fell apart, Dietz and Schwartz felt they didn't have to shove a good song into a dusty trunk. Into *Jennie* it would go.

Well, not *all* of it. Martin considered one of its lyrics smutty: "Before I go to meet my maker I want to use the salt left in the shaker."

Was there still a little Postulant Maria left in Martin? Dietz couldn't see her point, and Schwartz threatened to go the Dramatists Guild. Yet they knew they'd lose this fight. To paraphrase and embellish what Ethel Merman had said after her Rose lost the 1959–60 Tony to Martin's Maria, you can't buck an actress who has the mindset of a nun.

Battling with her husband was difficult, too. Many who'd previously worked with Halliday might have been inclined to call him "Four-Eyes"—not because he wore glasses (he didn't) but because he seemed two-faced.

Ah, well. At least the show's opening moments were promising. They replicated the type of mellerdrama in which Laurette Taylor had starred. Schulman had concocted *The Mountie Gets His Man, or Chang Lu, King of the White Slavers.* Jennie Malone, playing "Our Melissa," was literally out on a limb, for like Maria in *The Sound of Music,* she'd climbed a tree—but this one had been stretched across a waterfall. Melissa needed to rescue her baby from the rapids below, but wouldn't have if the weight on the tree branch hadn't conveniently lowered her (in the nick of time, of course).

Jennie may be the only musical to have been influenced by Hammacher Schlemmer. Martin bought an exercise wheel there and thought that it *had* to be in the show.

And so it went into *Escape from the Harem, or Omar and the Captive Virgin,* the show's second-act melodrama. Jennie was Shalamar, a Middle Eastern concubine who tried fleeing her shah. Once he captured her, he hung her upside down on that revolving wheel to torture her.

"I've always wanted to sing upside down," said the always game Martin, who'd washed her hair nightly in one of her previous musicals and had flown across the stage in another. But *Jennie* would in fact turn Martin's whole life upside down. Of the five musicals she did during the Tony era, it was the only one for which she didn't receive a nomination.

No one saw that coming as the show was being prepared. Wrote *Billboard*'s Boston stringer Cameron Dewar, "It will open at the Colonial on July 29, and bookings are reported to be even heavier than they were for *Mr. President,* which broke advance sales here."

(Yeah, and look what happened to that one....)

"In Detroit," wrote a *Look* magazine reporter, "tickets are as rare as rubies in a fistful of Cracker Jack." Nice publicity, but of the five weeks the show played in Boston and the four it did in Detroit, it could only boast one week in each city as a sellout. Was it true, then, that *Jennie* had the biggest advance of the season at $1,250,000 and that the show that was to open on October 17 was printing tickets for performances through April 1964?

Perhaps, for after Richard Rodgers dumped Alan Jay Lerner and *I Picked a Daisy*—thus freeing the Majestic Theatre that they'd booked—*Jennie* decided to "move" from its planned home, the 1,498-seat Winter Garden, to the 1,609-seat house. Martin was again having an influence on *Funny Girl,* which was now free to take that theater (and its glorious almost-block-long-sign).

That Martin had turned down *Funny Girl* for *Jennie* is ironic, because both had similar plots. Jennie, en route to stage fame, also married the wrong man: James O'Conner. In addition to being a gambler, he was a wastrel and drunk.

But her man, she loved him so.

A better man—British playwright Christopher Lawrence Cromwell—was waiting for Jennie to dump James. Unlike in *Funny Girl,* this Eddie Ryan character got the girl. But was it love or did Jennie feel he might write her a good play? (Taylor's second husband, J. Hartley Manners, did just that by penning *Peg o' My Heart* for her.)

There would be another analogy to *Funny Girl:* a trying, try-anything tryout. "High Is Better than Low" was originally the third song but became the twelfth. "Before I Kiss the World Goodbye" went from fifth to eighth place, and "Over Here" from ninth to sixth. (Time for a sentence that includes the words "rearranging," "deck," "chairs," and "*Titanic*"?)

Jennie's friends the Turnbull Sisters—Ethel and Stella—were separated soon after their birth. Ethel was excised, a decision that sent home ol' Broadway pro Constance Carpenter (who'd taken over for Gertrude Lawrence in *The King and I*).

But a character named Bessie Mae Sue was added. This was Martin's third tribute to her childhood friend Bessie Mae Sue Ella Yaeger. In *South Pacific*, she'd asked that a character be named Ensign Sue Yaeger. Martin trumped that with *The Sound of Music*, where she actually insisted that the list of actors include a Sue Yaeger who played "A Postulant." This resulted in some later chaos with the IRS, who wanted to know why the elusive Ms. Yaeger wasn't paying taxes.

Jennie did have its moments as a spectacle. Slips were inserted into *Playbills:* "Please note: there is a fire effect during the second act. It is completely mechanical. No fire is used. The effect is entirely safe."

They should have warned the audience about the bomb that *Jennie* was turning out to be. That many on the staff were unhappy with others didn't help. Crawford again, from her memoir: "I was the only contact among the various parties, spending nights until 3 A.M., going up and down in elevators to the various rooms trying to effect a compromise."

Martin decided to lose Dennis O'Keefe as James and get George D. Wallace in instead. She also apparently lost interest in the show as it wended its way toward Broadway. In Boston, she had six solos and was part of four other numbers. By Broadway, she'd shed three of those solos: "Dinner Is Served," in which she earned her keep at her mother's house, "On the Other Hand," in which Jennie rejected James, and "Close Your Eyes," when she all too predictably reconciled with him. While Dietz and Schwartz did write her a new song—"I Think I'm Going to Like It," referring to her sudden success—she chose not to add it to the show.

Also dropped was "O'Conner," James's song in which he aggrandized himself, and a choral number, "No Hope for the Human Race." In their place came—nothing.

What had been *Escape from the Harem, or Omar and the Captive Virgin* had now become *The Sultan's 50th Bride.* But a look at the dramatis personae shows each had the same characters. What's in a name?

That destruction by fire and water figured prominently in *Jennie* turned out to be apt, for some critics unleashed their fire on the show while others threw cold water on it. Martin went relatively unblemished: "expert and endearing" (Nadel), "piquant and ageless" (McClain), "a pleasure to watch" (Watts), "fine and appealing" (Chapman). Taubman, however, said, "My heart has belonged to Mary Martin. But *Jennie* does not make it easy to remain faithful."

Kerr was more blunt: "Martin forever, but not *Jennie,*" which he called "a woeful tale of some woeful people in a woeful way." Agreeing with him were Watts ("a dolorous story"), Chapman ("a tearjerker"), and Taubman ("a soggy saga"). Nadel started by referencing a show song of twenty-two years earlier: "Poor *Jennie.*"

McClain, however, while calling it "a good show" but not "a great show," predicted that "it will do very well for a season or two."

Wrong. *Jennie* did set a house record the week of October 27, raking in $91,847 thanks to standees who cracked the $91,700 capacity mark. Not even two months later, during its final frame—and Christmas week, yet—it took in $47,102.

It's an Ill-Wind Department: The Signet Players, a community theater in Cleveland, profited from *Jennie.* They bought from Halliday $40,000 worth of sets—for $2,000.

But wait! At *Our Hearts Belong to Mary,* just before the tribute came to an end, Martin sang "Before I Kiss the World Goodbye." She knew that it was the right song for a woman who was about to turn seventy-two and hadn't sung on Broadway in eighteen years (and, though she didn't know it, would be gone in five more).

Nevertheless, she didn't sing the lyric about the salt left in the shaker.

Fade Out—Fade In had a Great Parade, too—of lawsuits.

It certainly had the pedigree for success. The star would be Carol Burnett, whom the nation enjoyed each Tuesday night on TV as a down-to-earth, homespun girl with no pretensions. Burnett would often get a laugh by walking to center stage, clearing her throat with a loud "Ahem," as if she were summoning up phlegm, and then deciding at the last moment to keep it down. TV stars on variety shows usually displayed more elegance.

Burnett would deliver music by Jule Styne and a book and lyrics by Betty Comden and Adolph Green. It was the three writers' seventh show together, but their first original musical since their biggest hit: *Bells Are Ringing* in 1956.

Directing would be no less than George Abbott, who had staged Comden and Green's second- and third-biggest hits—respectively *Wonderful Town* and *On the Town*. What's more, Abbott had made Burnett a Broadway star after casting her in *Once upon a Mattress*.

When audiences entered the Mark Hellinger Theatre, the curtain was already raised to reveal a most entertaining scrim. Set designers William and Jean Eckart had replicated the cement expanse in front of Grauman's Chinese Theatre, replete with handprints and footprints of famous stars. Just seeing the names Fred Astaire, Jean Harlow, Jeanette MacDonald, and the Marx Brothers (including Zeppo!) whetted audiences' appetite for a return to '30s Hollywood.

They got it. Soon after the curtain went up on *Fade Out—Fade In,* a parade of movie stars—including Astaire, Harlow, MacDonald, and the Marxes—came forward to the delight of Hope Springfield (Burnett), the small-town girl who'd been summoned to Hollywood by FFF Studio founder L. Z. Governor. Now all her dreams of stardom were about to come true. Not bad for someone who only recently had been, as she sang, "The Usher from the Mezzanine."

For that song, Comden and Green wrote a lyric that they later dropped—but had they retained it, it would have taken on a much different meaning in eleven years: "Then she got a part in a chorus line on Broadway."

Hmmm, the gawky and awkward Burnett as a '30s movie star when glamour was the main requirement for success? There had to be a catch, and Comden and Green came up with a lulu. L. Z. had attended a Broadway show and was taken with the fourth chorine on the left; he had his minions sign her before he went off to Vienna to have a session with the eminent psychiatrist Dr. Anton Traurig.

There the good doctor couldn't help noticing that whenever L. Z. made a numerical list, he omitted the number four. As a test, Traurig asked him to recite the Gettysburg Address (which an Austrian wouldn't know, would he?), and Governor started *"Five* score and seven years ago..."

L. Z.'s lapse came because Ralph, the fourth of his six nephews, was an over-achiever who wanted to usurp the crown. The mogul went into a form of denial, which would now impact his business. He'd really meant to hire glamorous Gloria Currie (Tina Louise)—the fourth chorine—but inadvertently asked for the fifth, who happened to be Hope.

Most everyone at FFF was surprised at L. Z.'s choice, especially the studio's favorite leading man, Byron Prong. Devoted fans of the film *Auntie Mame*, whose screenplay was provided by Comden and Green, will recognize the name. He was the first actor billed underneath the title in Vera Charles's "terribly modern operetta" *Midsummer Madness*. Jack Cassidy, playing *this* Byron Prong in *Fade Out*, received the same billing.

Equally skeptical of L. Z.'s decision were five of his six nephews, headed most vociferously by Ralph. Only Rudolph saw something in Hope, the type of woman with whom he could fall in love—which he proceeded to do.

Once L. Z. returned, he canned Ralph and demanded that Rudolph fire Hope. Thus came one of musical theater's most underrated first-act curtains, replete with dramatic irony. Hope was in her bedroom celebrating that Hollywood had just rechristened her "Lila Tremaine." She joyously sang of parting with her dull name in favor of this glamorous one. Just as she was ending the song, Rudolph was seen opening her bedroom door en route to walking over and delivering the bad news. Curtain—and curtains for Hope.

Of course, there was a happy ending, and Hope did manage to become a star, leading to one of musical theater's most underrated *second*-act curtains: Hope is asked to put her smile in the cement at Grauman's, but gets her face stuck in the cement and is struggling to pull it out as the final curtain descends.

Considering the plot, *A Girl to Remember*, the show's first title, was its most logical. After the creators had flirted with *The Idol of Millions*, they landed on *Fade Out—Fade In*, probably because the tune they wrote by that name was so fetching. No, it wasn't "Hello, Dolly!," but it summed up what had happened in the story and was tuneful.

The score had other assets. When L. Z. decided he'd worked hard enough and was now on a sexual "quest for his youth," Styne wisely wrote a Charleston to reiterate just how far off L. Z.'s youth was. Burnett had a marvelous eleven o'clock number in which she portrayed Shirley Temple while Tiger Haynes played Bill "Bojangles" Robinson. "You Mustn't Be Discouraged" was a spoof of all those perky songs that Temple used to sing; here, instead, the message was "There's always one step further down you can go," with the Johnstown Flood and the San Francisco earthquake offered as proof.

The musical was originally set for a late November 1963 opening, but in June, Burnett announced that she was pregnant and due in December. She wanted to spend the winter at home, but would be willing to start rehearsals in the spring for a late May opening.

Producers Styne and Lester Osterman returned the $1 million advance, which was, as Daddy Warbucks would say fourteen years hence, "a lot of money in those days"—enough for 125 sold-out performances.

So *Fade Out* had to wait until May 26, 1964, to open. It was the seventy-fifth and final show of the 1963–64 season, but had it met its original schedule as the season's twenty-ninth production, it might well have turned out to be the season's biggest musical hit.

Taubman: "Spreads enough good cheer to suggest that it will be around for a while." Chapman: "I never stopped enjoying it." McClain: "It seems an assured smash." Nadel: "An exuberantly funny musical." Watts was a little less impressed: "It has enough enthusiastic relish to make it entertaining." Such enthusiasm was lost on Kerr: "I couldn't like it."

The producers weren't concerned once they saw the weekly grosses. The week of June 7 saw the show break *My Fair Lady*'s house record (granted, because of higher ticket prices): $83,958. That record lasted a week, for June 14's week brought in $83,969. Two weeks had to pass before that one was broken at $84,876.

If all this happened in November—soon after the opening of the quick flop *The Student Gypsy,* the disappointing *Here's Love,* the just-missed-the-bull's-eye *110 in the Shade,* and the awful *Jennie*—then *Fade Out—Fade In* would have been the first blockbuster musical of the season. With *Hello, Dolly!* still nine weeks away and *Funny Girl* nineteen, Burnett's musical would have had a solid head start on momentum.

The delayed opening also meant that *Fade Out* lost the publicity from the Tony Awards, which had an April 30 cutoff date that season. In hindsight, we now see that with those reviews and an on-fire box office, a November opening would have meant nominations for Best Musical and plenty of other categories. And while the Tonys weren't yet the glorified infomercial that's now broadcast each June to a national television audience, some positive publicity is better than none. Those six newspapers made the Tony Awards mean something, too.

As if the 1963–64 Best Actress in a Musical Tony race didn't turn out to be hot enough with Carol Channing, Barbra Streisand, Inga Swenson, and Beatrice Lillie, imagine Burnett in the mix. She certainly would have been nominated in place of Swenson—and might even have won. Failing that, she might have siphoned enough votes from Channing to make Streisand the winner.

None of that happened. What *did* happen in early June, however, was one of the greatest insults a Broadway musical has ever endured. Tina Louise, playing a studio starlet and object of L. Z.'s affection, would leave *Fade Out— Fade In* after a mere twenty-four performances to play Ginger Grant on *Gilligan's Island*. As Harry Rigby, a production associate on this season's *The Ballad of the Sad Café*, was always fond of saying, "Let's face it: Everybody needs money."

But that first fly in the ointment was a mere gnat compared to what would come. In late June, Burnett missed performances because of "an abdominal ailment," and in July, she said she needed minor surgery. She'd be unavailable for a solid week, so the producers went looking for a name replacement.

And settled for Betty Hutton.

It was probably the first good offer Hutton had had in a while. She hadn't done a Broadway musical in nearly a quarter century, in the era when Hollywood wanted her. But by 1964, she hadn't made a film in seven years, and her 1959 TV series couldn't last more than a season.

If there had ever been any doubt that the public had lost interest in Hutton, *Fade Out* proved it. She grossed $29,039.

The following week, when Burnett returned, the show was back at capacity.

This was sobering news to Styne, Osterman, Comden, and Green. Although their work had been lauded, the public seemed to want to see Burnett and not their musical.

So they knew they were in trouble in August when Burnett claimed that she'd aggravated an old neck injury during a taxicab ride. Ditto September, when she signed to do a new TV series, *The Entertainers*. Burnett stated to the press that "television is my first love." Perhaps TV, where she'd rehearse and improvise for a few days before performing live—and then starting the process all over again—seemed more creative to her than eight-a-week of a show set in stone.

Credit to Burnett, however: She did offer to buy out her contract for $500,000. That would have paid back all or almost all the investment. How foolhardy that the powers that be didn't agree, for this half million in the hand was worth billions in the bush. And why would anyone think that Burnett would simply return and give 100 percent to the show in which she'd clearly lost interest—nay, *discarded* interest? Styne and Osterman said they'd see her in court.

Burnett first spent some of October in a hospital, then in November made the brass-tacks statement that she'd been "unhappy and dissatisfied with the musical long before last July."

Perhaps Burnett felt that during early rehearsals, she hadn't received Styne's full attention, for he was still tending to *Funny Girl* during its forty-two-day delay in reaching Broadway. Burnett might have reasoned that Styne would have done better by *Fade Out—Fade In* if he'd only been available.

She undoubtedly noticed that Styne had given *Funny Girl* a far superior score, which may have been more unnerving to her considering that the two musicals were in some ways very much alike. Each had in its center a less-than-stunning young woman who desperately wanted a show business career. Both shows featured a big production number that replicated the opulent days of yore. And just as Fanny had had her Eddie Ryan, Hope had her champion in Rudolph Governor.

So why wasn't Styne equally inspired to write for *Fade Out* as for *Funny Girl?* If the torturous *Funny Girl* tryout had drained him, Burnett might have wondered why she should suffer. At the time, she was a much bigger star than Streisand, but Styne's musical wasn't doing the wonders for her career that Streisand's was. And to think that she'd turned down *Funny Girl*...

So even in May, Burnett had probably agreed with Kerr (that Styne's songs sounded "familiar"), McClain ("the music was good without being great"), and Watts ("I doubt if this stands among the unfailingly talented composer's notable scores."). Taubman cited the "attractive tunes," but that appraisal was a far cry from his view two months earlier that Styne's *Funny Girl* was "one of his best."

In fact, one reason why *Fade Out—Fade In* couldn't have been one of Styne's best scores involved Burnett herself. While Streisand could sing comic songs, she could also belt out a soulful ballad, and the public loved hearing her do both.

Burnett's singing voice is harsh and nasal. Would you want to listen to her for many minutes singing a ballad along the lines of "People," "The Music That Makes Me Dance," or "Who Are You Now?" *Fade Out* did give her one torch song—"Go Home, Train," in which Hope refused to retreat even after having been fired. And while Burnett poured on the emotion to compensate for her less-than-lovely voice, she didn't erase the memory of Streisand when Fanny turned her back on a train, too: "Don't Rain on My Parade."

Note that in her fifty-plus-year recording career, Streisand has always recorded for the same company. Despite all the changes that popular music has endured, her label has never come close to dropping her. As late as September 2014, she released a new album.

Burnett has gone through four different labels, was released by all, and last recorded an album in 1972. Most telling is that two of her LPs—one for Columbia and another for RCA Victor—were each called *Carol Burnett Sings*—as if the very idea of her attempting such an activity were an anomaly.

Over the years, Burnett and Streisand have each received two Tony nominations and multiple Emmys, but Streisand has won eight Grammys, while Burnett has been nominated for one—in the Spoken Word category.

So Styne had to write mostly "funny music" for Burnett, and actually did a good job. Comic songs, however, rarely have melodies as strong as their lyrics. Comden and Green did well by her, too, and included her already famous catchphrase "Yuck!" in "Call Me Savage," in which Hope was desperately trying—and failing—to convince Rudolph that she was a femme fatale. Yes, there was that terrific Shirley Temple eleven o'clock number, but Burnett had to share it; when Streisand sang her final song—"The Music That Makes Me Dance"—she was all alone center stage.

With Burnett claiming an inability to perform, *Fade Out* faded out on November 14. Had Burnett's pregnancy and disinterest not occurred, everyone on that date would have been instead preparing to celebrate the show's first anniversary on Broadway.

In December, the courts ruled in Styne and Osterman's favor, which must have made Burnett feel that indeed "there's always one step further down you can go."

But getting the show up again would cost another $100,000. Many on Broadway were uttering a famous expression that included the words "good," "money," "after," and "bad."

Imagine the mood when Burnett arrived at the theater on that late January day to begin re-rehearsing the show. Cassidy was gone, so there was a new leading man in Dick Shawn. But how did all her previous castmates, three months poorer from the layoff, regard her, knowing that she didn't want to be there? The star sets the tone for the show and captains the ship. There had to be some "Well, Carol won't be giving 100 percent, so why should I?"

Styne, Comden, and Green did their best to accommodate her and improve the show. They dropped "Lila Tremaine" and substituted their old unused title song "A Girl to Remember." They replaced "Go Home, Train" with "Everybody Loves a Winner." Perhaps to make Dick Patterson a little happier as Rudolph, they had him sing to Hope "Notice Me."

The term "spin"—meaning putting a positive sheen on a negative situation—hadn't yet been coined, but the concept had long been known to press agents. Veteran publicist Harvey Sabinson did his best to let the public know that unlike this time last year, there was no advance sale, so theatergoers would have their cream of the crop of tickets.

But too much press about legal matters had circulated. Who wants to see a star perform when you know that only a legal judgment is keeping her in place? Burnett's attitude gave the term "command performance" new meaning. Theatergoers decided that if Burnett wasn't having a good time doing the show, they wouldn't have a good time watching her slog through it.

When she sang her opening song "It's Good to Be Back Home" were her teeth gritted throughout? Some would-be ticket buyers decided against a purchase because Burnett might not be there when they arrived at the Hellinger.

Fade Out closed on April 17, 1965, only days before the 1964–65 Tony nominations were announced. That the show was now an unhappy memory for Broadway may be why it received no Best Musical nod. No, it wouldn't have beaten *Fiddler on the Roof,* but it could have held its own with the other three nominees: *Golden Boy, Half a Sixpence,* and *Oh, What a Lovely War.*

The show received all of one nomination—and it wasn't for Burnett. Why no acknowledgment of the star who'd been called "magnificent" by McClain and "extraordinary" by Chapman, and lauded for her "comic impudence" by Taubman and her "gift for character humor by Watts," not to mention Nadel's belief that she could "make everybody fall apart from laughter"?

Didn't Burnett belong in the company of Elizabeth Allen (*Do I Hear a Waltz?*), Inga Swenson (*Baker Street*), Nancy Dussault (*Bajour*), and newcomer (and winner) Liza Minnelli (*Flora, the Red Menace*)? Clearly she was being punished for not staying with the show.

(Let the punishment fit the crime.)

Ironically, Cassidy, who received the show's sole nomination, had bolted before the reopening. The Tony committee may have felt that he would have stayed with the show if there had been a show. Besides, he hadn't started the fire; everyone knew who was really responsible.

Burnett went back to TV and did better than ever with an eleven-year run of *The Carol Burnett Show*. A popular feature of the weekly series was a question-and-answer session with the audience. One night she was asked, "Are you coming back to Broadway anytime soon?" to which she gave a curt "No!" before stating, "Next question," avoiding any chance that the owner of the inquiring mind could ask "Why?"

And yet, Burnett did return—thirty-one years later, the way Betty Hutton did when no other branch of entertainment was courting her.

As for Styne, Comden, and Green, only three years later they tried again with *Hallelujah, Baby!* Apparently they had either blocked out the entire *Fade Out—Fade In* debacle or believed that their "Girl to Remember" show was one that no one remembered—for they recycled the melody of "Call Me Savage" and forged a new song called "Witches' Brew" with an all-new lyric.

Hallelujah, Baby! received reviews far inferior to *Fade Out—Fade In*'s, but it had a leading lady (Leslie Uggams) who was happy to be starring on Broadway. So it ran longer and—how 'bout this?—won the Tony as Best Musical, partly because the season in which it was competing had been a putrid one for song-and-dance shows.

As Styne was fond of saying, "You always win for the wrong one." As proof, he'd mention that his "Three Coins in the Fountain" should not have won the

1954 Best Original Song Oscar, but that Harold Arlen and Ira Gershwin should have won for "The Man That Got Away."

Fade Out—Fade In was the show that got away.

They respectively ran 478, 679, and 694 performances in England, so of course America would get to see *Stop the World—I Want to Get Off, Half a Sixpence,* and *Pickwick.*

So shouldn't a musical that ran 627 performances get its chance on Broadway, too?

The difference is that *Rugantino* was a smash hit not in London but in Rome. The 887-mile distance between the two cities is even wider culturally.

That didn't stop producer Alexander H. Cohen from importing it. He'd always viewed himself as master-importer David Merrick's main rival. Merrick felt he had no rivals at all.

(The latter was correct.)

After its Toronto tryout, Cohen's *Rugantino* would run 599 fewer performances than it had in Rome. Could one reason be that *Rugantino* remained in the Italian of bookwriter-lyricists Pietro Garinei and Sandro Giovannini?

Keeping the musical in its native language allowed the Italian cast to replicate their roles, which saved money on recasting. And while airfare from Rome for a cast of forty-six couldn't have been inexpensive, *Rugantino* was budgeted at $210,000 at a time when some musicals cost twice as much.

Opera fans were long accustomed to seeing productions in foreign languages; Broadway theatergoers were not. Thus Cohen filled the *Playbill* with seven columns of dense synopsis for avid readers and a more modest two-page condensation for lazier ones.

He didn't stop there. As *Billboard* oxymoronically reported, Cohen would provide "sub-titles flashing above the stage." So the producer does get credit for introducing the supertitles that have now become commonplace in opera.

Rugantino, the title character, had his problems as the curtain rose. His hands and legs had been locked into stocks as a punishment for "a minor prank" that Papal Law decried.

What he did was not made clear. This was a problem, for a theatergoer needed to be the judge of what was major or minor. If the offense was indeed minor, then *Rugantino* would seem to be an indictment against a Catholic Church that was too repressive and all too willing to humiliate those who didn't follow its laws to the letter.

Garinei and Giovannini must have felt that they'd answered this question when they soon described Rugantino as "a scoundrel." This allowed the audience to infer that the Church was throwing the book at him now that it had the chance—much the way that the U.S. government snagged Al Capone in the '30s for tax evasion when it couldn't quite pin him down for bootlegging, prostitution, and worse.

Rugantino saw a young couple stroll by. When he learned that Gnecco and Rosetta were married, he didn't care; he wanted the lady for himself. His friends doubted that he could seduce her, which led to one of musical comedy's favorite gambits: the bet. Rugantino would win a handsome sum if he could bed Rosetta by "Lantern Night," the annual festival that was only a day away. If he couldn't get her into the sack, he'd jump into a very different kind of sack—a large burlap one—and hop all the way to the Church of San Pasquale.

(The authors didn't say how great a distance that was.)

Mastro Titta, as short and roly-poly as any operetta's burgomeister, came on. He was established as the local innkeeper as well as the town executioner whenever the occasion called for it. The authors' giving him such an atypical sideline left little doubt that they would later have him use his power.

Many a character in many a musical has walked in at the wrong time or has all too conveniently eavesdropped in order to learn a vital piece of information. But *Rugantino* was the first to have a fettered hero overhear the sounds of a screaming fight between a husband and wife waft through an open window. Rosetta hated that Gnecco was a papal spy who turned in miscreants for money and had had one of her admirers killed.

Did Gnecco do this because his wife was interested in the devotee, too? That wasn't made clear.

Garinei and Giovannini would have done better if Rugantino had heard Rosetta complain that Gnecco had fingered him. What's more, if Rugantino had decided to seduce Rosetta only *after* he'd learned that she was in an unhappy marriage, he would have seemed a little less venal.

The next morning, after Rugantino was released, he committed another act that could have hampered his hands and feet. While he was passing the

Prince's mansion, he saw a dead cat in the street, so he took the liberty of throwing the animal's corpse into the Prince's open window. What made matters worse was that the family inside was in the midst of a wake.

Actually, the Prince and Princess didn't seem to be devastated by the loss of Grandpa. She suggested to her husband that after the wake had ended they would walks to the docks, where she would pretend to be a prostitute; once she landed a customer, she and he would allegedly set off to her place of business, only to have the Prince jump out of the shadows, beat the man, and throw him into the Tiber.

Some nobles aren't so noble.

The plot returned to Rugantino (and not a moment too soon). He saw Rosetta on the street and suggested that they take a stroll down the local Lovers' Lane. She countered with an offer to come up to her place. Rugantino was counting and spending the money he'd soon receive from winning the bet.

Wrong again. Rosetta lured him there so that Gnecco could pummel him. Rugantino's souvenir was a broken finger.

Arriving just in time to soothe Rugantino was Eusebia, his longtime mistress. In the past, they'd committed many a scam by pretending to be a brother and sister in distress and preying on sympathetic strangers who were willing to house them until their fortunes changed. In this case, Mastro Titta would provide the shelter.

Once they'd settled their housing concerns, Rugantino strolled by the docks, where he encountered the devious Princess. But she didn't take him to the Prince, because she was taken with him.

The Prince, in that tired plot device mentioned above, overheard her. So that night, he found Rugantino and invited him to the house for dinner. He served Rugantino the dead cat that had landed there earlier—and made him eat it, too.

This plot point couldn't have sat well with theatergoers who were still digesting their own pretheater meals.

After Rugantino had finished eating, he left and learned that Rosetta was posing for a sculptor who was creating a statue of a man and woman together. The authors conveniently made the male model ill so that Rugantino could volunteer to take his place. Rosetta refused to pose with him just as Gnecco was coming in. Rugantino ran for his life (or at least for his other nine fingers).

He took refuge in a nearby church. When Mastro Titta came in to give his confession, Rugantino pretended to be the priest. Among the wrongdoings detailed by Titta was his love for Eusebia. Why this would be a sin went unexplained, but "the priest" took the opportunity to tell Titta to be nice to Rugantino because he was Eusebia's brother.

Lantern Night arrived, so Rugantino was in grave danger of losing his bet. But he did convince Rosetta to take a walk with him, which led to an unintentionally funny song, easily the most inadvertently hilarious of the season: "Roma Nun Fa La Stupida Stasera."

Loosely translated, it means "Rome at Night Makes You Make a Fool of Yourself." Composer Armando Trovaioli indeed created a pretty melody, but it wasn't the magnum opus that he thought it was. A listen to it on the original cast album would challenge anyone not to laugh.

First the entire company sang the ten-line lyric.

Then the men's chorus repeated it word for word.

Then the women's chorus did.

Then both groups sang it together—again, the same ten lines.

Assume that it was done? No, for then Rugantino sang the same ten lines.

Followed by Rosetta doing the same.

It had to be over now, right?

No, Titta took his turn with the same ten lines.

Turnabout being fair play, Eusebia did, too.

Now it had to be over, right?

No—for then everyone joined in to sing it a capella.

Trovaioli apparently believed that this song was *so* beautiful that it didn't even need any musical accompaniment.

And after the audience heard the same lyric and melody nine times in a row, it saw the curtain fall with the requisite suspense: Would Rosetta give in?

Act Two began with Rugantino relating that indeed she did. However, because he'd come to genuinely love Rosetta (yes, of course), he'd tell his friends that he lost. That soon put him in the sack and hopping to San Pasquale.

But en route, Rugantino's friends taunted him so much for losing that he couldn't stand the insults and blurted out the truth—just as (surprise!) Rosetta walked in and heard him. She all too predictably said that she never wanted to see him again.

If that had only been Rugantino's biggest problem. Gnecco was stabbed to death near where Rugantino was standing. He walked over to the body and foolishly removed the knife just as a lawman entered.

Lots of inadvertent entrances in *Rugantino,* no?

Rugantino managed to escape. Rosetta, who assumed that he *did* kill Gnecco, publically announced that she was Rugantino's lover and proclaimed her love for him.

This didn't do any favors for the fugitive, who was captured and set for execution at Titta's hand the next morning. (No trial?) Rosetta came by and swore she'd always be faithful to him and his memory. That cheered Rugantino enough that he could go fearlessly to the guillotine.

When this show was first being readied for Rome, didn't anyone say "Sento odore di guai libro"—"I smell book trouble"? After it opened, wasn't there at least one critic who said of the antihero "Puoi attingere acqua dolce da un fallo bene?"—"Can you draw sweet water from a foul well?"

Chances are *Rugantino* passed muster with Italians because it was structured and sounded like a Broadway musical—song-scene-song-scene—which was an unfamiliar animal to a nation that had been brought up on opera.

As for the music, a listen to the Italian cast album suggests that Trovaioli had visited Manhattan in the late '50s, saw *West Side Story* and *My Fair Lady,* and said, *"Ecco come è fatto!"* ("So that's how it's done!")

Also helping *Rugantino*'s Roman run was its advertisement as "a musical spectacle," a promise on which it delivered. The atmosphere of a quaint Italian village was well replicated, and two concentric turntables—one traveling clockwise, one counterclockwise—were impressive for their time.

Every critic mentioned them, too—but they also had liabilities to note as well. Taubman: "Mixed into it like a rich sauce for a tasty pasta are impudent and bawdy comedy and maudlin melodrama." Kerr: "Largely irrelevant and sometimes quite sleepy." Watts: "Resolutely and resoundingly dull." McClain became jingoistic: "It doesn't do anything that we don't do better in the way of music, mounting, and certainly choreography."

"The music is a Roman equivalent of the old *Lucky Strike Hit Parade*," said Nadel, referencing the 1950–59 TV series that each week detailed the nation's bestselling records. As for Chapman, he used every critic's favorite's say-nothing euphemism: "Interesting."

Not with that book, it wasn't. On Leap Year's Day, twenty-three days after opening, *Rugantino* leaped into oblivion. The $210,000 musical wound up costing—and losing—$300,000.

Now we come to the shortest-running musical of the season.

And you thought at nine performances it was *Anyone Can Whistle*.

Café Crown ran a third as long. It opened on Friday, April 17, and called it a life on Saturday, April 18, after its third official performance.

That Friday opening wasn't arbitrarily chosen. Shows that didn't expect good reviews often opened on Friday, for reviews would be printed on Saturday—the day that newspaper reading was at its lowest.

One can see why Hy Kraft would think that his 1942 semihit comedy (also called *Café Crown*) would make a good musical. What a rich locale was Second Avenue in the '20s and '30s, when it was "the Jewish Rialto" lined with Yiddish-language theaters.

In the first third of the twentieth century, these houses were filled with Jews who had emigrated from Europe. They felt nostalgic for home, alienated by their accents, intimidated by the Gentiles' language, and starved for recreation. So what if immigrant impresarios routinely bowdlerized and changed the plots of classics? After a hard day at work, seeing Romeo and Juliet live happily ever after made for a nice night.

As a youth, Kraft had attended the shows and, more important, had frequented the Café Royale at Twelfth Street and Second Avenue. This was the hub of Yiddish theater that saw the hubbub of deals made, opinions shared, arguments fought, parts cast, and money raised.

As the '40s began, Kraft noticed that many children of Jewish immigrants now thought of themselves as Americans. They weren't responding as strongly to a theater that often suggested they stick to their own kind. Besides, every generation must put its own stamp on entertainment by finding and creating its own stars, so these young people were more interested in Bing Crosby than Boris Thomashefsky.

So Kraft had his theme: tradition vs. assimilation, a worthy one, as *Fiddler on the Roof* would ultimately prove twenty-two years later. He created Yiddish producer-director David Cole and his star Lester Freed, who wanted to go eight avenues west and forty blocks north to Broadway. Not only that, Freed planned to take David's grown ingénue-daughter, Norma, with him as his co-star and wife.

That scenario wasn't far removed from what the Adler family had endured. Luther and Stella Adler were reluctant to abandon their father, Jacob Adler, one of the greatest Yiddish theater stars. (How great? His funeral in 1926 saw streets clogged with an estimated 50,000 to 100,000 admirers.) And yet, brother and sister went uptown.

Cole had earmarked both Lester and Norma for his next opus, *The King of Riverside Drive*. Its plot: "A tired Jewish-American businessman-millionaire," said Cole, "wants to divide his fortune among his children and asks, 'Which of you loves me the most?' "

It was *King Lear*, all right, but Cole didn't dare credit the Bard. His investors, especially Café Crown's busboy Hymie, had seen Shakespeare fail before, so they were reluctant to give the writer another chance.

Lester's agent arrived with the good news that his client had been cast in a Broadway play. The actor was less thrilled when he heard that he'd been typecast as a rabbi. Norma, however, saw it as a foot in the stage door at the Selwyn.

Cole had something to say to the agent: "You steal our people and want Freed like all the others: Broadway, Hollywood, radios, jukeboxes." Lester ultimately decided to stay with Cole rather than appear in a stereotypical (and small) role.

Ah, but when a *Hollywood* offer came in . . .

Café Crown opened only forty-seven days after the December 7, 1941, attack on Pearl Harbor, when people needed to laugh, and yet it could only manage four months in a season in which *Blithe Spirit* would start a run five times as long. Now, in 1963–64, perhaps it could be more successful as a musical.

But the director was Jerome Eskow, who'd never directed anything on Broadway. The producer was Philip Rose, who'd always be venerated for having given the world *A Raisin in the Sun*, but he'd had less luck with musicals. His *Bravo, Giovanni* had died a quick 1962 death and lost $550,000, much of it from Columbia Records.

That *Café Crown* was the shortest-running musical of the season was no surprise to those who had noticed that its ads failed to proudly proclaim "Original Cast Album by [Label] Records." That every company passed on the rights to record the show meant that even before it went into rehearsal, it had two strikes against it.

What's wrong with the show?

How bad is the score?

Café Crown would be the season's only book musical that didn't have a recording deal in place, which caused Rose to nix even one out-of-town-tryout. He would take the still-novel route of staying in town for less costly previews—thirty of them.

Rose was able to sign some solid names: Theodore Bikel as the father (renamed Samuel Cole) and Sam Levene as Hymie. Tommy Rall would play David Cole, now Samuel's *son*, who was thinking of abandoning Second Avenue with his girlfriend, Norma.

More to the point, Kraft's play and its café setting seemed right for musicalization. Kraft had inadvertently given composer Albert (*Redhead*) Hague and lyricist Marty Brill a head start on one song, for in his comedy's opening scene he'd written a snippet, "Au Revoir, Poland—Hello, New York," which the Café Crown's waiters sang in between delivering latkes and seltzer. This was the title tune for the new Yiddish musical that would soon open across the street and in which they'd been cast.

Hague and Brill chose to present the number in rehearsal as opposed to opening night. They envisioned it as a showstopper, but once it played in front of an audience, the show went on.

The second act featured something unexpected, but "unexpected" didn't automatically mean "good." "What in the world is this musical doing with of all things a *King Lear* Ballet?" Taubman demanded to know in his pan. "It is hard to believe that a Yiddish theater would go for something as fancy."

Or as serious. It might not quite have been a dream ballet—again, a convention that was on its way out—but it passed for one. Choreographer Ron Field should have insisted on a big comic numba that showed the fast-'n'-loose way Second Avenue artists played with masterpieces—say, having Hamlet become a rabbi's son who's at yeshiva. (Don't laugh. One Yiddish playwright did precisely that to the Bard's biggest hit.)

"Opening up the show," a practice of which musicals are fond, may have helped close it down, for the rehearsal scenes didn't involve Hymie. "Sam Levene has been cast as a waiter," wrote Kerr, "and he has nothing to do but wait— wait on tables, wait for the author to give someone else a funny line. It's clear, after a time, that none is coming his way." At least Hymie got to sing "So Long as It Isn't Shakespeare" in the matter-of-fact, shoulder-shrugging way Levene always conducted business.

A subplot from the play got greater prominence here: Cole had once had an illegitimate son, who had grown up and wanted to meet his father. In the musical, he was played by Alan Alda, who'd portrayed the boyfriend in *Fair Game for Lovers*. Would he have believed that that four-performance flop would outrun his next one? As Kerr wrote, "For the second time this season and for the second time in a disaster, special mention must be made of Alan Alda," who "should be noted by people who have better shows in mind."

Was *Café Crown* "too Jewish"? Lord knows, another 1964 musical—next season's smash *Fiddler on the Roof*—centered almost exclusively on Jews. No, Hague and Brill's score couldn't compete with Bock and Harnick's, any more than Kraft's book could rival Joseph Stein's.

But *Café Crown* might have reminded contemporary Jews of their parents who reveled in their own little world and seemed to resist assimilation. *Fiddler*, set in a more distant time and place, essentially dealt with their grandparents, to whom children often give more indulgence and affection. They could applaud Tevye for at least trying to move with the changing times; they weren't happy that Cole &Co. didn't want to.

The Second World War had hastened the end of Second Avenue. Jews and Gentiles who'd fought in the trenches now had new feelings for each other that ranged from tolerance to genuine love. As Alisa Solomon wrote in *Wonder of Wonders*, her study of *Fiddler*, "Where one American in five told pollsters in 1948 they wouldn't want a Jew as a neighbor, by 1959 such antipathy was expressed by only one in fifty."

By then, the Café Royale had closed and turned into a dry-cleaning establishment. Philip Rose closed *Café Crown* after having been taken to the cleaners.

So when we count up 1963–64's book musicals, we see only one made from a movie—that would change in the seasons to come—in addition to three originals, two inspired by real people's lives, one based on a novel, and five inspired by plays.

No—make that *six* book musicals adapted from plays. There's another produced by a name we've already encountered. The time has come to give him a little more time.

CHAPTER THREE

*

The Showman

He brought four productions to Broadway in 1957–58 and six in both 1958–59 and 1960–61. And yet, the producer formerly known as David Margulois never before or after would have as busy a season as 1963–64. "David Merrick presents" were the first words on the window cards of eight shows: five plays and three musicals. (And, of course, he would have had his ninth production and fourth musical of the season had he stayed with *Funny Girl*.)

Juggling projects must have been particularly busy the week of November 10. While Sunday was then a day of rest for many, Merrick was up early getting the weekly financial reports for his currently-running attractions.

Hmmm. *Stop the World—I Want to Get Off* had dropped from $28,806 to $26,962. On the face of it, that seemed terrible, given that capacity at the Ambassador was $61,000. But the week before this was the much-heralded star Anthony Newley's final frame with the show that he'd co-written and had directed. Merrick had chosen not to replace him with a star, but opted for the unknown Joel Grey in hopes that the eye-catching title would keep attracting theatergoers.

So far that seemed to be the case. Besides, the entire enterprise had only cost $75,000—easily the lowest budget for a major musical in the '60s (and probably the '50s and '40s)—and had repaid in a few weeks. So why hire a costly star and risk losing the money that had already been made?

Alas, *Oliver!* was a different story. Merrick had expected this to be a smash and get him his first Best Musical Tony. Not only did it lose to *Funny Thing,* but it also hadn't had a sold-out week since June 30. The previous week it had grossed $47,672 out of $69,000.

What's more, Merrick had to endure the expense of putting in a new Oliver now that Bruce Prochnik had grown too tall. Ronnie Kroll, who'd spent the last six weeks on Broadway in *Here's Love*, now had the part. (He, his parents, and/or his agent were no dummies; they knew he had to get out of that turkey.)

Those were the holdovers. The new shows? *110 in the Shade* did $57,371 out of a potential $59,000—up for the third week in a row since opening, and now at 97.2 percent capacity. Yes, but that still meant hundreds of tickets hadn't been sold. Merrick knew that one empty seat didn't simply mean one vacancy; it meant that hundreds of playgoers weren't fighting to see his new show.

Everyone but Taubman had liked it. Maybe, Merrick had to think, he shouldn't have gone on national TV last spring and called Taubman "an incompetent hack" and "a blind idiot."

On the other hand, Taubman had liked Merrick's two nonmusical London imports, but seats were available for those, too. At least John Osborne's *Luther* was selling solidly. But what would happen when rising glamour-boy star Albert Finney left in mid-January? Merrick wondered if he should sign a new star, let understudy John Heffernan take over, or simply close it. At the very least, he'd have to move it, for another show was coming into its theater.

That was the St. James, and the show was *Hello, Dolly!* So Merrick the landlord would be evicting Merrick the tenant. (Merrick loved the St. James, to which he brought eight out of the eleven attractions that the theater housed during the '60s. It was in the same building as his office, so dropping in on a production was nice 'n' easy.)

Alas, Merrick's other import, Jean Anouilh's *The Rehearsal*, wasn't doing well. Merrick probably hadn't done the math that would reveal that eleven previous Anouilh plays on Broadway had averaged a scant eighty-five performances. He probably felt loyal to the author of *Becket*, which had brought him his first Best Play Tony Award after nine other plays hadn't.

Becket, however, was a straightforward history lesson. *The Rehearsal*, although dealing with one of Broadway's favorite themes—adultery—would never be confused with *The Seven Year Itch*.

Instead of a modest New York apartment, the setting was the Chateau of Ferbroques in rural France, where every spring a group of minor nobles enjoyed presenting a play just for the fun of it. This year, the choice was Marivaux's *The Double Inconstancy*, which, in Anouilh's insouciant way, had a double meaning; the chicanery in the play mirrored what was happening in these nobles' lives.

To truly appreciate the nuances of the Anouilh play, one had to know the Marivaux one, too. Alas, Pierre Carlet de Chamblain de Marivaux (1688–1763) had only been to Broadway by virtue of four imported limited engagements by classical impresario Sol Hurok, and none was *The Double Inconstancy*.

Later in the decade, Merrick had Broadway writers Americanize other French plays into *Cactus Flower* and *Forty Carats,* and experienced far more success than he would have with *The Rehearsal*. Although it ran a healthy forty-three weeks in the West End, it would do only fourteen here.

Merrick put the figures aside and looked ahead. He was now facing his busiest week of the season. First would be Monday's opening of *Arturo Ui*—abbreviated from its full title, *The Resistible Rise of Arturo Ui*. Bertolt Brecht's 1941 play, reportedly written in a mere eighteen days, told of a thug who rose to power in gangland Chicago and cornered the vegetable market. That the brute was made to resemble Hitler was no coincidence.

Brecht, in his five other Broadway chances, saw his best showing with the previous season's fifty-two-performance run of *Mother Courage and Her Children*—and that production, directed by Jerome Robbins, starred Anne Bancroft, who'd won an Oscar during the run. Even that extra publicity couldn't keep it alive.

That failure must have pleased the always competitive Merrick. Robbins, you'll remember, wanted Bancroft as his *Funny Girl* when he was planning to direct and when Merrick was co-producing it. *Mother Courage* was the property he had chosen instead.

Arturo Ui had a future Oscar winner in Christopher Plummer. Tony Richardson would direct, starting rehearsals after only two weeks' rest following the opening of *Luther*.

Richardson was the reason this production was happening. Even before *Luther,* he'd done well by Merrick in staging *Look Back in Anger, A Taste of Honey,* and *The Entertainer*. As he saw it, Merrick owed him the chance to do a show he was hot to do. (And they said he had no heart!)

If *Luther*'s cast of twenty-five seemed overwhelming, what of *Arturo Ui*'s thirty-seven? They included established star Madeleine Sherwood, future star James Coco, eventual Negro Ensemble Company co-founder Robert Hooks (who was calling himself Bobby Dean Hooks at the time), and ten people who'd never again appear on Broadway.

Opening night was Monday, November 11, and by Tuesday morning, November 12, Merrick had read such phrases as "An evening of excitement and stimulation," "Quite a theatrical stunt, all right," and "A stunning and spectacular show."

Does this sound as if it's a play that will close on its first Saturday? One wonders if Merrick even saw these quotations respectively given by McClain, Chapman, and Watts. There's a better chance that Merrick looked through Kerr and saw the words "tedious," "obvious," "heavy-handed," "half-hearted," and "drone" jump out at him, and from Taubman's review such phrases as "less worthy of respect," "the wrong tone," and "the trouble is everywhere." If he'd bother to read Nadel, he wouldn't have been happy with him, either: "Not all the drama of the late Bertolt Brecht is deathless" was his lede.

Merrick couldn't dwell long on *Arturo Ui,* because on the following night, Wednesday, November 13, he had another opening. Although Merrick was twice as likely to import a foreign play than produce a home-grown one, *One Flew over the Cuckoo's Nest* belonged to the latter category.

The story is now familiar from the famous film made a dozen years later. After Randle P. McMurphy's scrape with the law, he was judged a psychopath. He wasn't unnerved at the prospect of being placed in a mental hospital, for he assumed he'd have it easier than he would in a work camp.

Hardly. Randle immediately caused trouble by refusing to take a shower, telling the aides that he first wanted to meet his fellow inmates. They included Chief Bromden, a mostly silent and brooding Native American, and Billy Bibbit, a stuttering virgin.

(The latter was played by Gene Wilder. In a few years, he'd become famous as Leo Bloom, partner in crime with Max Bialystock in the film *The Producers*. One wonders if he picked up a few tips on sleazy producing while working for Merrick.)

Randle persisted, but Nurse Ratched wouldn't have it. "You must realize that our policies are engineered for *your* cure, which means cooperation....You must follow the rules."

"That," said Randle, "is the *exact* thing somebody always tells me about the rules—just when I'm thinking about breaking every one of them."

So breaking *him* was Ratched's plan. Never mind that Randle found a way to eliminate Billy's stutter, albeit by bringing a prostitute into the hospital and paying her to have sex with the lad. Ratched didn't feel that the end justified the means.

Randle's loopholes drove Ratched loopy. One of them had to lose, and the nurse ensured it wouldn't be she by arranging for McMurphy's lobotomy.

Nevertheless, the play managed to go out on an exhilarating high note. Once Chief Bromden saw how far Ratched would go to maintain order, he escaped from the hospital en route to a better life. Randle P. McMurphy had not died in vain.

Was maverick Merrick attracted to this play because he identified with Mc-Murphy's antiestablishment stance?

If it didn't have the makings of a crowd-pleaser, it had a name to bring in the crowds: Kirk Douglas as Randle. What an asset to have this genuine movie star commit himself to a run-of-the-play contract. What a difference from to-day's film stars, who come in for twelve weeks, win their Tony, put it next to their Oscar, Emmy, and perhaps Grammy, close the show, and forget that Broadway exists.

Although Douglas would never return to the New York stage, he fully committed himself to *Cuckoo's Nest*. He had, in fact, bought the rights to Ken Kesey's countercultural novel and had hired as his writer Dale Wasserman, who'd helped bring Douglas's 1958 Hollywood hit *The Vikings* to the screen.

Merrick probably would have chosen a different writer if this hadn't been Douglas's baby all along. The producer was even forced to accept a 50 percent partnership with Edward Lewis, who'd produced each of the four Douglas films from the previous four years.

Douglas was obviously loyal. That Malcolm Atterbury had a small role as a mental patient seemed to be a Douglas payback; in 1938, Atterbury was running the Tamarack Playhouse in Lake Pleasant, New York, where he gave young Douglas his first professional job.

After all this goodwill, reporting that *Cuckoo's Nest* was a smash would be nice. Not to be. About the characters, McClain said, "We don't care too much what happens to them." Watts found it "confusingly designed," and Nadel felt it was "so unlikely that it borders on fantasy." Kerr concurred: "So preposterous a proposition for the theater that it could be dismissed very briefly if it weren't for the extraordinary tastelessness."

Taubman agreed with Kerr, stating that the jokes were "either embarrassing or in appalling taste. How can a thread of compassion stand out in a crazy-quilt of wisecracks, cavortings, violence and histrionic villainy?" Only Chapman responded positively: "Funny, touching and, as it moves swiftly toward its end, exciting melodrama."

They were all entitled to their opinions, but why did Kerr, Watts, and Nadel reveal the ending by actually using the word "lobotomy"? (McClain slightly obfuscated the procedure by calling it "brain surgery.") Perhaps they felt that their notices would discourage readers from attending, so they might as well tell them how the play played out.

So as of Thursday, November 14, the future didn't look bright for *Cuckoo's Nest*. Still, Merrick reasoned, where there was life and Kirk Douglas, there was hope. *Arturo Ui* had neither, and so Merrick would close it after eight performances on Saturday, November 16—the same day he'd fly to Detroit to see the first performance of *Hello, Dolly!*

En route he also had to give some thought to the play that would open two weeks before *Dolly* and the musical that would open a month after.

That Merrick was producing them was even more of a surprise than his sponsoring *Cuckoo's Nest*, because he'd never before produced a revival. Now here he was planning two, starting with Tennessee Williams's recent play *The Milk Train Doesn't Stop Here Anymore*.

The Williams play brings to mind a poem by Andy Logan that was published in the March 16, 1963, issue of *The New Yorker*. The twelve-line *The Milk Train Stops at Tiffany's* referenced not only *The Milk Train Doesn't Stop Here Anymore* but also Truman Capote's *Breakfast at Tiffany's*, which had recently enjoyed success as a film.

Logan's opening was "Says Holly Golightly to Flora Goforth," respectively citing the heroines of Capote's and Williams's works. After they exchange compliments, the poem concludes:

We're two-for-the-show girls,
The forthlightly Go-girls;
And, wrongly or rightly,
(Golightly tells Goforth)
"We'll both sell out nightly,
on stage, screen, and so forth."

Really? On that precise cover date of March 16, producer Roger L. Stevens was closing *Milk Train* after sixty-nine poorly attended performances.

That it opened during a newspaper shutdown was literally one strike against it. Oh, the critics did their best during that 114-day arid span by pooling their resources and publishing a glorified brochure called "First Nite," which offered all their reviews.

(Interest was that high then in what the critics had to say about the latest openings.)

Still, not enough people knew that Chapman felt that *Milk Train* involved "great excitement" or that Coleman believed that it was "an important play, a milestone."

On the other hand, fewer people than usual learned that McClain said that the milk train had "stopped far short of its destination" or that Kerr found it a "disappointment"—not to be confused with Taubman's calling it "disappointing." And given that this serious play was about Flora Goforth dictating her memoirs to a secretary (at least before an Angel of Death could arrive), not only Watts but also Nadel pointed out that its multimarried heroine seemed to be reminiscent of Belle Poitrine in the previous season's slam-bang musical comedy *Little Me.*

That is hardly what Williams set out to write.

Who would have expected that only 290 days after closing, *The Milk Train* would stop again on Broadway? Merrick decided to offer more star power than Hermione Baddeley (Flora) and Paul Roebling (the Angel). Give 'em Tallulah Bankhead and Tab Hunter, she as a would-be-sexy sexagenarian, he as her half-her-age love object.

With its January 1 opening, it would be the first Broadway offering of 1964.

Happy New Year?

No. Cougars were not yet in fashion.

Actually, this was a *revisal* (although that term hadn't yet been coined), for Williams had reworked his script. That caused Taubman to use the word "improved"—before reprising his "disappointing."

His unenthusiastic review turned out to be the best of the bunch. Chapman: "Simplified and rather awkwardly stylized." Watts: "The play remains pretty much as it was." Nadel: "The previous production was infinitely superior." Kerr: "Now worse than before." McClain: "Williams should have torn up *Milk Train*."

And suddenly, Merrick's 1958 five-performance run of *Maria Golovin*—an opera, yet—had to settle for a tie as his shortest-running production out of the thirty-eight that had sported his name. (His closed-in-previews musical version of *Breakfast at Tiffany's*, foreshadowed in Logan's poem, was still three years off.)

Only six weeks after the *Milk Train* stopped came *Foxy*—the musical that Stephen Sondheim must have avoided because it bore the nickname of his mother, with whom he had, shall we say, issues.

Foxy was a musical version of Ben Jonson's 1606 comedy *Volpone* (Italian for "sly fox," which Larry Gelbart chose as the name of his 1976 straight-play adaptation). Volpone pretended to be deathly ill, assuming that once his servant, Mosca, spread the news, his so-called friends would come bearing expensive gifts, all in hopes of being remembered in his will.

At least *Milk Train* had made it to Broadway on its first attempt; *Foxy*, despite the presence of Bert Lahr, had closed eighteen months earlier after its tryout in Dawson City in the Canadian Yukon.

Talk about going out of town...

Actually, *Foxy's* bookwriters, Ian McLellan Hunter and Ring Lardner Jr., had moved *Volpone* from seventeenth-century Venice to the Yukon during the late-nineteenth-century Gold Rush, so trying out there would seem to have been one of Merrick's famous publicity-grabbing stunts.

But Merrick wasn't at all involved with that 1962 production; it was co-helmed by the esteemed Robert Whitehead, whose previous outing was the Tony-winning *A Man for All Seasons*, in a producing career that had also sponsored Arthur Miller, William Inge, Eugene O'Neill, Terence Rattigan, and Jean Anouilh, as well as Friedrich Duerrenmatt's *The Visit*, the last play that Alfred Lunt and Lynn Fontanne performed.

Whitehead's co-producer wasn't as esteemed. Stanley Gilkey was best known for co-producing the trio of revues *One for the Money, Two for the Show,* and *Three to Get Ready* without bothering to mount *And Four to Go*. Gilkey had opened the third one at the Adelphi, the former name of the unlucky 54th Street Theatre, but moved it to the Broadhurst as soon as he could. When he was evicted from there, he did something unprecedented and, some would say, downright stupid: He moved back to the Adelphi.

Gilkey's final Broadway credit in 1958 had a title befitting a producer who can no longer get the job done: *The Day the Money Stopped*.

In 1962, Dawson City's population was around 700—fewer than the number attending a performance of *Arturo Ui*. But Dawson City played host to 50,000 or so visitors each summer, and the Dawson City Festival Foundation did have that Palace Grand Theatre with nothing to play in it. So, with a little help from the Canadian Theatre Exchange, *Foxy* played from July 3 through August 18, 1962.

Most seats were empty. That would seem to have been the end of that, but Billy Rose was interested in producing if Gower Champion would direct and choreograph. Champion, of course, instead elected to do *Dolly,* but Merrick optioned *Foxy* on the condition that Lahr stay with it.

He did, if for not the most enthusiastic of reasons. In *Notes on a Cowardly Lion,* John Lahr's biography of his father, he baldly stated that "Lahr, facing a new season with a daughter in college, a son at Oxford, and no other offers, signed."

The bookwriters were smart in how they began their musical. Larry Blyden came out and told those in attendance that they were about to see a show about greed and that he would play a character named Doc (based on Mosca) who worked for Foxy. With this it's-only-a-play framework, theatergoers could consider the smarmy characters they'd soon meet as mere actors presenting a play. They didn't need to identify with them or moralize against them.

A better idea still: Instead of having Volpone initiate the idea of bilking his friends while Mosca had no choice but to go along with it, here, the scheme was Doc's brainstorm. That allowed Lahr to play innocent, which he always did so well.

For all the talk of how well Merrick exploited publicity, one wonders why he didn't endeavor to sign Ray Bolger and Jack Haley to play two of the sharpies who'd try to become Foxy's beneficiary. With *The Wizard of Oz* now an annual television event, most everyone knew Lahr, Bolger, and Haley. The crowds at the box office would have resembled the Yukon Gold Rush.

Given that *Foxy*'s lyricist was Johnny Mercer, he, too, could have suggested Bolger, with whom he'd worked on the film *The Harvey Girls*, and Haley, who sang a Mercer lyric in "When Are We Going to Land Abroad?" in the 1941 film *Navy Blues.*

Granted, that last one wasn't one of the songwriter's greatest achievements. But Mercer's lyrics had enhanced pop hits ("I Wanna Be Around," "Satin Doll") in between his receiving fourteen songwriting Oscar nominations and winning four times. In fact, as *Foxy* entered rehearsals, Mercer was on a consecutive win streak, thanks to "Moon River" and "Days of Wine and Roses," both with composer Henry Mancini. Many thought that their newest hit—the title song of *Charade*—would give them a hat trick.

Ah, but Broadway? Mercer's six attempts had resulted in five failures, although two of his songs became standards: "Come Rain or Come Shine" from the 1946 failure *St. Louis Woman,* and "Jubilation T. Cornpone" from his one hit, *Li'l Abner* in 1956.

Now, with *Foxy,* Mercer would be reunited with composer Robert Emmett Dolan, with whom he'd written the 1949 Broadway flop *Texas, L'il Darlin'.* As before, there was very little music of note in Dolan's work. Affable, pleasant, and, yes, nice—which, of course, is different from good.

One must wonder what melodies were inside Mercer's head when he was writing the lyrics. He was an occasional composer, having a near-hit with *Top Banana* in 1951 and writing a few melodies for *Saratoga* in 1959 when composer Harold Arlen was indisposed. More to the point, Mercer wrote both music and lyrics for his Oscar-nominated "Something's Gotta Give."

But Mercer must take blame for his uninspired song ideas. Beware when a musical's song list contains a clichéd title (cf. *Ari*'s "The Lord Helps Those Who Helps Themselves"); Mercer had "Money Isn't Everything," "Rollin' in Gold," "Many Ways to Skin a Cat," and "This Is My Night to Howl." Worse, none of these songs moved the action forward, no more than "S.S. Commodore Ebenezer McAfee III," which did little more than announce the arrival of a ship. But there'd been a lot of water under the bridge—more than thirty-five years—since a certain show boat had come onstage while a song celebrated it.

Giving Lahr a number called "Bon Vivant" sounds right, but Dolan's melody seemed like an up-the-scales, down-the-scales piano exercise. The pseudo-elegant approach kept it from being a showstopper, and instead allowed it to receive only the politest of applause.

One song added after the Dawson City run got staff members nodding and stating, "*That's* the single." It was given to young lovers John Davidson, the future *Hollywood Squares* host, and Julienne Marie, the future first Mrs. James Earl Jones, and called "Talk to Me, Baby." (He was a prospector in love with her, unaware that she worked as a prostitute, and—well, you know.)

"Talk to Me, Baby"? If only everyone connected with the show could have talked to each other—or at least civilly. Starting with the tryout in Cleveland and continuing in Detroit, there was substantial rancor.

While the theater has always been the writer's domain (as opposed to Hollywood, where the director rules supreme), collaboration is nevertheless the key. In an instance of what might well be the most petty behavior known to Broadway, Hunter and Lardner gave Lahr a line that ended with "ha-ha." After a performance in which he said "ha-ha-*ha*," they came backstage and complained about the extra syllable.

Lahr threw them out of his dressing room. To be fair, however, this happened after Lahr had been improvising a good deal of the text.

Merrick suddenly found himself fielding a few unwanted phone calls from Cleveland.

But really, in the scene in which Foxy entered a saloon and saw a painting of a nude spanning the bar, was the authors' "How far out!" really preferable to Lahr's suggestion: "Mmmm. Whistler's sister"?

Director Robert Lewis couldn't win. When he told Hunter and Lardner that Jerome Robbins was willing to take a look at the show, they rejected the offer. He did no better with Lahr. As he wrote in his memoir, "Whenever I agreed with the writers on cuts or additions to the script, my stock went down a bit with Bert. Whenever I couldn't agree to his suggestions for strait-jacketing his partners in scenes, my stock plummeted sharply."

Blyden claimed that Lahr told him point-blank, "If they end the show the way it is now, it's going to be your show. It's not going to be your show. It's going to be mine."

Merrick suddenly found himself fielding substantially more unwanted phone calls from Detroit after *Foxy* had opened there on January 13. Four days later, Merrick was receiving a very different kind of phone call—congratulatory—on *Dolly*'s unanimous raves. With a cash cow—nay, cash bull—to tend, Merrick decided to close *Foxy* without keeping his opening date at Billy Rose's Ziegfeld Theatre on February 16, 1964. Only after his investors balked did he reluctantly bring it in.

In those days, *Variety* summed up the critics' reaction to productions: "*Barefoot in the Park* opened to six raves." "*Café Crown* opened to six pans." *Foxy* got a sui generis reception: "All six approved as a vehicle for Lahr."

Indeed. Taubman: "If you admire Bert Lahr—and it's un-American not to—*Foxy* is for you." Kerr: "Bert Lahr should be preserved like a fine old wine." Nadel: "We should be—and are—grateful for anything that brings Bert Lahr to the New York stage." McClain: "If you are not a Bert Lahr fan, you should first have your head examined." Watts: "A musical comedy that is dedicated to hilarity and puts Bert Lahr in charge of the laughter has a particularly good head start." Chapman: "I had a high old time Lahrfing at Bert."

Those are enough to fill a large display ad, no? But if it ran, Merrick would have had to deal with some of *Foxy*'s warring personalities on a day-to-day basis. Some say that at *Foxy*'s opening-night party, Merrick made the grand gesture of selling the entire enterprise to Billy Rose for a dollar; others said the selling price was five times as much.

(After that incident, Rose apparently flipped the show to Max Bialystock. Look closely in the 1968 film *The Producers* and you'll see *Foxy*'s window card on the wall of his office.)

The name on everybody's lips was not to be *Foxy*. Oh, well. As Mercer had reiterated, "Money isn't everything." He had to be somewhat mollified six days after the opening when "Charade" did result in his third consecutive Oscar nomination.

Only thirty-six days after *Foxy* had closed after its seventy-second performance, Lahr got his Tony at the Hilton, which happened to be directly across the street from the Ziegfeld, where the show had been the only booking for the entire 1963–64 season. The glorious Joseph Urban–Thomas W. Lamb structure on Sixth Avenue at Fifty-fourth Street was seeing its penultimate show. Nineteen months would pass before *Anya,* a 1965 musical version of *Anastasia,* became its last tenant; then it was razed in 1966. (Today's Ziegfeld, a half block west on Fifty-fourth Street, is a different building.)

The 1,660 seat theater—which today would be coveted for its large capacity—can still be seen for a few seconds at the 3:10 mark of the 1965 film *How to Murder Your Wife.* Where's the documentary called *How to Murder Your Theater* starring Billy Rose, who sold the showplace to developers? For that matter, David Merrick could have been the main attraction of *How to Murder Your Musical.*

In baseball, when a pitcher is doing exceptionally well, he occasionally throws a lousy pitch in hopes that the desperate hitter will swing at it. This is called "wasting one." David Merrick wasted one with *Foxy.*

Still, at season's end, Merrick had managed to do what no producer had done before: He'd won the Tony Award both for Best Musical (*Dolly,* of course) as well as Best Play, *Luther.*

Merrick had indeed moved Osborne's play to the Lunt-Fontanne Theatre, where he'd promoted Heffernan into the lead. As the producer had secretly feared, *Luther* ran out of steam and business. At 211 performances, it couldn't even surpass the modest London run of 239 showings.

Luther was only the second play to win the Tony after it had closed. The first, incidentally, was Merrick's *Becket*—another play about religious turmoil. Note that *J.B.* in 1958–59 and *A Man for All Seasons* in 1961–62 each won the Best Play Tony; thus, four out of the six Tony-winning plays from 1958–59 through 1963–64 had religious themes. And while future Tony winners *Amadeus, Angels in America,* and *Doubt* would touch upon religion, no other Tony-winning play has had religion as its main theme.

Broadway became a place where the saints went marching out. True, much of America would soon join the Christian Right and the Republicans who loved them, but members of the Moral Majority and the Christian Coalition were not among Broadway's prime ticket buyers. These were not the customers who made *Agnes of God*—in which a young nun is accused of killing her illegitimate child—one of the ten longest-running Broadway plays of the '80s.

Osborne, who had created the character and idiom of "the Angry Young

Man," was now writing about a Famous Angry Young Man. Martin Luther (1483–1546) started off wanting to be a good monk, and fully agreed to the demand "You are not to throw off the yoke of obedience." That he agreed to this and so much more greatly upset his father, who didn't see much difference between a monk's cell and a prison cell. As he bitterly told his friend, "He could have been a man of stature." The audience enjoyed some dramatic irony when the friend responded, "And he will, with God's help."

Not that Martin looked promising at this point. His suffering from epilepsy was dwarfed by self-esteem issues. ("I am a worm.") His paranoia ranged from "The birds seem to fly away the moment I come out" to "All I can feel is God's hatred" to "I'm like a ripe stool in the world's straining anus."

His colleague Johann von Staupitz (1460–1524) dryly noted, "You're always making up sins you've never committed." The Church, however, would soon accuse him of ones that Luther believed were no sins at all.

That bring us to John Tetzel (portrayed by Peter Bull, who'd played one of Finney's tormentors in *Tom Jones*). This friar (1465–1519) was also a salesman, who addressed the audience as if they were his customers.

Peter Bull made a move that was quite unexpected in this theatrical era. He broke the fourth wall when encouraging the audience to answer him with an occasional "Yes!" or "Amen!" Many people did in this early and primitive version of audience participation.

"What I bring you is indulgences," he said. "The Pope himself has sent me." Tetzel promised that those who bought from him would see their spiritual fate immeasurably improved. "There isn't one sin so big that one of these letters can't remit it," he insisted. "Not only am I empowered to give you these letters of pardons for the sins you have already committed; I can give you pardon for those sins you haven't even committed."

(Buy now; sin later.)

If there were no such thing as religion, Tetzel would have given Signor Pirelli a run for everyone's money by selling miracle elixir. "Letters aren't just for the living, but the dead, too," he averred. Certainly: That allowed for many more money-making opportunities.

Martin had vowed to obey God, but he didn't necessarily believe that his promise included the Pope. Soon Staupitz was accusing him of "preaching against indulgences again." Osborne would have done better to show Martin in action. Instead he wrote a later conversation in which Luther complained to Staupitz about the sale of "a feather from the wing of the angel Gabriel." Staupitz in turn urged him not to sermonize on such things on All Saints' Day, the sixteenth-century Roman Catholic equivalent of Black Friday, in that it was the biggest day in the number of sales of indulgences.

Luther's cogent response: "You can't strike bargains with God." He saw a disparity between a religion that preaches the virtues of poverty while also looking to make money. Pope Leo X (1475–1521) needed St. Peter's Basilica rebuilt, and Martin Luther was bad for business.

Theatergoers eventually heard a sermon in which Luther criticized his congregation's purchases of indulgences. "You'll sleep outside with the garbage in the streets all night so that you can stuff your eyes like roasting birds on a scrap of swaddling clothes, eleven pieces from the original crib, one wisp of straw from the manger," he roared.

A little more than three hundred years had passed since the Magna Carta had limited a monarch's powers; the Catholic Church was moving in the other direction, for in a little more than three hundred years it would proclaim that its Pope was infallible on matters of faith and morals. But, as Osborne pointed out, many in those days already believed in papal infallibility.

If Luther had been alive in 1870 to witness that proclamation, he would have been doubly infuriated. Even when he battled with the worldly and willing-to-compromise Cardinal Cajetan (1469–1534), Luther held fast. His pleas to meet with the Pope—to "take his case to the Supreme Court," if you will—were refused. Instead the Cardinal demanded, "You must admit your faults and retract all your errors and sermons.... You must promise to abstain from propagating your opinions at any time in the future.... Confess your errors; keep a strict watch on your words."

Well, is there any Lutheran alive today who assumes that Martin agreed?

Pope Leo X did make an appearance deep in the second act; he was on a hunt for big game and was dressed to kill in a most unpontifical hunting outfit. He read a letter aloud that Martin had sent him, alluding to "my disputation" and "nailing it on the door of the Castle Church." Again: Osborne would have done better to show Martin in action earlier rather than tell us about it later.

"Cunning German bastard," the Pope said of Martin, but he gave him one last chance. Martin rejected it and was excommunicated. So he took to his pulpit and told his congregants about "a latrine called Rome, the capital of the devil's own sweet empire."

Luther was the ultimate fundamentalist who believed in every word in the Bible. That had its own silver lining: Because he wanted his countrymen to read the Good Book, which only had Latin and Greek editions, he translated it into German. Staupitz, now a Lutheran, gave Martin credit for this during a visit to his home. There theatergoers met Luther's wife, the former Katharina von Bora, who wouldn't be a favorite of Catholics, either; she was a nun who broke her vows and left the convent.

If it doesn't sound worthy of a revival, today's producers would agree with you. Some Best Play Tony winners receive frequent Broadway revivals: *Death of a Salesman; Long Day's Journey into Night.* Some are revived once: *Marat/Sade; Equus.* Some settle for off-Broadway revivals: *Angels in America; Rosencrantz and Guildenstern Are Dead.*

But as of this writing, *Luther* has never again seen a professional New York production.

CHAPTER FOUR

*

The Comedies

L*uther* was the eleventh show that Merrick either had imported or had seen overseas and then commissioned an American adaptation. During the late '50s and '60s, he could be seen on various TV talk shows displaying the passport that he carried with him at all times so that if he got a tip on a good European show, he could rush to the airport, catch the next plane, and beat out the other producers who were still asking their mates, "Honey, have you seen my passport?"

Of course, Merrick didn't import every hit that had played London. Take *The Irregular Verb to Love,* the first comedy of the 1963–64 season, which ran nearly a year in London, and *Roar like a Dove,* the last comedy of the 1963–64 season, which played over 1,000 West End performances.

Merrick didn't stand in the way of Alfred (*The Voice of the Turtle*) de Liagre Jr.'s producing the former and the newly formed partnership of Fryer, Carr, Harris, and Herman taking on the latter.

Wise, wise David.

Actually, if audiences thought that the characters in *Anyone Can Whistle* were crazy, what did they think of the heroine of *The Irregular Verb to Love?*

And yet, like *Whistle,* Hugh and Margaret Williams's play was ahead of its time.

Never mind the terrible title or that "love" is in fact a regular verb. Instead, center on how the London *Theatre World Annual, vol. 12* captioned a picture of the 1961 West End production:

"Joan Greenwood as Hedda Rankin, a champion of lost causes and campaigner against cruelty to animals, who has been serving a prison sentence for trying to blow up a furrier's with a home-made bomb!"

And *yes,* that exclamation point was definitely the punctuation included by editor Frances Stephens, who obviously found the plot audacious.

The Williamses deserve credit for anticipating a cause that would take hold in the '80s. Today *The Irregular Verb to Love* might do substantially better, especially if enterprising producers opened it on the day after Thanksgiving now known as "Fur-Free Friday." Back then, however, the play could muster less than a third of its 360-performance London run, even with Oscar winner Claudette Colbert as the bomber.

Although Colbert had appeared in a dozen Broadway plays in the '20s, her live appearances were far rarer once she became a Hollywood star. After she made what would be her penultimate film in 1955, she settled for theater. *Irregular Verb* was her fourth Broadway play in the previous eight years.

Colbert may have preferred films because the camera could hide the right side of her face, of which she was deeply ashamed. As a youth, she'd injured her nose; a bump was the constant reminder of the accident.

But Colbert's facial irregularity was not what killed *The Irregular Verb to Love.* Audiences simply couldn't believe a high-bred woman could resort to terror. Decades would have to pass before they would.

Lesley Storm's *Roar like a Dove,* Chapman reported, "ran three years in London. It ran damn near that long Thursday evening."

Emma (Betsy Palmer) was an American who in 1949 had married Robert, a Scottish lord, and thus became Lady Dungavel. She'd assumed that she'd have "a romantic life in a romantic castle" on his farm overlooking extensive property in the Western Highlands of Scotland. So imagine how excited she was when she and Robert were invited to Queen Elizabeth II's coronation.

And imagine how devastated she was to miss it because she was in the hospital delivering a child.

Emma had hoped to be constantly mentioned in the society pages because she'd attended one posh event after the other. Instead, Emma was cited six times total—and always in the columns announcing births.

"That isn't news," she said. "That's monotony."

Emma now yearned to be back on Fifth Avenue, where "maybe I'd hear a wolf whistle from somebody who didn't know I was a married woman with six children." She said she'd even settle for "Italians who mutter at you in the streets."

Her cousin Edward reminded her that Robert was a good provider. Emma responded with "In America, all men work and all women enjoy themselves."

If that sounds unfortunate to your twenty-first-century ears, you ain't heard nothin' yet. Robert wanted another child because the six he already had were girls.

"Seven's my lucky number," he said.

So Storm wrote a more benign variation of the Henry VIII story. Robert genuinely believed that it was "time Emma had another child to keep her occupied. There's a whole wing of rooms we don't know what to do with."

No wonder Emma mentioned suicide—and she was only half-joking. What she did instead was call her parents in California. Soon Tom and Muriel were on the premises, and in-law trouble loomed. American theatergoers in 1964 no longer wanted to see senior citizens freely dispense advice to their middle-aged children who not only welcomed it but often abided by it.

At least Muriel wasn't the typical doting grandmother. "It's like passing a memory test to get their names straight," she moaned before tartly telling her son-in-law, "You keep hanging millstones around my daughter's neck. America could teach you plenty. It doesn't give women the status of rabbits."

Robert stayed myopic throughout the speech. "But what a son Emma could have!" he responded. "A biological inspiration!"

There was another Henry VIII parallel. Without a male heir, the Dungavel land would be inherited by Bernard Taggart-Stuart, Robert's second cousin. Never was there any discussion that any of the six girls would have a right to the property. No suggestion was even made that any lass would take an interest in it. And while audiences met only one child—cast size was becoming a genuine concern in play producing—Jane at eight was already precocious and adventurous.

Too bad Lesley Storm wasn't. If she'd lobbied for Jane and the other children to get what was rightfully theirs, she'd have had a play that would have better pleased its Broadway audience.

Robert had misgivings about Bernard, who'd never expressed any interest in running the farm. But as Tom said, "Men have to give up their dreams when they have women in their lives. Compromise means 'Do it their way.' " So Robert invited Bernard to give the farm a try.

Bernard took to animal husbandry like a duck to water torture. He was repulsed by the "stinking creatures"—manure was *not* his favorite perfume—and yet he was sensitive to the plight of animals. He felt terrible when a horse had to be put down and worse when he learned that the cute goose he'd seen walking around that morning was now earmarked for that evening's dinner. Bernard soon left the farm faster than Garth Drabinsky bolted from the United States when the securities regulators wanted to have a chat.

Tom and Muriel, let alone Emma, feared that Robert would revert to Plan A and impregnate. Tom had other opinions, too: "Women want to visit Paris and go shopping. We die of thrombosis, they drop $100 wreaths on us—our own dollars—then they're off on a spending spree 'round the world on our insurance policies."

Before any women in the audience could either laugh or gnash their teeth, Storm immediately had Muriel talk of Paris, the posh Hotel Le Meurice, and "a shopping list as long as my arm." Emma interrupted with a "Me, too!" before Muriel resumed with a promise "to spend money like crazy."

Tom's reaction: "Muriel just has to produce a hoop and I jump through it for the sake of peace." He insisted that "the only countries with happy women keep them in a state of obedience or duty." After he asked the inevitable "Are we men or mice?" he wasn't surprised when Robert immediately answered "Mice."

So Tom suddenly switched to Robert's side on the pregnancy issue; at least one man would get what he wanted from marriage. Tom genuinely believed that "in ten years, you'll be blaming Emma for the son you never had."

And the next night Emma seemed to capitulate. She wore her nicest negligee, asked for brandy, downed it, and complained that Robert hadn't poured enough. When she asked for a kiss, Robert gave her one—on her forehead. He was apparently willing to abandon his male-heir plans, but Emma was now angry at his lack of romance. A flare-up soon erupted into a forest fire of emotions, and the prospect of divorce was very much looming as Act Three, Scene One ended.

If the title *Two for the Seesaw* hadn't been already taken, it would have served this play well.

Emma and Muriel took the six girls to America, which left Robert and Tom to do little but drink their nights away while moaning some you-can't-live-with-them-and-can't-live-without-them sentiments.

And then suddenly, without any advance word, Emma and Muriel returned. Muriel asked Tom, "Have you enjoyed your freedom?" and when he said "It's been hell," she said she'd "enjoyed every minute" and that Emma seemed "ten years younger. Sons of millionaires are praying she'll file for divorce."

When Jane told her father that her mother's first observation on coming home was that the hedges needed cutting, my, did Robert spring to action to see that the servants pruned them. Men on first dates may bring flowers, but long-married abandoned husbands cut shrubs.

However, another issue had brought Emma home: She was indeed pregnant. Now she wanted "the VIP treatment you hand over to your pedigree cows." Robert quickly agreed, and said of the impending baby, "If she's a girl, she's just as welcome."

But happy ending! It's a boy!

Nadel was the play's only advocate: "It will please many people" was one of the season's worst predictions. *Roar like a Dove* did run into the 1964–65 season—but without a roar and for all of six days. Both Taubman and Watts were more gracious than Chapman in actually using the word "polite," while McClain was a tad harsher with "listless." When describing the plot, Kerr was more blunt than the rest: "I'm sure this makes no sense to you at all. It doesn't to me, either."

Theatergoers of each sex may have disliked the way that they were portrayed. Husbands were tired of hearing that they'd be lost without their wives, and wives didn't like seeing that they'd best succumb to their husbands' wishes—especially with the implication that six girls aren't nearly as worthy as one boy. Moreover, to establish that women really enjoy being unfettered from husbands only to have them return seemed to bring the play back to square one—and an oh-so-square conclusion.

Women's view of the world had changed in the seven years since the comedy had had its West End debut in 1957—coincidentally, the same year that Betty Friedan had begun her research for the book that would become *The Feminine Mystique*. By the time *Roar like a Dove* opened in New York, Friedan's study of the real feelings of housewives and mothers had enjoyed fifteen months' worth of readers and had spent many weeks on the *New York Times* bestseller list.

So Mrs. London Theatergoer of 1957 had a different reaction to *Roar* than Mrs. (soon-to-be-Ms.) American Theatergoer would have in 1963–64.

Even before Friedan, another momentous incident had taken place. On May 9, 1960—only forty-four days after *Roar like a Dove* had closed in London but more than four years before it opened on Broadway—the birth control pill was introduced. Broadway's female theatergoers may have wondered why Emma didn't surreptitiously use it. If she had without Robert's knowledge and he later found out about it, this would have been a more compelling comedy.

But, you say, that would mean a deception, and audiences wouldn't have wanted to see Emma resort to that. Ah, but what Storm did in her penultimate scene was have Emma tell Robert that the doctor said this pregnancy could kill her. In her final scene, she admitted that she'd lied just to worry him.

Twenty performances sounds about right.

If you add up the number of performances of the fourteen new comedies produced in 1963–64, they'd total only four performances more than the season's biggest comedy hit.

One of Neil Simon's first stage directions for *Barefoot in the Park* stated that Corie Banks Bratter was "lovely, young, and full of hope for the future." Audiences first met her when she entered the apartment where she and her new husband, Paul, would start their marriage.

It was a dump. Exacerbating that was its having been painted a color that looked good as a swatch but terrible when Corie got it home.

But theatergoers remembered their first love nests after they'd moved away from home. They understood why Corie was oblivious to a place where, as Simon wrote, "a ladder, a canvas drop cloth, and a couple of empty paint cans stand forlornly in the center of the room."

All Corie needed was four days, and when the curtain went up on Act Two, the apartment "is now a home. It is almost completely furnished, and the room, although a potpourri of various periods, styles, and prices, is extremely tasteful and comfortable."

And the audience went "Ooooooooooooooooooo!"

(Simon obviously liked the sound of that, for in his next two plays, *The Odd Couple* and *The Star-Spangled Girl,* he had the Act Two curtain rise on a much-improved apartment—and an "Ooooooooooooooooooo!")

One thing Corie couldn't change was that this was a fifth-floor walk-up. Love for her new place kept Corie from even noticing. Upstairs neighbor Victor Velasco appeared not to care, but he was merely putting on a brave front. The dashing Lothario was actually working hard to battle his biggest enemy—age—in hopes of not becoming a Lothari-old.

Two other characters, however, were quite daunted by those dozens of stairs. Rookie director Mike Nichols made his audience feel the brunt of those five flights by having Paul make his first entrance breathing murderously hard and working substantially harder to catch his breath. Adding to the fun was seeing an unmindful Corie cut off his air by passionately kissing him nonstop. The not-very-well-known Robert Redford was hilarious in trying to frantically extricate himself from her lips, showing that he genuinely feared he would die from a lack of air.

If a twenty-something had such trouble with the climb, imagine how Corie's middle-aged mother, Ethel Banks, would do. Mildred Natwick wheeled into the apartment as if she'd just gotten off a carousel Billy Bigelow had sent into overdrive. But as uproarious as Mrs. Banks was in this scene, she and Paul split more theatergoers' sides at the top of Act Two, Scene Two.

The four had just spent a night on the town. Corie and Victor stormed into the apartment laughing and reminiscing about the great time they'd just had. And as they headed upstairs to his apartment for nightcaps, Paul came in carrying Ethel. He flung her on the couch before collapsing next to her.

Forty-five seconds may not seem to be a great length of time, but in stage time it's an eternity. Nichols had Redford and Natwick just breathe heavily, in-and-out, out-and-in, wondering if their next breaths would be their last, eyes wide open in disbelief over what they'd endured. Some nights, they just sat there and heavily breathed for more than a minute—because they had to wait for the audience to stop laughing.

Also having a hard time with those stairs was the play's unsung hero: Herbert Edelman as telephone installer Harry Pepper. He created a genuinely nice guy who liked his work; after he installed the Bratters' phone, he said to Corie in a heartfelt manner, "Have a nice marriage—and may you soon have many extensions."

Edelman also scored hilariously in his second scene, after Harry had arrived to reattach the phone whose cord Paul had yanked out in anger in a fight with Corie. Edelman could feel the unmitigated antagonism between the two, so he sped up his work to a frenetic pace in order to get the hell out of there.

Then Paul rose from his chair and walked toward him—just to get a drink on the table that was next to Harry, but Edelman wasn't sure if Paul was about to take out his displaced hostility on him. He let out a moan of genuine and full-blown fear as he backed himself against the wall, certain that Paul was coming over to kill him.

Barefoot received the best reviews of any play that season. McClain: "The funniest comedy I can remember." Chapman: "A hurricane of hilarity." Taubman: "A bubbling, rib-tickling comedy." Watts: "Simon's comedy deserves every bit of success it is certain to achieve." But after Kerr proclaimed it "easy, breezy, amiably idiotic and irresistibly funny," he did use one adverb that turned out to be inaccurate: "Mike Nichols has temporarily abandoned Elaine May."

Barefoot stayed parked at the Biltmore for nearly four years, finishing up as the eighth-longest-running nonmusical in Broadway history. Its 2006 revival couldn't last even four months. Yes, it was atrociously cast and directed, but the problem wasn't that the audience might not have recognized such 1963 touchstones as the Toni Home Permanent, the *Andrea Doria, McCall's* magazine—or the $125/month rent for a one-bedroom Manhattan apartment. *Barefoot* took place in an era when a young miss would live at home until she married. Once Corie Banks wed, she was pleased to be "Mrs. Paul Bratter." She apparently never gave a thought to going to work, but was content to stay at home and (presumably) clean and cook while Paul went out to make a living as a lawyer. Of course, even in those days, there was more to marriage than that, so Corie's wise mother, Ethel, was there to dispense sage advice: "Make him feel important." Such sentiments now cause some stomachs to churn.

But Betty Friedan's book was very much in evidence when *Barefoot* opened, so why did it score when *Roar like a Dove* didn't? Emma was a middle-aged woman who should have been wiser as well as older; Corie was just a kid, so her innocence was bearable. As Sondheim would write in one of his most famous musicals, "Everybody has to go through stages like that." Trouble is, Emma had and wasn't doing a damn thing about it.

Simon also showed that husbands and wives need to learn how to fight; such knowledge doesn't come easily. Indeed, the first real contretemps between Corie and Paul resulted in her demanding a divorce.

To be sure, she overreacted, but theatergoers knew that the couple would be all right. Seeing Corie and Paul come to understand what they'd learned long ago was part of the enjoyable ride. And while Mrs. Banks's marital advice now sounds dated at first hearing—"You've just got to give up a little of you for him"—most anyone in a serious relationship knows that he or she does wind up compromising. That's part of the price one pays to be in love. (Whether it's worth it is for each theatergoer to decide.)

In its heyday, *Barefoot* was produced internationally, en route to paying back its angels 667 percent on their investments. However, when a production was being readied for France, Simon was urged to change one detail. Because so many apartment buildings in Paris were built before the dawn of elevators, climbing five flights to reach an apartment was considered nothing extraordinary.

So Simon moved the Bratters to a *ninth*-floor walk-up.

Take a look at the first ad for *Any Wednesday* that was published in *The New Haven Register* on December 22, 1963.

Then check out the title page of the Broadway opening-night *Playbill* on February 18, 1964.

Three different names are there.

Having a trio of staff changes in fewer than two months is harrowing for any management. But a four-character comedy couldn't do much worse than losing half its cast—both the male star and male supporting player—not to mention its director, too.

Any Wednesday didn't limp into town after its New Haven and Boston tryouts; it crawled in. Even *The New Yorker* made fun of the show when announcing its opening: "Produced by George W. George, Frank Granat, Howard Erskine, Peter S. Katz and Edwin Specter Productions, Inc.," it stated, before wryly adding a parenthetical expression: ("Have we got them all?")

Today, of course, if a mere five producers brought a play to Broadway, there might be a feature in the *Times* on their amazing achievement. But in 1963–64, that many producers—especially for a one-set, four-character comedy—was unheard of. Of the season's seventy-five productions, fifteen did have the credit "in association with." But forty-seven shows had only one producer listed over the title; twenty had two; six had three, and one had four. Only *Any Wednesday* had five.

Playwright Muriel Resnick, in her postmortem book *Son of Any Wednesday,* said that when neophytes George and Granat first agreed to do her comedy she thought "two producers were too many." Little did she know how many more she'd need.

Resnick's name didn't inspire check writing. The high school dropout's biggest success was *Life Without Father.* Not *Life WITH Father,* Broadway's longest-running play, but *Life Without Father,* a modest-selling novel. So how could the $85,000 be raised?

As it turned out, *Any Wednesday* came in at $110,000. During its tryouts, most Broadway observers assumed it wouldn't come in at all.

Even Resnick admitted that it was a slight work. John Cleves was a Manhattan mover-and-shaker who'd shaken up his own dull life by telling his wife, Dorothy, that he took a business trip every Wednesday. His true whereabouts were right in New York at his company's executive suite that he used as a tax write-off.

It's also where he allowed his mistress, Ellen Gordon, to live full-time.

All went well for two years, until Cass Henderson arrived from Akron to confront the mogul. Cleves had swallowed Henderson's company in a hostile takeover, and the young man wouldn't take it lying down.

He wasn't able to lie down, either, because New York hotels were crammed during this exceptionally busy convention-filled week. Cleves's new secretary took pity on Cass and offered him the executive suite—unaware that it was nothing of the kind. So when Henderson arrived and found Ellen there, he inferred that she'd been hired for his carnal pleasure.

To make matters worse, when Dorothy dropped by Cleves's office to tell him about a new coat she wanted to buy, the new secretary said that John had just called from the executive suite, so she sent Dorothy there. When Dorothy arrived, she assumed that Ellen and Cass were a married couple. Almost two acts passed before Dorothy fully understood what had been going on; by then, Ellen and Cass had fallen in love.

Would such a whirlwind courtship lead to a marriage that would endure? That's a question that few commercial comedies dared to pose.

A year earlier, George and Granat had offered Ellen to Barbara Harris, but she was committed to that oft-spoken-of surefire hit: Rodgers and Lerner's *I Picked a Daisy*. Once that fell through, Harris preferred to spend 1963–64 in the off-Broadway musical *Dynamite Tonight*. ("Tonight" was right; it ran one performance.)

From legends (Geraldine Page) to newcomers (Zohra Lampert), most actresses declined to play Ellen. When George and Granat suggested twenty-six-year-old Sandy Dennis, Resnick was dead-set against her—and not simply because Ellen was supposed to be turning thirty as the play began. Resnick had seen Dennis in *The Complaisant Lover* two seasons earlier and thought her "fat." Never mind that Dennis had recently won a Tony as Best Featured Actress in *A Thousand Clowns*.

Then Resnick happened to drop by the Actors Studio when Dennis was working with an improv group. The actress's energetic and inventive moves changed Resnick's mind. Dennis was signed even before a director was.

The producers offered Dorothy to Greer Garson, only to be told by her agent that "Miss Garson doesn't do comedy." That decision was probably made after Garson was terribly received as Rosalind Russell's replacement in *Auntie Mame*.

Anne Bancroft, Joan Fontaine, Arlene Francis, Dorothy McGuire, and Patricia Neal also declined to play Dorothy. But far many more actors—twenty-one all told—said no to playing John Cleves. Joseph Cotten, Richard Crenna, Peter Lawford, Walter Matthau, David Niven, Tony Randall, and Gig Young all preferred to wait for other phone calls. James Daly opted to play Sacco and Vanzetti's lawyer in *The Advocate*.

Meanwhile, a similar number of directors were refusing Resnick. Because she was friendly with Mike Nichols, who told her that he wanted to move from stand-up comedy to directing, she suggested him to George and Granat. They pooh-poohed the suggestion because he'd had no experience.

Nichols certainly would rectify that four months before *Any Wednesday* opened when *Barefoot* received unanimous raves. That's when George and

Granat suddenly thought that Nichols was a good idea. Alas, by then Nichols had decided that *Any Wednesday* was too similar to *Barefoot* and that he didn't want to be typecast as a director of four-character, one-set comedies.

Yes, Nichols's next show was *Luv*—a *three*-character, one-set comedy. But *Luv* was much edgier than *Barefoot* or *Any Wednesday* and bore no resemblance to them.

George and Granat's bigger problem was raising money. Hence they welcomed first Erskine, then Katz, then Specter. They approached Marguerite Cullman, then Broadway's most famous investor (who even wrote a book on her theatrical adventures, *Occupation: Angel*). Cullman did give George and Granat a check—but for the other production that they were doing that season: *Dylan*.

However, Cullman did give Resnick some advice. The playwright had originally stated that Ellen and John had been lovers for four years, but Cullman felt that the longer the illicit union, the less sympathetic Ellen would seem. Resnick took the tip and halved the length of the relationship.

Finally Jack Smight, a TV director whose credits included one episode of *Route 66*, two *Dr. Kildare*s and four *Twilight Zone*s, said yes. Then, only days before rehearsals were to begin, he decided he was better off in Hollywood.

Michael Gordon, who'd recently spent his time directing Doris Day in *Pillow Talk* and *Move Over, Darling,* gave Resnick and her producers the same early encouragement before coming to Smight's conclusion and retreating to California.

If they couldn't get the director of Neil Simon's second comedy hit, they'd take the one who'd helmed his first: Stanley Prager, who'd staged *Come Blow Your Horn*.

He at least showed up for auditions.

There Resnick was quite taken with an unknown actor whom she thought ideal for Cass: Gene Hackman. Neither Prager nor Dennis agreed with her. Prager, however, was ultimately no barrier, because he soon quit.

Management was so desperate that it approached John Newland, whose total Broadway experience was appearing in a twenty-one-performance comedy nine years earlier. He deigned to direct, but only if he could play John, too. When the producers said no, so did he.

Having less Broadway experience than Newland—literally none—was

George Morrison. But he came highly recommended by the now-hot Nichols, so he was given the directorial reins.

Resnick asked Morrison to audition both Hackman and Rosemary Murphy; the latter had been with the play since its very first reading. George and Granat believed that Murphy was "all wrong" for Dorothy, but Resnick insisted.

And then Murphy showed up thirty pounds heavier than when Resnick had last seen her. The actress was understudying Colleen Dewhurst in *The Ballad of the Sad Café* and, good Method actress that she was, she wanted to look the part of the butch Miss Amelia.

All right, Resnick reasoned, Murphy could lose the weight. But Morrison simply didn't like Hackman—and Dennis hadn't changed her mind about him, either. Morrison cast an actor who wasn't much better known: Dick York.

Better news was that Michael Rennie had agreed to star as John. Today the urbane actor is best remembered for being ill the day the earth stood still in the first line of *The Rocky Horror Picture Show*. But in 1963, Rennie was a well-known name who'd just come off an important role in the still-running *Mary, Mary*.

Yes, Rennie demanded custom-made suits and insisted that footlights be used, too. But at this point, he was a bigger name than Dennis and York, so he was awarded top billing. And Rosemary Murphy was losing enough weight to win the role.

All set—until York decided to stay in California. He had a chance to be in a new series called *Bewitched*. With little time left before rehearsals were to start, Morrison and Dennis had little option other than to accept this Gene Hackman.

And the ads for New Haven had already stated that Dick York would be in the show....

The joy of getting the Music Box Theatre, a prime house, was greatly tempered by Morrison's quitting after insisting to Resnick that the play should go in a more serious direction. Dennis felt he had a point, and she stopped talking to Resnick.

Co-producer Howard Erskine took over as interim director. He at least had some Broadway experience as a director. After all, he'd guided *The Happiest Millionaire* to an eight-month run in the 1956–57 season. His directorial skills may have been less influential in getting him the *Any Wednesday* job than his co-producing and coming up with the extra much-needed monies.

Management seriously considered Robert Altman to stage the play. Can you imagine the future director of *M*A*S*H*, *Nashville*, and *Gosford Park* directing a commercial comedy about adultery? If Altman hadn't unequivocally stated that all performers but Dennis be fired, he might well have been hired.

All this happened before New Haven. During rehearsals, George suggested a few changes in Rennie's performance, which made the star stop talking to his lead producer. Resnick also recalled overhearing Murphy calling her agent and screaming, "Get me out of this!" That no more than three hundred tickets had been sold for the two-balcony Shubert didn't inspire confidence.

Neither did the reviews from the New Haven papers. No, they weren't bad; the critics from the *Register* and the *Journal-Courier* each called it "amusing." But that isn't so hot when one considers the old adage: "What New Haven laughs at Boston smiles at—and New York regards with no response whatsoever."

(Then why even bother with New Haven?)

At least during this tryout they picked up a director who'd join them in Boston: Henry Kaplan.

Who?

He'd directed *Gentlemen Prefer Blondes* in London, and although management would have preferred someone else, they could find no one else.

They went to Boston, mostly to hear the opinion of Elliot Norton, the *Boston Record-American* critic who'd been reviewing pre-Broadway tryouts for more than thirty years. Impressing the critics from the *Globe*, *Herald*, and *Traveler* would be nice, too, but Norton, the savviest of them all, was the one they wanted.

Elinor Hughes in the *Herald* praised "the bright, unexpected turns of wit by which the playwright has sparked an amusing"—there's that adjective again—"but thin play."

Oh.

Alta Maloney in the *Traveler* liked this "bright new comedy" much more than Hughes. She reported that "the audience sat back and laughed all the way through" and concluded that "it's like a healthy dose of tonic on a never-ending winter day to find an evening of laughs."

Yes, but these two were Boston's most indulgent critics. What would the sterner Kevin Kelly say in the *Globe*?

"It is predictably plotted in a slight, rather quietly amusing manner."

(There's that adjective once again....)

But Kelly insisted that work needed to be done to keep it from being "an early spring flop."

And that all-important review from Norton?

"*Any Wednesday* is a better play than it seemed at Monday's opening performance at the Wilbur. Not, alas, much better, but at least a little."

Uh-oh...

Norton decided that the actors "need a different text, or a totally different approach."

Hmmm, was George Morrison right in wanting to make it serious?

Not according to Norton. He insisted that "there is only one conceivable way of telling Miss Resnick's story, and that is as a farce of the broadest possible sort." Then he felt compelled to add that it was "a tenuous comedy idea which might have been made to seem attractive as a short story in a ladies' magazine but has to be stretched and strained and teased and bedeviled into a semblance of theatricality."

Oy.

Of course, some people don't read reviews carefully. In those days, newspaper reviews often had subheads that were printed in bold type and interspersed between the paragraphs so that the casual reader could get a gist of the entire review.

Norton's sub-heads said, "Tenuous Comedy Idea," "Little Wit," and "Text Against Her."

As for Rennie, Norton believed that he "acts without any real force or conviction" and "looks ill at ease. What a waste of talent!"

Kelly concurred, although he was harsher in claiming that *Any Wednesday*'s "leading man had been left behind," that he had "all the worst lines when he has any," and that he had "very little to do as the roué other than pose in his well-pressed suits while arching a romantic eyebrow."

At least Rennie's custom-made clothes got a good review.

Maloney was better. She said, "Rennie looks very wealthy and as if he had the bad back he's supposed to"—but that's all she said. The usually easygoing

Hughes wrote that Rennie had "an impossible assignment" because he had been "called upon to sulk and snarl far more than to smile" before concluding that "Rennie doesn't snarl very convincingly."

That's when Rennie decided to leave. Wasn't that, along with the Norton pan—and a total of fifty people in the Wilbur the night after the reviews broke—enough to make producers close in Boston?

No. Even in the theater, where there's life, there's hope—even if the producers had to hire Don Porter, an actor with no Broadway experience. True, he was a small seminame, having played Ann Sothern's boss eighty-four times in both her TV series. But the last episode had aired three years earlier. That he was willing to learn the part in a hurry was enough for the producers.

Under these arduous circumstances, one might have expected Sandy Dennis to quit, too. While she wasn't a name—yet—she had at least won that Tony. Hadn't she realized that she'd made a mistake in choosing *Any Wednesday* as her next vehicle?

But Dennis *was* getting the reviews. New Haven called her "engaging" with "a special charm." Boston then saw Maloney decree that Dennis had "wonderful appeal," while Hughes called her "an increasingly charming and gifted young actress who has made an art of daffiness and conquers your heart with her innocence, honesty, and vulnerability." Even Kelly's negative review made room to say that Dennis was "wonderfully winning" with "an artful style—and delightful." And while Norton thought that Dennis played Ellen as a "tiresome neurotic" and "just plain stupid," he called her "a natural comedienne with an instinct for the truth."

Maybe Dennis stayed because she assumed that it would all be over very soon anyway.

Not at all. Soon after the Broadway premiere on February 18, the Music Box sported a sign that proclaimed, "All six critics cheer *Any Wednesday*. Smash comedy hit!" As proof, they offered:

"For a long time to come, the Music Box Theatre is going to be full of happy people. *Any Wednesday* is there to stay" (Nadel). "A success! Makes everyone laugh a great deal. Sandy Dennis is something very special" (McClain). "*Any Wednesday* has a delightfully fresh charm, a bright and engaging humor, a gay spirit and a sympathetic heart. Richly comic" (Watts). "A captivating funny, light-hearted comedy. It has an expert touch. Sandy Dennis is irresistible, a girl who manages to be extraordinarily and charmingly funny" (Chapman). "Romantic merry-go-round. Newcomer to playwriting Miss Resnick is remarkably sure-footed. *Any Wednesday* juggles its sinful elements with a weather eye for honest sentiment and virtue" (Taubman).

(That adjective "sinful" was more valuable to management than "amusing.")

And here was Kerr with another of his charming ledes: "Let me tell you about Sandy Dennis. There should be one in every home." The sign outside the Music Box went on to quote Kerr's "The girl is enchanting. The comedy is attractive. The occasion is trim, bright."

Any Wednesday didn't receive a Best Play Tony nomination; such acknowledgments rarely go to light-hearted fare, and *Barefoot*'s better reviews made it the token comic nominee. But Sandy Dennis was not only nominated but also won—no small feat, given that her competition was *Barefoot*'s Elizabeth Ashley, *Sad Café*'s Colleen Dewhurst, and *Marathon '33*'s Julie Harris.

Who expected that half the cast would go on to win Oscars? Dennis did when directed by Resnick's first choice, Nichols, in *Who's Afraid of Virginia Woolf?* Hackman, who Watts said was "a good and promising actor," made good on that promise by winning his Academy Award for *The French Connection.*

And while Rosemary Murphy had to settle for a Tony nomination and lost to Barbara Loden of *After the Fall,* she must have been very glad that her agent did not indeed get her "out of this."

When *Any Wednesday* closed after twenty-eight months and 983 performances, only thirteen comedies in the entire history of Broadway had ever run longer. Even today, more than fifty years later, it's only slipped to twentieth place.

The movie rights were sold for $750,000. Jason Robards, who opened *After the Fall* two nights after *Any Wednesday*'s disastrous Boston debut, would have never guessed then that a film version would result or that he'd play John Cleves in it. The "all-wrong" Rosemary Murphy reprised her role, too.

Before that happened, Lord knows how many sleepless nights were had by those who bolted from *Any Wednesday.* George Morrison didn't wind up directing on Broadway for nearly five more years—and then only with a play that lasted five performances.

Many of the dozens of directors who turned down the play didn't have an auspicious 1963–64. Jerome Robbins, Robert Lewis, and Reginald Denham all had quick failures. Norman Jewison and Garson Kanin respectively opted for *Here's Love* and *Funny Girl*, and we saw where those got them. Fred Coe and Robert Altman staged off-Broadway flops. Morton DaCosta cast his fate with the 1964 World's Fair, where his revue *To Broadway with Love* (which was as dull as it sounds) did two-a-day for five weeks.

Some of the actors who thrust their thumbs down at playing John Cleves suffered in 1963–64, too. Chester Morris played a Greek harassed by loan sharks in *The Tender Heel*, which had a four-day run in San Francisco before closing there. If you add the performances that James Daly played in his early-season entry (*The Advocate*; eight) and his late-season effort (*The White House*; twenty-three), they'd only reach the number of performances that *Any Wednesday* played in its two tryouts.

Oh, well. If everything *had* gone smoothly, Muriel Resnick certainly wouldn't have got *Son of Any Wednesday* out of it. She must have known she was lucky, because she never seriously pursued Broadway again. There were rumblings every now and then of her working on a play or providing a new book for an old musical, but *Any Wednesday* was her only time on Broadway.

That decision pretty much set the tone for her colleagues, although they didn't stop trying. Henry Kaplan staged the aforementioned *The White House* and followed it later that year with *P.S. I Love You*, which proudly advertised that its director "turned *Any Wednesday* into a hit." (P.S.: That's more than he could do for *P.S.*, which ran twelve performances—four times the run of his final Broadway credit in 1967, *A Minor Adjustment*, which apparently needed substantial adjustments.)

George and Granat, thanks to *Dylan* as well, turned out to be two-hit wonders. They later co-sponsored three Broadway shows, all flops, before the latter stopped producing. George had an additional four more Broadway tries ranging from the disastrous *Via Galactica* to the almost-hit *Night Watch* and the prestigious money-loser *Bedroom Farce*. He did give Joe DiPietro the idea that turned into the 2010 Tony-winning Best Musical *Memphis*, but he died two years before it opened.

And yet, George and Granat turned out to be far more successful than their three *Any Wednesday* partners, each of whom only produced once more on Broadway. Edward Specter co-sponsored *Henry, Sweet Henry*, which lost every dime during its eighty performances. But that was almost four times as long a run as Peter S. Katz's *Peterpat,* which rang in at twenty-one—which was more than *five* times better than Howard Erskine could manage with his four-performance flop *A Minor Miracle.*

Erskine had already had his major miracle. And Broadway tends to be miraculous in very small doses.

Although many who work on Broadway perversely need the competition to fail, Louis S. Bardoly and Alexander Doré must have been seriously rooting against Muriel Resnick. For Bardoly had written a play that Doré was now about to direct: *The Sunday Man*—about a businessman who visited his mistress not every Wednesday, but (of course) every Sunday. Chapman, Kerr, and Nadel weren't above mentioning *Wednesday* in their *Sunday* reviews.

There's rarely room for two shows with the same plot in the same season. *The Sunday Man* opened on May 13, 1964, and closed that same night.

It wasn't a Sunday, which one might have expected, given the show's title. But given its similarity with *Any Wednesday,* one must wonder why the management chose a Wednesday as its opening night.

For the record, in a season when the cutoff date for the Tony Awards was April 30, *The Sunday Man* was the first show ineligible for the 1963–64 awards. It would have to wait for the following season's Tonys.

It was not in contention for an award, although Kerr's lede deserved one: "*The Sunday Man* is a play in which three of the male actors lose their pants. I leave you to guess what is going to happen to the producers' shirts."

This was one of a half-dozen 1963–64 productions—three comedies and three dramas—that decided to call it a day after opening night. Never had so many shows closed after one performance. *The Billboard Index of the New York Legitimate Stage* in both the 1926–27 and 1927–28 editions counted 302 Broadway productions in each—the most ever in one June-to-May semester (and just before the movies started talking, you'll notice). But even those two chock-full seasons didn't have six one-night stands.

Remember *Once for the Asking* (November 20)? Of its author Owen G. Arno, Kerr wrote, "God forgive him."

Arno's plot had Ashley Robbins as a copywriter for Hollingshead, Inc., an advertising agency. He hadn't come up with any new ideas, and of course time was a-wasting. Lucky for him, his new next-door neighbor turned out to be a good fairy who could grant one wish, albeit for only twenty-four hours.

That's more time than Cinderella got, but not much. Kerr complained that Ashley used his wish to get a great idea that would please his boss; he harkened back to a time when men "wanted to be Lindbergh or Babe Ruth or Ben Hecht or Dracula."

The good fairy didn't neglect Ashley's family. He wasn't pleased, however, when his wife said she wanted "to spend some time in Gregory Peck's bedroom." No matter; when she was whisked there, Peck was filming in a far-off land. The joke was feeble because it depended on the wife's stating her wish to spend some time "in Gregory Peck's bedroom" without specifying sex, so that Arno could get a punch line out of it.

Ashley's daughter was young enough to want to be a goldfish, and soon her parents were talking to the little *Carassius auratus* in the bowl. If that wasn't enough, Ashley's boss had always envied his little sister, so he soon showed up in an outfit that went from a head full of pigtails to toes in Mary Janes, with a cute taffeta dress in between.

Watts: "There actually was a time when plays as abysmal were a fairly common occurrence on Broadway. Things have at least improved to an extent that it now stands out as a misfortune of virtually unique proportions."

Next!

Experienced globe-trotters have always been wary of travel articles that sport a double byline from a couple with the same last name. The two obviously enjoyed a free press junket, and would therefore accentuate the positive to ensure that they'd be invited on the next complimentary cruise.

Similarly, veteran theatergoers had to be wary when they saw that *Have I Got a Girl for You!* (December 2) was "a play by Irving Cooper based on a story by Helen Cooper"—his wife. Taubman pointed out that "it would have been more gallant of him not to mention her."

Joe Garfield was thirty-five but still living in his boyhood bedroom. One of his reasons might have been economic. High school football coaches were then getting only a few thousand a year.

Joe's mum was not one to keep mum. She tried fixing him up with a Park Avenue rich girl who ultimately was as uninterested in Joe as he was in her.

Joe had instead been attracted to Helen, an equally poor high school teacher, and she would be the one he'd choose. To make for an even happier ending, Joe was offered a coaching position with the New York Giants.

Really? The Giants would be *that* interested in a high school coach? Isn't there a pecking order where they'd first recruit a successful college coach? There's a profound difference between coaching in college and with the pros, let alone between high school and the big leagues.

No matter. Joe turned down the job because he was so dedicated to good ol' Fremont High. We don't know that the opening- (and closing-) night audience groaned when they heard this too-good-to-be-true scenario, but we can infer that Chapman and Nadel at least cringed over one line, for both cited it: when Momma said of Helen, "She'd rather curdle up with a good book."

A comedy that fared much better had both Taubman and Nadel calling it "hilarious," which Watts virtually did when citing its "hilarity." Most accurate was McClain: "People will be laughing at this one for months."

Yes, but not years. *Nobody Loves an Albatross* lasted six months and a day.

One theory will later be advanced for its inability to pay back after solid reviews. For now, let's look at Ronald Alexander's satire, which may have been the first insider's look at the still-new world of mass-market television.

In the dozen or so years that the tube had been around, executives had learned some major lessons that resulted in radical decisions. NBC, CBS, and distant runner-up ABC were now offering more sitcoms and fewer Shakespeare adaptations and Carnegie Hall concerts than they had in the '50s.

When *Albatross* debuted, *The Beverly Hillbillies* was the nation's No. 1 television show for the second consecutive year. It was the inspiration for *Petticoat Junction*, which spawned a spinoff, *Green Acres*.

Those two series weren't as good as their forebear, as impossible as that may sound.

All made money, which is how such people as Alexander's writer-producer Nat Bentley could live *L.A. dolce vita* in Hollywood. It was also a place for morals tomorrow, comedy tonight. Nat told his eleven-year-old daughter, Diane, early on that his most recent wife "was a female impersonator." If that confused her, it wouldn't matter to him as long as he got a laugh out of her.

Nat was busy reading *A Child at Heart*, a recent Broadway hit that his boss,

Hildy Jones, had outbid Disney to acquire. Would the story of a little orphan girl who'd been corrupted by terrible people make a good series?

Privately, Nat thought, "Why would anybody want to make a series about the purity and tenderness of a child when every parent knows they're our natural enemies?" Publicly, he declared, "I'm a man of very definite opinions— and frankly, I don't know."

He had no idea how oxymoronic (and moronic) he sounded. How could he? Other *Child at Heart* adaptors had already changed the story to center on a kid who lived in the forest and whose best friends were animals.

"This," said Nat, "could bring back radio."

Yet he'd agree to be this show's executive producer, for it could be the right stepping-stone to his becoming the network's creative head. To be sure, the script needed work, but Nat would fix it à la Sammy Glick: by hiring someone to stooge for him. Phil Matthews would do the writing, and Nat would appropriate the credit.

"How come you let me write under your name?" Phil naively asked. Nat really believed he had a valid answer when stating, "Do you think that if I didn't have faith in you that I'd put my name on your script?"

But Hildy wanted Nat to use Sean O'Laughlin, who did "all the big live hour-and-a-half shows adapted from old movies." (Indeed, '50s TV did this quite often; even such musicals as *Bloomer Girl, A Connecticut Yankee,* and, yes, the twenty-one-performance flop *Shangri-La* were abridged for television. Alexander himself had condensed *The Man Who Came to Dinner* and *The Royal Family.*)

Yet Alexander undoubtedly didn't pattern Sean after himself, for his stage direction said, "No one can tell what he's thinking. This is mistaken for depth of character."

Then there was Sean's agent, Mike Harper, who "smiles as he cuts your heart out." He wouldn't allow Sean to respond to questions but answered for him, down to "Fine" after Nat asked Sean how his flight had been.

There was discussion on whether the show should have canned laughter, because "live people never sound real." The surprise was not that Nat said this but that L. T. Whitman, the network's general manager, did.

Nevertheless, Nat immediately said, "You know, he's right."

The canned-laughter machine was the brainchild of the quite proud Victor Talsey. "We shape the humor of the American television audience," he insisted. "Millions of people in millions of homes think shows are funny 'cause we say so."

(As Nat would say: "You know, he's right.")

Hildy didn't tell the audience anything it hadn't already learned when she said to Nat, "You're a man of five-minute loyalties." But she may have surprised the audience by stating, "And I'm a woman of no loyalty at all."

And what would a 1963 commercial comedy be without sexual harassment? After Nat hired Jean Hart as his new assistant, he told her, "I demand only two services: absolute loyalty and occasional sex." He actually offered to pay her overtime if she'd spend the night. And in those male chauvinistic days, Jean was neither surprised to hear him talk this way nor furious that he'd said it. Even if she had had the courage or inclination to call him on it, he'd have said that he was merely joking; back then, that passed for enough of an apology.

Would that were Nat's only flaw. "People are liars, and they like to be lied to," he told Jean. That apparently included himself, for despite the talk that Nat gave about doing "an important series called *Injustice* about all the things that happen to minorities and underprivileged people," audiences knew he wasn't serious, even if he didn't.

Nat used the word "broad" to mean a woman, but so did Hildy. She obviously thought that being "one of the boys" was a necessity for success. So did Marge Weber, "a woman comedy writer who feels she must assert herself on every level." Long ago she beat down her husband and co-writer Bert Howell, who was totally submerged by his dynamo wife; his greatest contribution to the partnership was fetching drinks for her.

Marge didn't worry about offending Nat when meeting Phil. "Nat put his name on so many of my scripts," she said, "that he once told somebody I was Nat Bentley."

The culmination came when Phil would no longer help Nat, which forced him to write his own script. Everyone adored it, save for Marge, who pointed out that it was plagiarized from a Shirley Temple film.

And Nat unabashedly admitted that was true. "I figured I'd fool you for ten to twelve weeks, but you're smarter than that."

Can't you hear Robert Preston, Broadway's favorite lovable con man, saying these lines with his arms akimbo? Indeed, the *Playbill* cover even showed him in this stance. And critics did call him "delightful" (McClain), "distinguished" (Nadel), "likeable" (Kerr), "marvelous" (Taubman), "the best" (Chapman), and "brilliantly funny" (Watts).

With such solid pros (and future stars) as Barnard (*Da*) Hughes and Richard (*Soap; Empty Nest*) Mulligan, *Albatross* seemed in. Even Robert Brustein, who had as much use for Broadway as the Prozorovs had for Italian in their small Russian town, wrote in *The New Republic* that "*Albatross* is the stage equivalent of an underground film, for it has been smuggled past the customs designed as a conventional and trivial Broadway 'hit.' "

Indeed, Brustein put "hit" in quotation marks to demean the word. In another manner of speaking, "hit" in quotation marks was just right, for *Albatross* did not return its investment to its backers.

The ol' theory that audiences aren't inherently interested in show biz problems could be a reason. But an argument can be made that theatergoers weren't interested in a play "as cynical as a Restoration comedy and almost equally cold-hearted" (Watts), "ruthless in its account" (Taubman), and "mean" (Kerr).

One might infer that Alexander was enacting revenge for the tough time he'd had working in television. Although he wrote for *The Dick Van Dyke Show*, *Walt Disney's Wonderful World of Color*, and two others, he never did more than two episodes of any series. We can only hope that he worked the bile out of his system by writing *Nobody Loves an Albatross*.

One final note: No actor appeared in both *Luther* and *Nobody Loves an Albatross*.

That sentence may seem unnecessary, but in 1967, some readers of a runaway bestseller went checking to see if any actor had.

For Ira Levin had created Guy Woodhouse, the father of Rosemary's Baby and an actor who, Levin had fabricated, had appeared in both of those plays. And although we're here to celebrate Broadway, may we give some credit to Robert Nelson, who decorated the set for the 1968 film version? At the 31:40 mark, the actual window cards for both *Luther* and *Nobody Loves an Albatross* can be seen framed and hanging on Rosemary and Guy's living room wall.

Unanimous pans.

They were given to eleven productions in 1963–64. Because *Bicycle Ride to Nevada* opened in September, when the *Mirror* was still publishing, it earned the humiliating distinction of being the final show to receive seven pans from seven critics.

Producers of the other ten obviously felt that six pans were bad enough. Nine of those shows amassed a total of thirty-seven performances, but the tenth was one of the hottest tickets of the season. It ran 148 sold-out performances and could have played hundreds more if its stars had wanted to continue: Paul Newman and Joanne Woodward.

Newman, really. *Baby Want a Kiss* started previews on April 6, 1964—the day after Newman's performance as Hud lost the Oscar to Sidney Poitier's Homer Smith in *Lilies of the Field*. But *Hud* had taken in $10 million—the nineteenth-highest-grossing film of the year—to *Lilies'* $2.5 million.

Hud had cemented Newman's reputation as a genuine sex symbol. So when he announced that he'd come to Broadway for the first time in five years, theatergoers paid attention and money.

That Newman would co-star with his beloved Oscar-winning wife was a nice bonus. What theatergoers didn't know was that if it weren't for her, they wouldn't have seen Newman, for Woodward was the one intent on doing James Costigan's play.

Costigan's two previous Broadway efforts had lasted a total of twenty-four performances, which didn't bode well for the new play. So why was Woodward interested?

Well, she *was* once engaged to Costigan in her pre-Newman days. While she might have loved the play, such factors as guilt, let-me-show-you-how-big-I-can-be, or the fact that the plot involved husband-and-wife movie stars could have fueled Woodward's interest. Less enthusiastic but dutiful husband Newman agreed.

Their first motivation was to help the Actors Studio, where they'd both studied early in their careers. Both felt that the organization had helped them immeasurably. Newman was now getting close to a half million a picture and Woodward a few hundred thousand, but in order to help the Studio, they offered their services for what was then Equity minimum: $117.50 a week. Considering that the play would sell out at $37,350, the Actors Studio would make a tidy profit, even with the Newmans bolting after four months.

The Actors Studio could have made a substantially bigger killing if it had chosen a theater other than the aptly named Little. It was Broadway's small-

See? Carol Channing could be serious when she wanted to be. Here as Dolly Levi she's offering one of her many business cards to Cornelius Hackl (Charles Nelson Reilly), which establishes her as a dance teacher. And he's ready to learn, as many a Cornelius was during the then-record 2,844-performance run of *Hello, Dolly!*

Neil Simon (left) and Mike Nichols (right) look a little cocky, don't they? You would be, too, if your new show had a Great Parade outside its theater the way *Barefoot in the Park* did on the morning of October 24, 1963. Such a rush at the box office was common when a show uncommonly opened to six raves from the six critics. Phoning for tickets, let alone ordering them online, was far in the future.

Carol Burnett is Hope Springfield—no, make that Lila Tremaine, as Hollywood has just rechristened her. Now that she has her movie-star name, she's imagining the Oscar that will soon be between those hands. Ultimately, what you see between those mitts is precisely what the Tony committee awarded Burnett for her role in *Fade Out—Fade In*: not as much as a nomination, despite great reviews. That's what you get when you try to get out of a show and turn a smash into a money-loser that closes well before its time.

At first glance, you thought this was Barbra Streisand, didn't you? Seconds later, you realized it was Fanny Brice. That's how similar Streisand was in those days in looks and demeanor to the former Fania Borach. Streisand was one of the luckiest people in the world to be in the right place and time—and have the right talent—to play a *Funny Girl*.

District Attorney Thomas Mara (Larry Douglas, right) looks shocked, but Judge Martin Group (Cliff Hall, left) has apparently seen and heard everything, because he looks unfazed at the assertion by R. H. Macy (Paul Reed, center) that "That man over there is Santa Claus!" It was Reed's big number in *Here's Love* and the first job he had following his three-year stint as Captain Block on *Car 54, Where Are You?*

Does Angela Lansbury look a little glassy-eyed to you? Was this photograph shot during the infamous *Anyone Can Whistle* performance in Philadelphia when Lansbury looked into the audience and saw Nancy Walker, whom she suspected was being considered as her replacement? As it turned out, Lansbury stayed although the show didn't. Would she have ever guessed then that she'd become one of Broadway's biggest stars in a five-decade, five-Tony career?

When was this picture taken of Noël Coward on the set of *The Girl Who Came to Supper*? His smile suggests it could have been immediately following the reviews of the Boston tryout, when the critics raved about his music and lyrics. Or was it a grand gesture he gave after the closing performance, which came only three months after New York's critics and audiences were less impressed? Oh, well— there was always *High Spirits,* which Coward would direct until he decided he needed help from Gower Champion.

Florence Henderson (left) was the title character in *Fanny,* the first show that David Merrick (center) ever solely produced. But that was in 1954. Ten years later, Merrick had what was then his biggest hit—*Hello, Dolly!*—with Carol Channing (right), so he knew which side his cake was frosted on. Henderson was *The Girl Who Came to Supper* that season, but that didn't necessarily mean that Merrick would include her in dessert.

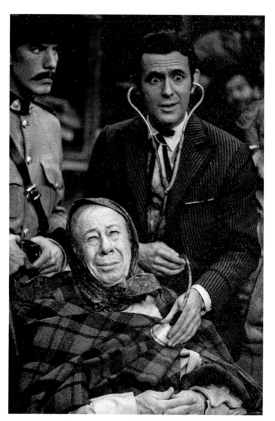

AT LEFT: Here's Bert Lahr (center) pretending to be deathly ill, and getting that phony diagnosis from his confederate, Doc (Larry Blyden). Their musical, *Foxy,* turned out to be the terminal patient, dying after only seventy-two performances. It would have run longer, however, had producer David Merrick taken better care of it. Lahr's Tony-winning performance wasn't even preserved on an official original cast album.

BELOW: It's been said that if you want something done, ask a busy man. Jule Styne certainly qualified in 1963–64 with a Great Parade of assignments. Not only did he compose for *Funny Girl* (which sported some of his finest music) as well as *Fade Out—Fade In* (which featured some of his funniest), he also found time to compose the incidental music for Brecht's *Arturo Ui.*

Yes, you can see her in the film of *The Sound of Music,* but there, as Sister Sophia, Marni Nixon is all swaddled up in an old-world nun's outfit that shows only a portion of her head and very little of her body. So here's a better representation of Nixon in late 1963. Once again, she's learning music, this time so she can provide Audrey Hepburn with a better voice in the film of *My Fair Lady.* And if that isn't enough of a favor to Alan Jay Lerner and Frederick Loewe, the following May Ms. Nixon gave voice, body, and soul to Eliza Doolittle in a City Center revival of the legendary musical.

As Starbuck (Robert Horton) tries to curry favor with Lizzie Curry (Inga Swenson), we have to wonder along with her if he's on the level. Instead, he could be trying to stop her from throwing cold water on his claim that he can bring cool rain to the parched Texas Panhandle, where temperatures have reached *110 in the Shade*. Broadway audiences enjoyed both Swenson and Horton, unaware that they'd see her only one more time (the following season in *Baker Street*) and him never again.

est, with just over the 500-seat minimum that a house needed to be considered a Broadway theater.

With the premature closing of *The Girl Who Came to Supper,* the theater that was generically named the Broadway—the street's largest with over 1,700 seats—was suddenly available. But in those days, theaters with 1,000 seats or fewer seemed destined for plays, while those with more than 1,000 were the ones for musicals. And because this was a mere three-character play, management felt that it certainly required an intimate house.

(Compare this to 2004, when Billy Crystal brought his one-man show to the 1,218-seat Broadhurst and in 2013 to the 1,435-seat Imperial.)

Costigan received not only royalties as a playwright but an extra $117.50 a week for playing Edward, who set up exposition nicely by talking to his dog, Barney, while preparing for his two visitors. He hadn't seen Emil and Mavis for fifteen years, although the three were quite close when they were starting their careers. But with short story writer Edward not achieving nearly as much as movie stars Emil and Mavis (no last names), they had grown apart.

Once the couple arrived, Barney ran off, his job done. To establish that Emil and Mavis were beautiful people, they were bathed in "a flood of unnatural light" as "a royal fanfare" played. But both urged Edward not to come too close, lest he see them at their worst.

Indeed, those who came to stargaze Woodward had to be disappointed that her face was obscured by a veil for the play's first forty minutes. She'd had no fewer than twelve facelifts—or so claimed Emil, who wasn't above disclosing this to Edward in order to aggrandize himself.

And how did you get to be you, Mr. Emil? "Everything I've done," he insisted, "I've accomplished with my God-given looks and personality, my belief in the democratic system and sheer gall." Oh, what hard luck stories he handed Edward, referring to childhood poverty, time spent in an iron lung, and an artificial leg. When Edward couldn't understand the last claim—he'd seen both of Emil's legs when they used to swim together—Emil smiled and offered that as proof of his success: He could afford doctors who could make an artificial leg look 100 percent natural.

"But," said Emil, "just because we have a stunning home and a successful marriage and a fabulous career, I don't want to give the impression that we're not affected by what's going on around us." Mavis believed she'd prove his point by telling of the antibomb symposium they'd recently held, where they served "curried crabmeat, rice, salad and scooped-out watermelon filled with five kinds of rum. Everyone said it was the best symposium they'd ever been to."

Both said that they didn't like it when the press called them "immortal," for they preferred "royalty"—because kings and queens do eventually die. In this same quasi-modest vein, Emil droned, "It's vulgar to say how much you've been getting," but not much time passed before he mentioned his $3,500 watch, $250,000 house, and his $18,000 car that he got for $16,500. "We got a fabulous discount on account of who we are," he explained.

Add *Baby Want a Kiss* to the ahead-of-its-time list. Emil and Mavis were health-obsessed, claiming to be staunch teetotalers and vegetarians—until Edward offered them alcohol and meat, and they rationalized that because they didn't *kill* it, they could eat it.

They brought with them a record that was the current No. 1 hit: "Baby Want a Kiss." Actually, it was a song meant to teach parakeets how to talk, but the teenagers had embraced it because it had a good beat and they could dance to it.

Once again Costigan was prescient—and not simply because two months after his play closed, "Do Wah Diddy Diddy" was atop the nation's charts. Emil and Mavis were emblematic of adults who were starting to embrace youth at any cost. In the years to come, baby boomers would take this to extremes: "I *like* Eminem," they'd say, even indignantly, for saying otherwise indicated old age. Costigan gave Emil and Mavis a head start.

But Edward had his flaws, too. He told of once losing interest in a woman for having a body that wasn't nearly as appealing as her face. Here Costigan rounded out Mavis by having her show some sensitivity and intelligence: "Men expect too much," she said. "Her face was beautiful. You should have been satisfied with that."

Then, when Edward got specific and mentioned "her big behind," Mavis's compassion and acumen disappeared quicker than "Sleep Now, Baby Bunting" after the first preview of *Funny Girl*. "Why didn't you say so?" she snorted. "The one thing in the world that I cannot forgive is a big behind."

The three reminisced about how they used to interpret each other's dreams. Here the play got too serious for its own good and seemed to be parodying *Who's Afraid of Virginia Woolf?* The line of dialogue that must have been the hardest for Woodward to say was "I never looked at another man since I met

Emil, and Emil never again slept with any other woman, not even his wife."
Six years earlier, Woodward had come between Newman and Jacqueline Witte,
his wife of eight years.

At least the Newmans became poster children for the perfect marriage. In
1968, *Playboy* readers would learn how Newman felt about one-night stands,
let alone extramarital affairs: "Why go out looking for hamburger when you
have steak at home?" became an oft-quoted remark.

So Newman must have enjoyed what Emil had to say about their marriage:
"We are sensational in bed together . . . and that is the greatest success story of
all." Where the Newmans apparently parted company with this couple could
be found in the way Emil concluded the statement: "because basically we don't
like each other."

Mavis reiterated this when she told Edward, "Divorce is against our faith.
You know how devout we are," seconds before citing California's community
property laws. However, she knew that Edward had loved her for years, and
said she wanted him to keep worshipping her.

"You mustn't ever stop," she commanded after Emil had left the room. "I
need that kind of love—that kind of blind, selfless love that gives and gives
and asks nothing in return."

Emil, on the other hand, was more interested in making money from endorsements, especially "Celebrity Seed," an artificial insemination company. He then got a kick out of delivering what he imagined might be the
product's commercial: "Why settle for second best? Now you can have a baby
by your favorite actor," he said, before listing eleven more august occupations.

Maybe the play genuinely spoke to Newman and Woodward after all, for
they had the chance to spoof stars and pseudo-stars whom they'd undoubtedly met during their many years in Hollywood. They'd come to know people
who believed that superstardom automatically resulted in knowing everything about everything. The Newmans had seen that stardom was a homonym
for "star dumb."

In real life, the Newmans would have kept their feet on the ground if they
were in the middle of a 9.5-on-the-Richter-scale Los Angeles earthquake.
Instead of "Celebrity Seed," Newman and Woodward would eventually create
such charities as the Hole in the Wall Gang Camp and the Committee Encouraging Corporate Philanthropy.

We must wonder, however, if Newman got an idea after Edward said, "The only wonder to me is that somebody doesn't put you up in packages and sell you in all the supermarkets." Is that how Newman's Own was born?

Baby Want a Kiss more than once turned blackly comic. Mavis implied that Emil had rented a boat, taken his first wife, their four children, the nanny, and their dog out to sea, and drowned them all. Costigan tried to lighten the situation: "After a suitable period of mourning," Mavis said, "we were married the following afternoon."

Harder to take was Emil's telling Edward about his son's death—which, he claimed, he learned from reading the obituary in the newspaper. He matter-of-factly implied that Mavis ignored the fifteen-pound child soon after she'd delivered it. "I can't have a fat baby," he quoted her as saying. "It's bad publicity." A startled Edward asked if he thought Mavis had killed the infant. He shrugged and said, "All I know is what I read in the paper."

Once again, Costigan was ahead of his time, here stressing that being fat was the ultimate disgrace. And once again, he tried to ameliorate the situation with a *Virginia Woolf?* parody, at least suggesting that the child never existed. We may yet see a revival of *Baby Want a Kiss*.

While Costigan was offering Broadway a *Kiss,* Anita Rowe Block concentrated on both *Love and Kisses*. It opened on December 18, 1963, but couldn't make it to 1964. Its plot does suggest that it was only worthy of thirteen unlucky performances.

The Pringles resided in the fictional Elmsdale, Michigan, said to be a suburb of Detroit. For months, Jeff and Carol had been consumed with the upcoming wedding of their daughter, Elizabeth, to Freddy, already a junior partner in a law firm but someone who, according to Jeff, "sounds like the Encyclopedia Britannica."

Just before the invitations were mailed, Buzzy Pringle trumped his sister's ace by announcing that he'd recently married his girlfriend, Rosemary. Given that Buzzy was just about to be graduated from high school, the family was appalled. They were too young to marry! And where would they live?

Right in the Pringle home, as it turned out, and right away, for a honeymoon wasn't mentioned even by the newlyweds.

An outsider thrust into a new household would cause problems, but one flaw of *Love and Kisses* was that Rosemary didn't cause nearly enough. The unexpected twist was that she and Buzzy were virgins who seemed to have no particular interest in sex. Before Rosemary retired on the first night, she asked her new husband, "Does the wife get the upper or lower bunk?" *Love and Kisses* was an apt title, for those two items were all that seemed to interest the couple. For that matter, the older Elizabeth and Freddy were later revealed to be virgins, too.

Rosemary certainly wasn't interested in a career, which was odd given that her mother was then in Afghanistan on an anthropological expedition. Wouldn't such an achiever bestow on her daughter some values about work and independence? But Rosemary was a cipher who stayed at her nonhome while her husband went to work. Yes, by the third act, she'd decided to look for a job, until she was forbidden by Buzzy, whose old-world mindset was of the "No wife of mine is going to work" mentality.

Both son and daughter eventually sought advice from Jeff, whose good deed of giving it went punished when he was accused of meddling. Carol banished him to the living room couch, which forced a couple of bursitis jokes. After that, *Love and Kisses* inextricably turned into not-so-glorified TV fare, an episode of a series that could have been called *Father Knows Nothing.*

Parents of baby boomers knew that their teens had more carnal goals than Buzzy and Rosemary. Some kids had already discovered that aforementioned birth control pill. So Block's premise was downright naive, somewhere between wishful thinking and utopian.

And yet, *Love and Kisses* managed to get a movie sale. The 1963–64 season was the tail end of an era when Hollywood was willing to buy quick Broadway failures (the 1934 Katharine Hepburn vehicle *Spitfire*, which in 1927 was a forty-seven-performance flop called *Trigger*) or even plays that had never reached the stage (*Everybody Comes to Rick's,* which was reworked and renamed *Casablanca*).

The *Love and Kisses* film was the brainchild of a name far more famous to Americans than any studio mogul's: Ozzie Nelson, the power behind the perennial sitcom *The Adventures of Ozzie and Harriet*, then in its twelfth season and destined to go four more. Given that the series was so vanilla—not even vanilla ice cream, but vanilla ice milk—we can see why the notion of nonsexual teens appealed to Nelson.

So when he happened to be in New York between December 16 and 28, Nelson wouldn't have been expected to see *Spoon River Anthology*. *Love and Kisses* was more his style. It would be, he reasoned, a good vehicle for his younger son, teen idol Ricky; what's more, the elder Nelson would not only produce it, but direct and write the screenplay, too.

Interesting note: Buzzy in the play was said to have an A average, but Nelson changed that to B+—perhaps thinking that palming off his guitar-strumming son as such a brain would alienate the teen audience whose grades weren't nearly as high.

Ozzie Nelson would have been better off that December if he'd just gone to see the Christmas tree at Rockefeller Center. The picture was as big a dud as the stage play. Ozzie may have been titillated by the semisexual nature of the piece, which was far more frank than anything he would unleash in his sitcom's 435 (!) episodes. Ricky was even allowed to say "damn" and "hell," each of which had yet to be heard on network TV. Perhaps the picture would have done better if it had used an ad campaign not unlike the one *Anna Christie* used in 1930—"Garbo Talks!"—by stating "Ricky Swears!"

CHAPTER FIVE

*

The Dramas

We've already seen shows about those whose real names were used (Fanny Brice, Martin Luther) and those who had them obfuscated (Laurette Taylor, Boris Thomashefsky, and Adolf Hitler). Finally, depending on your point of view, there was also Kris Kringle.

Dramas in 1963–64 certainly portrayed many actual people, some named by names, other masked. But back then, when people heard the name Dylan, the real person who immediately came to mind was a poet surnamed Thomas and not a singer whose first name was Bob.

Over the last fifty years, that has changed. But Dylan Thomas (1914–53) was the most famous poet-cum-bad-boy of his era. No wonder that Sir Alec Guinness was willing to portray him.

Playwright Sidney Michaels centered on the last year of Thomas's life, when the poet was thirty-eight and his wife, née Caitlin Macnamara, was thirty-nine.

Those are the statistics. Emotionally speaking, Caitlin (Kate Reid) was more than a year older. After Michaels's three-hour drama *Dylan* had concluded, many theatergoers came away thinking Dylan's level of maturity was around thirty-eight months. What endurance Caitlin had to remain married to him for sixteen years; she might have even stayed longer had he not died only two weeks after turning thirty-nine of 1) pneumonia, 2) pressure on the brain, and, of course, 3) a fatty liver. (His daughter, Aeronwy, swore till the day she died that the doctor attending him had administered a morphine overdose.)

Audiences might not have sided with Caitlin from the outset, given that her first line was "So here you are, you scum." When she brought up her father's friendship with painter Augustus John, Dylan vaingloriously said, "I'll come off better'n he will in a thousand years."

If we can judge by Google, Thomas was correct. As of this writing, the score is Dylan, 539,000 hits; Augustus, 276,000.

When Caitlin said he wasn't as famous as he thought he was—that "nobody in your home town even knows who you are," he corrected her. "In my home town," he grandly proclaimed, "I'm known as the drunk."

The couple was living in Laugharne, Wales, but Dylan had undoubtedly made a trip to Ireland to kiss, hug, and pet the Blarney Stone, for he made many witty observations. When Caitlin asked where he'd been the previous night, he said he was with "Fishermen. Whores. The kind of people Christ used to pal around with."

"You don't give an f'ing damn about me," Caitlin said. True, she only used the first letter of that four-letter word, but for a woman in that era, the contraction was potent. Caitlin was no shrinking violet when she became purple with rage. When Dylan accused her of being with "seven truck drivers," she responded, "I have to have *some* fun." When he was away—as he often was—she bemoaned being stuck with "three Dylan-aping time-sucking brats." Again, love vs. career: Caitlin had been a model and modern dancer until motherhood took over.

Now she'd have no help, for Dylan would enjoy six months of lucrative poetry readings in America. Yes, but would Caitlin and the kids see any of the money?

Dame Edith Sitwell had proclaimed that Dylan was "the only lyric poet of the twentieth century," a statement that filled him with white-hot air. When Caitlin seemed unimpressed, Dylan slapped her. Like (too) many other wives of the era, she accepted it along with much of the audience. Worse, a few lines later she was saying that "I love you the way you are."

Dylan came to the United States courtesy of American poet John Malcolm Brinnin (1916–98), who booked him into New York's YMHA. This would essentially be an audition; bookers attending would decide whether Thomas was worth representing on the college circuit.

So a trip to the White Horse Tavern beforehand was not a good idea. Alas, Brinnin enabled Dylan's drinking, calling the man "a frightened child." Meanwhile, his (fictitiously named) publisher, Angus Marius, procured women for "the oldest man alive."

A drunk Dylan approached Meg, an assistant editor, and pinched her breasts. When she didn't respond arduously, he called her a lesbian, then followed that up by bragging that he could "play 'Alexander's Ragtime Band' on his little tin balls with his own leather dong," before announcing, "I have to pee now," in an era when plays never acknowledged bodily excretions.

Miraculously, the bombed Dylan didn't bomb at the Y. Even Katherine Anne Porter was impressed, and Dylan rewarded her by piggy-backing her around the room.

A child? Dylan agreed when deconstructing "Baa Baa Black Sheep," starting with the admission that he was both the black sheep of his family and "the little boy who lives down the lane." Chapman, McClain, and Watts were enough impressed with the scene to devote paragraphs to it.

Not long after, Dylan's immaturity returned when he failed to mail home money that would pay his son's tuition. When time came for him to return home, he made one last attempt to bed Meg.

"A sailing party is a time for whoopee," he said.

"Then where," she asked him, "are you always sailing?"

To the grave, of course. The play ended with Caitlin tending to his coffin. Has anybody ever had more apt initials than Dylan Thomas?

Although Nadel didn't even mention Alec Guinness until the twelfth of his fifteen paragraphs, Kerr spent his first six paragraphs speaking of no one else and offering unmitigated praise. So did McClain ("a towering performance"), Watts ("brilliant"), Chapman ("a masterly demonstration of the actor's art"), and Taubman ("an actor who makes you forget that he is acting.").

Taubman also said that "one must turn to Alec Guinness rather than to the author for satisfaction." Kerr said that Michaels's play "does not grow in wisdom or grace." Nadel: "It only reports and provides no new insights." McClain was more sympathetic: "The author faced a challenge beyond his or perhaps anyone's capabilities."

On the credit side of the ledger, Watts saw it as "an absorbing study in human disintegration," while Chapman went all-out in proclaiming it "one of the beautiful plays of our time."

Maybe *his* time; *Dylan* hasn't passed the test of time. One little off-Broadway revival in 1972 lasted six weeks. No first-class theater has seen it since.

Did Pope Pius XII do little to nothing to protest Hitler's systematic "final solution" to rid the world of Jews?

John Cornwell alleged just that in *Hitler's Pope: The Secret History of Pius XII,* the most controversial book of 1999.

This indictment was old news to anyone who'd paid attention to Broadway in 1963–64, when Rolf Hochhuth's *The Deputy* made the same claim.

Hochhuth's title referred to the Pope's position as a deputy of Jesus Christ. However, the playwright felt that Pius XII abrogated his responsibilities while he was on the throne.

When Hochhuth sat down to write *Der Stellvertreter,* he was a thirty-year-old German Protestant who had actually been a member of the Hitler Youth. Some would later allege that one reason he wrote the play was to diminish the guilt of his people by turning attention to the Pope instead.

It would hardly be the only objection to the play.

Hochhuth made a bold choice in deciding to write in free verse. One reason, he said, was to avoid sounding "as if one were merely quoting from documents." Another was his noticing that high Church dignitaries don't speak in everyday language; "they express themselves in a more ceremonial manner."

So free verse it would be. And if that convention weren't enough, whenever Pius XII spoke, Hochhuth capitalized "Us" and "Our."

Two other characters figured prominently in Hochhuth's drama. First was a young German named Kurt Gerstein who in 1941 was told to start delivering gas to the Nazi camps. He thought nothing of it until a year later, when he discovered how that gas was being used. What he learned immediately turned Gerstein anti-Nazi. He decided to use the system to beat the system: He joined the SS and became a double agent.

Once Gerstein had incontrovertible proof that Jews were being systematically massacred, he brought word to Father Riccardo Fontana, a young Jesuit diplomat at the Vatican. Although he was a fictional character, Hochhuth closely based him on both Bernhard Lichtenberg, a Berlin provost, and Maximilian Kolbe, a Franciscan friar.

Fontana was horrified to hear that 1,800,000 Jews had been murdered. This fact was one of the play's most powerful, for audiences knew by then that the final total of "the final solution" was more than three times that. The implication was that Hitler was just getting started en route to murdering 1,000 Jews an hour.

So stricken was Fontana that when he learned of Jacobson, a Jew in hiding, he gave him his passport to aid his flight. Jacobson, in a gesture of solidarity, gave Fontana the yellow Star of David that Germans had been forcing each Jew to wear.

When Fontana brought news of the atrocities to those above him in the Church hierarchy, he was aghast to find that they did not want to address Gerstein's eyewitness reports.

Part of the problem stemmed from the fact that Pius XI, the previous Pope, had signed a concordat with Hitler in 1933. (In fact, the future Pius XII, then Eugene Pacelli, had worked on it.) Pius XI had even praised Hitler as the first statesman to join him "in an open disavowal of Bolshevism."

That was the crux of the matter. The Vatican feared Bolsheviks and Communists far more than Nazis—and certainly less than Fascism. The Church saw Hitler as the lesser of two evils and Stalin as far more dangerous. After all, Hitler wasn't persecuting Catholics, while Stalin was torturing members of all religions.

The Vatican was further intimidated after the Soviet Union's victory in Stalingrad, when its armies were advancing in Eastern Europe and taking over churches. Pius XII saw Hitler as his best chance of stopping it.

Thus Fontana was thwarted by the papal nuncio, who called the concordat "socially acceptable," and a cardinal who felt that "any anathema against Hitler will become a fanfare of victory for the Bolsheviks."

Meanwhile, Hochhuth had the Germans use the concordat to their own advantage. The fictional SS Captain Salzer said to one of his captives, "If those stories the hate-propagandists tell were true, do you imagine the Pope would give such friendly audiences to thousands of members of the German army?" That statement mollified the prisoner's fears, but audiences already knew the terrible fate awaiting the detainees.

Hochhuth alternated the many discussions and debates with other sobering scenes. Families were seen captured, separated, and displaced. Even Italian Jews who had converted to Catholicism were rounded up for "resettlement" right in front of the Vatican and only a few hundred feet from the Pope's throne. More than a thousand were brought to the camps; fifteen returned alive.

That led to Hochhuth's creating a woman of Italian Jewish origin who'd been engaged to an Italian Catholic soldier; thus, she would have been spared from the Germans once she'd married him. But the soldier was killed in the war, so the woman's anticipated dispensation was suddenly null and void.

Hochhuth also imagined that an Italian manufacturer brought in for questioning was so frightened that he said he approved the extermination of the Jews. The Nazi told him to prove it by spitting in the face of a Jew who'd been detained with him. When the manufacturer could only bear to spit on the Jew's coat, the officer sent him to be detained in the local dog kennel.

Why, Hochhuth asked incredulously, did the Pope still do nothing when these Italian Jewish captives were literally paraded in front of his windows? Salzer pooh-poohed any possible strife. "Berlin won't take a chance of roasting the Jews from Rome immediately," he told an ally. "If the Pope starts kicking up a fuss, they can always be sent back home. They won't be roasted until it's certain that he isn't worrying any more about them."

What Fontana did hear was that a cardinal said, "I have prayed for the Jews," and that the Pope's "heart is with the victims." He found that little consolation and would now break into the sanctum sanctorum and blatantly confront Pius XII.

Now, at last, in the play's eighth scene, Hochhuth introduced Pius XII, who soon started talking about Church finances. One could argue that as "CEO," he had a responsibility to see his "company" survive. And the Pope did condemn the recent Allied bombing of nearby Monte Cassino, which the Nazis had occupied. While he released a statement about human suffering, he didn't include the word "Jews," lest, Hochhuth assumed, he offend someone.

The playwright stopped short of specifically saying that the Pope was anti-Semitic. Instead, he characterized the Pope as a man with a large ego; he was quite insulted that Hitler hadn't apparently deemed him important enough to broker a peace treaty with the United States. Hochhuth surmised that wasn't the extent of the Pope's interest in America; he wanted to know the amount of donated money that had come from the States. How pleased he was with the contributions from Cardinal Spellman of New York City.

When confronted by Fontana, the Pope pointed out that many priests were secretly harboring Jews. This, he felt, was a good solution because such clandestine activities could be hidden from Hitler. Fontana was startled that such a "solution" was enough for the Pope, but he truly became infuriated when he learned that Pius XII knew in advance that Italian Jews would be rounded up and sent to camps. Would Pius XII ever take any action?

Yes: He would reassign Fontana to a nearby library, where the priest would catalog books "and take long, contemplative walks."

And while the Pontiff was pontificating, Hochhuth showed a line of Jews at the back wall of the stage, all going to their deaths.

Fontana began ranting, to which the Pope responded, "Obedience, unconditional obedience is the Jesuit's first commandment!" In response, Fontana pinned Jacobson's Star of David on his chest, left the room, was captured, and went to Auschwitz to be murdered.

History shows that more than a thousand priests martyred themselves in protest against the Pope's inaction—including Fontana's prototypes Lichtenberg and Kolbe. Some alleged that these priests went to the concentration camps simply to see what was going on, and initially didn't have martyrdom on their minds. Whatever the case, their martyring themselves had as much effect as a hunger strike.

Once Hochhuth finished the play in early 1962, he knew that his manuscript, although written in dramatic form, was substantially longer than the average play. Thus, he sought a publisher instead of a producer. He received a couple of rejections, but Heinrich Ledig-Rowohlt of the famed Rowohlt Verlag publishing house was impressed. Everyone in his employ who had read it, he said, "had been profoundly shaken."

Ledig-Rowohlt so believed in the play's stage potential that he sent it to noted director Erwin Piscator. What most affected him was that "it reminds all the participants they could have made their decision, and in fact they did make it even when they did not."

Or, to quote the expression that became much said in America later in the decade, "Not to decide is to decide."

"This play makes it worthwhile to produce theater," Piscator said. Initially he was undeterred by its length, asserting it was "a matter of complete indifference how long a play is if it is a good and necessary play. The span of *The Deputy* is fully justified."

He changed his mind once he truly realized that an uncut *Deputy*, depending on direction and pacing, might take as long as *nine* hours. Piscator directed an abridged production that premiered in Berlin on February 23, 1963—coincidentally, the same date on which Ledig-Rowohlt published the unexpurgated text.

At the back of the playscript were sixty-five additional pages. Hochhuth knew that he'd be open to vast criticism, so he included an appendix with documentation to prove he was accurate and not exaggerating.

Some would find the appendix more compelling than the play itself. But productions of *The Deputy* proliferated in London, Paris, Vienna, Stockholm, and Athens, all prior to its being optioned for Broadway.

Does *The Deputy* seem to be the type of attraction that would entice the producer of *Jumbo, The Great Magoo,* and the eponymous *Billy Rose's Crazy Quilt?* Yet Rose optioned it. To be fair, those attractions were Rose's productions in the '30s. His producing *Carmen Jones* in the '40s, an adaptation of Andre Gide's *The Immoralist* in the '50s, and a 1960 dramatization of John Hersey's *The Wall*—about Nazis terrorizing Poland—suggested that over the decades the showman had acquired more social consciousness.

However, Rose let his option lapse. Herman Shumlin, the noted producer and director of *Grand Hotel, The Little Foxes, The Corn Is Green,* and *Inherit the Wind,* would now work in the same two capacities for *The Deputy*. He considered presenting the unexpurgated script over two or three nights, but in the end, he decided, as Piscator had, on a single night's presentation.

Shumlin hired noted translator Jerome Rothenberg to adapt the play into English and work with him on the cuts. They wound up with a play that was still nearly three hours long.

Some familiar with the original play regretted that Rothenberg had eliminated so much of Gerstein and had minimized the Doctor, the play's unquestioned villain, whom Hochhuth had described as a "handsome and likeable" man who just happened to love to torture and kill Jews. His prize possession was a glass jar filled with the brains of young Jewish twins.

This detail came from August Hirt, a University of Strasbourg professor whose hobby was collecting skulls. But the real inspiration for the doctor was the notorious Dr. Josef Mengele. In bragging that he had sent Sigmund Freud's sister "up the chimney," he blithely claimed that he was "provoking God to answer."

(With the ultimate Nazi defeat, God could be said to have done just that.)

Although the role of Pius XII was comparatively small, Shumlin was able to entice distinguished British actor Emlyn Williams to portray him. Two ironies here: Williams, who'd now play someone criticized for his silence, had recently appeared on Broadway in a play called *Daughter of Silence*. Before that, he'd replaced Paul Scofield as St. Thomas More in the decidedly pro-Catholic play *A Man for All Seasons*.

Hochhuth won Germany's Young Generation Playwright Award not long before Shumlin booked the Brooks Atkinson Theatre for a February 26, 1964, Broadway debut. When that night arrived, two groups picketed: Catholics and the American Nazi Party, the latter dressed in full storm trooper regalia. First-nighters were told not to leave their seats during intermission, which was a difficulty in this era when many smoked.

While Taubman and Watts had their say, their newspapers had even more to add through editorials. "Silence" was the title of the one in the *Times*, as it levied blame on all—not just the Pope—who stayed quiet during those terrible times. Similarly, the *Post* editorial said, "To avoid the subject would make our generation guilty of the same kind of silence."

The *Herald Tribune* didn't offer an editorial but let Francis Cardinal Spellman do the talking. "An outrageous desecration of the honor of a great and good man," he insisted. A publication called *America*—arguably mislabeled, for it didn't deal with the entire nation but was aimed at Catholics—called the play "character assassination." Tom F. Driver, the critic for *The Reporter*, who would later be a staunch advocate for James Baldwin's *Blues for Mister Charlie*, called the play "an anti-Catholic tract of almost no subtlety."

Richard Gilman of *Commonweal*—a converted Catholic writing for a Catholic publication—wrote, "Its attempt to locate guilt instructs us in the supreme difficulty of the task." Here Hochhuth agreed, insisting that "Pius is a symbol not only for all leaders but for all men: Christians, Atheists and Jews."

After all, Vatican City wasn't the only country to avoid the issue. The reason the United States fought the Nazis wasn't to aid the Jews but to keep the Germans from conquering the world. Said Hannah Arendt, the German American political theorist, "The Pope did what most, though not all, secular rulers did." Indeed, what did FDR and Chamberlain do? The Allies might well have feared that they would have to house displaced Jews. As I. F. Stone wrote in his *Weekly,* "Expediency came before humanity."

However accurate Hochhuth was, he must be commended for not characterizing Fontana's adversaries as foppish bureaucrats. They gave solid rebuttals why a Vatican action might be disastrous. Many at the time indeed worried that if the Pope had spoken out, he might well have infuriated Hitler to the point where the madman would have had the Pontiff captured.

Historically speaking, there was merit in this fear. Albrecht von Kessel, attaché to the wartime German embassy, said that "the idea of taking the Pope prisoner had entered into Hitler's calculation. We had specific information that if the Pope resisted, there was the possibility that he would be shot while trying to escape."

Under those circumstances, how much more dramatic *The Deputy* would have been.

Von Kessel also believed that "a fiery protest from the Pope in 1943 would not have saved the life of a single Jew." He noted that the Archbishop of Utrecht condemned Hitler's policy, and soon after, the Nazis began capturing even Jewish converts to Catholicism, including the illustrious philosopher Edith Stein.

To those who thought the Pope did absolutely nothing, Von Kessel rebutted that Pius XII "prayed day by day, week by week, month by month for the answer."

Had Hitler killed the Pope or even abducted him, he might have lost the support of Germany's thirty-five million Catholics. On the other hand, because so many were staunchly behind their leader, these pro-Nazi Catholics might have opted to leave the Church instead. (Actually, the Catholics who were pro-Hitler could have been said to have already left the Church.)

Such arguments wouldn't have swayed Hochhuth if he'd heard them before writing the play. "If one takes one's religion seriously," he said, "if one measures the sincerity of the Church by the claims it makes, the silence of the Pope was a crime." He felt that even if the Pope's speaking up had had no effect, he still should have established where he stood.

And while noted critic Robert Brustein condemned *The Deputy* as "neither...good history nor...good literature," he applauded Hochhuth, who'd "certainly proven himself as a man of discriminating moral intelligence and outstanding courage, which makes him rare and valuable enough in the moral world."

Nevertheless, the play contained (at least) one instance where Hochhuth took substantial dramatic license. Pius XII had said, "As the flowers of the countryside wait beneath winter's mantle of snow for the warm breezes of spring, so the Poles must wait, praying and trusting that the hour of heavenly comfort will come."

Hochhuth retained the entire quotation except for one word; he changed "Poles" to "Jews."

On the other hand, Piscator cut the word "Russian" from Hochhuth's line "The prisoners in Auschwitz were freed by Russian soldiers." We all have our prejudices.

Pope Pius XII, who died in 1958, couldn't defend himself, but Cardinal Montini, the future Pope Paul VI, had a good amount of criticism in a letter he sent in 1963 to *The Tablet*, a Catholic periodical. The esteemed Eric Bentley drolly noted, "Surely this must be the first time in history that the premiere of a play has been noticed by the Vatican."

Bentley stated this in the foreword of *The Storm over "The Deputy,"* the only play this season (or most others) to warrant a second paperback. *The Storm over "The Deputy"* was Bentley's compendium of thirty-four articles from such writers as John Simon, I. F. Stone, and Susan Sontag. These pieces only filled the book's first 236 pages; the other 18 were sheer bibliography. It revealed that a startling *524* articles had been written about *The Deputy* in 1963 and 1964. Anyone who wanted to discount Bentley's statement "It is almost certainly the largest storm ever raised by a play in the whole history of the drama" would have had a hard time.

The Deputy did even more impressively in hardcover. In Germany, 40,000 copies were printed in 1962 and almost 200,000 in 1963. In America, it became only the second play to reach the bestseller list. (Eugene O'Neill's *Strange Interlude* had been the first in 1928.)

Shumlin was able to keep the play alive for 316 performances, making it the second-longest-running drama of the season behind *The Subject Was Roses*.

From 1962–63 through 1964–65, a Tony was given to Best Producer of a Play. Shumlin won for *The Deputy*. Considering that this was the only instance in those four years that the winning producer did not have his production nominated as Best Play, we can infer that his production was not the only reason he was selected; his great courage in bringing this to New York was obviously the deciding factor.

The Deputy was so thoroughly controversial that one profane word got lost in the miasma of criticism and defense. Had this been any other play, the word would have provoked intense outrage, but so much else was going on that it was metaphorically swept under the stage.

Captain Salzer, faced with a belligerent detainee, told him, "You'd simply disappear, reported missing, or maybe fall down a manhole or in the cunt of some Via Appia whore."

That certainly trumped Hapgood's "merde."

By 1963–64, Broadway knew Peter Shaffer. His *Five Finger Exercise,* about a young German who came to England to tutor a girl and found himself getting too involved in family matters, ran ten solid months. It also won the 1959–60 New York Drama Critics Circle Award as Best Foreign Play.

Now—was Shaffer a one-hit wonder?

He'd have two chances to answer that question when his double bill entitled *The Private Ear and The Public Eye* came to Broadway after a sixteen-month London run.

Alas, Maggie Smith, who appeared in both plays in the West End, didn't travel with them.

The Private Ear referred to Bob, who spent his free time in his rented room, where he incessantly played classical music. Only occasionally would he go to a concert, where he'd listen intently and talk to no one.

The previous night had been different. Doreen, sitting next to him, dropped her program; when he retrieved it for her, their eyes met. Whether this was love at first sight would depend on the next night, for Doreen had agreed to come to his room for dinner.

(A woman would go to a man's place on the basis of one chance meeting? Yes, the world was a safer place back then—or at least perceived to be.)

While Shaffer didn't specify whether or not Bob was a virgin, he made clear that the twenty-something didn't have much experience with women. Bob knew it, too, so he sought advice from Ted, his boss, who was quite the ladies' man. When Ted started to reveal his seduction secrets, Bob made clear that he was only interested in how to make a woman fall in love with him, not bed him. He likened Doreen to his framed print of Botticelli's *The Birth of Venus,* and used such words as "love," "charity," "dignity," "modesty," "grace," and "beauty" to describe her. If Bob ruled the world, women would be more interested in entering an *inner* beauty contest.

Ted also offered to show up, cook dinner, serve it, and at the "last swallow of coffee, I'm away. Nine-thirty you'll see me; nine-thirty-one you won't."

Even those attending their first play might have guessed that Ted was there not in order to help, but solely to show off how suave and experienced he was in order to win the lady for himself. Bob, however, wasn't aware of that possibility. When Doreen arrived—surprised to see a table set for three—Bob even sang Ted's praises while the Lothario was still in the kitchen.

Then Bob made the mistake of waxing rhapsodic about the virtues of his stereo system. He made clear that he'd invested a good deal of money in it, especially for a "glorified office boy," as he labeled himself. Audiences might have appreciated that he was willing to tell the truth and offer no illusions; Doreen instead said, "I like people who want to get on, who have drive."

Bob realized his error and started to talk about classical music, which did seem apt; after all, Doreen had attended a concert. Alas, she later disclosed that she'd been given a free ticket and went because she had nothing better to do.

Thus Bob's beautiful story of how he one day suddenly came to love Bach was wasted on her. When he told her the story of *Peter Grimes,* his favorite opera, he cited the lonely man that no one understood and who wasn't "good at expressing himself." Bob didn't realize that he was telling Doreen what could be included in his biography in the unlikely event that someone would ever want to write it.

Give Bob credit, he endeavored to show her exactly who he was: "I love to see the lines on people's faces. I mean, that's their life, isn't it? It's what happened to them."

Such sentiments were lost on Doreen, one of those people who don't know how to respond to unique perceptions. She could only relate to concepts that she'd heard before. Doreen was more socially adept than Bob (not by much, incidentally), but Ted would turn out to be more her speed, what with his surface gloss and lampshade-on-your-head type of humor.

How pathetic Ted was when he unashamedly flirted in a supposedly witty way while serving what he egocentrically called "Chicken à la Ted Veasey." "I left out the garlic," he said. "You never know how this evening might end."

And Doreen laughed. She did see through him to some degree—even telling him (while Bob was in the kitchen) that Bob was "a blooming sight more better mannered than what you are." And yet, not unlike Caitlin Thomas, she was attracted to the bad boy. So while she and Ted chatted away, Bob kept reaching for the wine bottle.

Ted did make good on his promise to leave at 9:30, but by then Bob had realized that his "best friend" was no friend at all. While Doreen was in the bathroom, he told him, "You're the organ grinder and I'm the monkey." And Bob hadn't even seen the scene the audience did: While Bob was in the kitchen, Ted had clandestinely asked for Doreen's phone number.

After Ted left, Bob sympathetically commented on her mundane job: "Complicated things like eyes weren't made by God just to see columns of pounds, shillings, and pence written up in a ledger."

Doreen's response: "What's the time?"

Bob didn't get the hint. When he opened up enough to tell her that he pretended to conduct an orchestra in the privacy of his living room—down to every arm gesture and stab—she said, "I really have to go now."

Once he saw that being himself was failing, he tried to be Ted. To use a Sally Bowles expression, he pounced. Doreen pounced back by slapping his face.

Now Bob had to save what was left of that face. He bragged that he had a fiancée and simply wanted Doreen as a new conquest. She saw through the ruse but didn't challenge him on it, for she actually felt sorry for him as she left.

Bob, realizing that music could not substitute for love, displaced his hostility on one of his most beloved records, purposely scratching it from edge to label and then listening to it in its new sabotaged state.

In 1963–64, before the era of CDs, downloads, and Spotify, people would say, "You sound like a broken record." By play's end, Bob felt like one.

With a downer such as this, could people really be expected to return for the second play? Those who did were rewarded with *The Public Eye*, a pointed comedy-drama that, along with its bit, provided not only charm but also a hint of the unique imagination that Shaffer would later show in *Black Comedy, Equus, Amadeus,* and *Lettice and Lovage.*

"Men of forty shouldn't marry girls of eighteen," middle-aged accountant Charles now acknowledged after some months of marriage. "Is there anything so utterly boring and ridiculous as the modern worship of youth?"

(Little did Shaffer know how much more pervasive that mindset would become.)

When Charles was courting the naive and uneducated Belinda, he loved teaching her about the cultural riches of London and beyond—and she loved learning. Once they were married, only then did he seem to notice how vast her ignorance was. The humdrum routine of everyday marriage was helping to sink them, too.

So Belinda was spending an inordinate amount of time out of the house. Charles suspected an affair and hired Julian, a private detective whom Shaffer described as having "a gentle eccentricity," as opposed to Charles, who was "exact and finicky"—qualities that have been said to be an accountant's occupational hazards.

Julian tailed Belinda day after day, leading to Shaffer's marvelous plot twist: Once Belinda noticed that a man was following her, she automatically assumed that he must be an admirer.

Not that she wanted to cheat on Charles. She just enjoyed the nonstop attention this man seemed to be giving her, in a more benign version of what Mavis had with Edward in *Baby Want a Kiss.*

When Charles confronted her about him, Belinda told him, "He just pops up ... in a coffee bar or a cinema or out behind a statue in the park." Although this stranger had followed her into cinemas to see horror film after horror film, he eventually led the way and brought her to see Ingmar Bergman's *Wild Strawberries,* which she adored.

The upshot? "When I'm with him," she said, "I live."

Belinda never said a word to her "admirer" because she'd learned from Charles what could happen when talking starts: Language can lead to castigation.

Charles was furious to learn that his "rival" was actually his employee, but when he finally told Belinda the truth, she was far more incensed. Shaffer managed to save the situation by having Julian intent on being "the first detective to cement a marriage." He taught Charles that one can never let the romance go, and that marriage should be a freeing adventure where one party is constantly courting the other instead of "wedlock."

There was one unpleasant ingredient: Shaffer established that Charles occasionally visited prostitutes. (Accountant, heal thyself!) Despite this sordid detail, the appeal and surprise of *The Public Eye* probably carried the double bill to a 163-performance run—not enough to make money, but enough to be respectable.

Still, the evening of one-act plays was on its way out. While the half century before 1963–64 had seen more than fifty evenings in which two or more one-act plays would be presented, the half century after has witnessed fewer than two dozen. As of this writing, there hasn't been a dramatic or comedic double bill on Broadway in the past twenty years.

Given what we hear about Americans' ever-diminishing attention spans, one-act plays should now be quite popular. Perhaps today's theatergoers feel that at 9 P.M. or so, dealing with a new plot, theme, and characters is simply too much work. Yes, people are used to seeing half-hour sitcoms on TV, but they've been following those shows for weeks, months, or even years, and they come to these programs already knowing the characters well. Confronting new individuals and starting a story from scratch just might be too daunting.

That may be why now, when plays of ninety minutes or even fewer are presented on Broadway, they're done as stand-alones. Theatergoers are getting less for their money, but as workaholism has increased—with wives as well as husbands having jobs to attend to the next morning—they're just as happy to get out at 9:30 and go home when Ted did.

"Here is an event of major significance to the theater and to television," bragged the advertisement. "A Broadway opening on television."

Indeed, on October 14, 1963—the very night that the new play *The Advocate* was opening at the ANTA Theatre—viewers tuning in to WJZ in Baltimore, WBZ in Boston, KYW in Cleveland, KDKA in Pittsburgh, and KPIX in San Francisco also saw Robert Noah's new play.

These five stations belonged to a consortium called Group W, which was intent on bringing its eight million viewers a taste of New York theater.

The Advocate, by first-time (and, as it turned out, only-time) Broadway playwright Robert Noah was their choice to debut a new series called *Opening Night on Broadway.* Its powers that be boldly stated that they would broadcast four to six Broadway openings a season.

If only.

Actually, *The Advocate* needed Group W more than Group W needed *The Advocate.* Michael Ellis and William Hammerstein wouldn't have had the money to bring the $100,000 production to Broadway if Group W hadn't invested an undisclosed but high sum. There was no longer much interest in once again stating that Sacco and Vanzetti didn't receive a fair trial in 1921 and how that continually frustrated and angered their defense attorney. (While Sacco and Vanzetti's names were used, Noah had "Warren Curtis" stand in for their actual lawyer, William Thompson.)

The Advocate might not seem like summer fun, but Ellis and Hammerstein premiered it at their Bucks County Playhouse in July 1962. They believed that it belonged on Broadway, but Alfred Drake, who directed, didn't.

Ellis and Hammerstein were undaunted. They signed Drake's old *Oklahoma!* castmate Howard Da Silva to stage it, and then, when they learned from a newspaper that Group W was hunting for a show to launch their series, they quickly got on the phone.

What those five cities saw wasn't *quite* what was seen at the ANTA Theatre. Group W didn't just haul cameras into the Fifty-second Street theater and start broadcasting live. The ANTA wasn't even used. Instead, the crews went out to Mineola, where the show had played a two-week tryout. They didn't even use the stage set that Ralph Alswang had designed, for it was deemed too large for taping purposes. A smaller set was built.

How strange that must have been for the cast of twenty-two (!), to be on the regular set on September 29 and on a different but similar one when rehearsals began on October 1 and when taping commenced on October 4 for three days. What's more, the actors were given direction not from Da Silva but from TV director Marc Daniels, who, if he was true to form for directors, undoubtedly changed a thing or two (or more) from what Da Silva had ordered.

Noah had to do a little script changing, too. As we've seen, TV hadn't yet allowed "hell" and "damn," so "bastards" and "son of a bitch" just wouldn't do.

After the taping, the cast returned to the ANTA for a week of previews on the original set. Dialogue was certainly reinstated, but one wonders if Da Silva had much to change back from Daniels's direction.

Still, the lead actors had to be pleased. Because of Equity demands, negotiations, and compromises, those who worked the entire three days of rehearsing and three days of taping received what would have been a month's worth of their Broadway salary.

Henry Fonda appeared—not in the play (more's the pity, the producers must have said) but as the host of the TV broadcast. Onstage, Curtis was portrayed by James Daly, esteemed by peers and critics, but not a star.

Group W gave it its all. Only eleven minutes of commercials were peppered between a thirty-three-and-a-half-minute Act One, a forty-seven-minute Act Two, and a twenty-nine-minute Act Three.

Not long after the 8–10:30 P.M. broadcast had finished, the reviews came in, letting everyone connected with *The Advocate* know that it was finished, too.

Daly's daughter—Tyne Daly—recalled that her father greatly believed in *The Advocate*. She related the excitement of the family's dressing up for the opening, attending the play, which they all loved, going to Sardi's, and enjoying the party—until, of course, the reviews came out.

Kerr said he'd been "wholly uninvolved." The same might be gleaned from the reviews from Watts ("suffers from a lack of sustained power"), McClain ("it just isn't very exciting"), Chapman ("more interesting technically than emotionally"), and Nadel ("of only intermittent interest").

And the *Times*? "The play was a welcome relief from domestic comedies, cowboys, and hospital corridors."

But, as you may have inferred, that came from the paper's TV critic. Taubman called *The Advocate* "a flawed document rather than a drama with fresh insights."

"My little sister was so brave," Ms. Daly said mournfully. "She waited until we had left the party and were safely in the car before she started to cry."

Dad had to be assuaged by Coleman's stating that "James Daly gives one of the best performances of the season." But how many were reading the *Mir-*

ror? It would shutter on Wednesday, even before *The Advocate* did on Saturday after eight performances.

Group W did not broadcast three to five other shows that season or any other. It should have waited a week and aired *Barefoot in the Park* instead.

There was another factor in *The Advocate*'s failure.

"It may be unfair, but it is impossible not to compare *The Advocate* with *A Case of Libel*," wrote McClain. "I'm afraid *The Advocate* comes in second-best."

It also starred Oscar winner Van Heflin, a far more bankable name than James Daly.

A Case of Libel was based on *Reynolds v. Pegler,* the 1955 lawsuit in which Quentin Reynolds sued famous right-wing columnist Westbrook Pegler for libel. Reynolds won a single dollar for compensatory damages, but $175,000 in punitive damages from Pegler ($100,000) and the Hearst Corporation and Consolidated Publications ($75,000).

The latter had published the offensive piece in the *Journal-American* in 1949—two years before McClain had joined the paper. At the time, *Reynolds v. Pegler* was the largest-ever judgment of its kind.

Theatergoers in 1963 could be expected to be more interested in a court case that took place nine years earlier than in the Sacco-Vanzetti trial that was now more than a third of a century old. Better still, *Reynolds v. Pegler* had actually experienced a renaissance in the previous two years. Louis Nizer, Reynolds's lawyer, wrote about his victory in his 1961 memoir *My Life in Court,* which spent more than a year on the *New York Times* bestseller list, often in first place.

Playwright Henry Denker changed Nizer's name to Robert Sloane (Heflin), Pegler's to Boyd Bendix (Larry Gates), and Reynolds's to Dennis Corcoran (John Randolph, who knew a good deal about having his reputation ruined from his many years on the blacklist).

One can infer that Denker changed the names because he veered greatly from the facts. Actually, he stayed pretty true to them. Was Denker, who held a law degree, intent on staying on the safe side? A better guess is that his fictionalizing the names might make an audience forget the original case, and would therefore keep the verdict in doubt.

Like any good dramatist, Denker made his audience care for his main character. Theatergoers had to be impressed that Sloane's associates spoke fondly of him when he wasn't around. All of them were glad that he was about to embark on a vacation because "he needs a rest—badly" after being "in court for 197 days in the past year." They also expected that soon he'd be busier than ever; his most recent triumph suggested that a judgeship would be his.

Denker also humanized Sloane when, soon after he entered, he said he'd "stopped to pick up something for his wife." That's when his secretary told him that Dennis and Anita Corcoran had showed up unannounced. "I suppose I'll have to be polite," Sloane told his associates.

What he ultimately had to do was take the case after Corcoran had explained it. Bendix had called him "an immoral yellow-bellied degenerate who masqueraded as a big brave war correspondent." The irony is that Bendix and Corcoran were once friends, until the latter wrote a positive review of a book that was decidedly anti-Bendix. That prompted Bendix to write that Corcoran had "gas where a man should have guts" and that he sold "his country and its freedom down the river by picking up the Commie chant."

Those were fighting words, to be sure, and fourteen million readers saw them in eighty-six papers that had been carrying Bendix for as many as nineteen years. *Time* magazine had made his name into an idiom; to be "Bendixed" was not what anyone wanted to be.

Corcoran had been. His newspaper had fired him because of Bendix's statements. Now he wanted to sue.

Sloane warned Corcoran that "libel is one lawsuit in which the plaintiff is on the defensive all the time." To prove his point, he imagined cross-examining a certain native of Nazareth who'd relocated to Jerusalem circa A.D. 33: "Isn't it a fact that from the ages of thirty to thirty-three, three whole years, you didn't work at *anything,* just wandered the countryside as a vagrant? And during that time, did you drink? Only wine. Uh huh. And did you ever commit assault against a group of moneychangers? And did you have frequent contact with a known prostitute?"

Actually, Corcoran had to be buoyed by the demonstration. If Sloane could make Jesus Christ seem guilty, he should be able to do the same with Boyd Bendix.

"It won't be just a case!" Stone sternly told Corcoran. "It'll be a way of life."

Corcoran wasn't scared—not yet—and decided to press on just as Sloane learned that he'd get that judgeship. As noble as all men are in such plays, he refused it in order to right a miscarriage of justice.

Denker made the stakes progressively higher when, six months later, Sloane was told that he was neglecting his far more important clients to the point where his firm might lose them. He now wondered if the sacrifice was worth it. "Does Bendix know something about your past that I don't?" he asked Corcoran, who assured him that he didn't.

Bendix did, or at least alleged to: "Corcoran was nude, performed sexual vulgarities, a spectator at debauchery in which partners of different colors engaged in drunken orgies." Denker didn't invent this. The transcript of *Reynolds v. Pegler* stated "that Reynolds and his girlfriend of the moment were nuding along the public road" and that "Reynolds and his wench were strolling along together, absolutely raw."

Bendix was written as the quite cocky type who felt that a medal would be the only thing they'd ever pin on him. In print, he'd proclaimed that he was "not part of that soft, fashionable elite of the intellect which will undermine this country with Freud on one hand and Marx on the other."

When Anita tried to broker a settlement, Sloane flatly refused. "If he's allowed to silence Corcoran today, tomorrow it's someone else. And the day after that, the whole country. I can't let it happen."

The speech was a passionate enough one to bring down the first-act curtain; the other two acts would take place in court. Not until now did theatergoers learn what Corcoran had actually written: "Boyd Bendix is a prime example of the once-great newspaperman who has become so enchanted with his own opinions that he will distort any fact to suit his purpose" and "Bendix believes in one God and one Country, provided both believe in Boyd Bendix."

Of course everyone knew as sure as God made Perry Mason that Sloane was going to win. That Bendix referred to himself in the third person helped audiences to hate him. Bendix's hubris also had him disregard the advice of his lawyer, for he assumed midtrial that he could do a better job. (He couldn't.) As Kerr wrote, "Should a villain speak so much cant and pose so smugly in the very first moments you meet him that you can never again be in any suspense about the proper outcome?"

So Denker tried the usual complication of the witness who'd clear up everything but couldn't be located; then, when he was finally found, he couldn't precisely corroborate what Sloane had expected.

Denker also added the throwaway line in Act One that turned out to be vital in Act Two. In addition, Sloane later led Bendix to believe that a statement he read was from Corcoran, but after Bendix quickly damned it, Sloane revealed that it was a quotation that Bendix had actually written.

Both Sloane and the defense attorney (Sidney Blackmer) got to make eloquent and fervent summations. Then came the wait for the verdict. In what might have been a nod to inflation, Denker had the court award Corcoran $500,000 from the newspaper syndicate and $100,000 from Bendix himself—and, yes, that dollar for compensatory damages.

What undercut the victory—at least for the audience—was that Bendix wasn't around at all to react or comment.

Hmm, John McClain—was *The Advocate* really the lesser work?

Chapman had a good point when noting that "the play only involves a claim for civil damages and not a crime. In most of the trials which have been put on our stages, the question has been a more exciting one. Is the hero or heroine going to be found guilty and sentenced to death or prison—as always seems to be likely up to the last moment—or will he go free?"

No, the stakes weren't high enough. Besides, the aforementioned Perry Mason already had six seasons behind him of never losing a case (although a loss would soon follow), so the audience had become complacent about lawyers who emerged victorious. As Taubman wrote, the audience "loses the pleasure of being in doubt about which way the jury will go."

Eight years earlier, *Inherit the Wind* had been a twenty-six-month hit that was based on the famous Scopes Trial of 1925; the difference was that the defendant was found guilty, and theatergoers, most of whom were on his side, could mourn his fate and yet be assuaged that time would vindicate him.

Fewer than six years after *A Case of Libel*, *1776* proved that if a playwright is skilled enough, he can turn a story with an inevitable ending into one filled with doubt. The best Denker could do was, as Coleman wrote, "a workmanlike job." His investors didn't even make the dollar that Reynolds and Corcoran were awarded.

* * *

With the possible exception of a James Joyce work, is there any book more difficult to read than a Russian novel?

"Ah, Anna Mihalovna Drubetskaya, allow me to introduce you to Maria Dmitryevna Akhrosimova and Vasily Sergeyevich Kuragin."

As onerous as that is, at least a reader can take his time, go back a few pages whenever he wants, and refresh his memory: "Hmmm, have I already come across Vasily Dmitrich Denisov or he is a new one?"

But hearing a peck of Russian names coming from the stage? That had to be a problem for theatergoers attending Paddy Chayefsky's *The Passion of Josef D.*—meaning Joseph Stalin. Where the "D." came in was never explained, although in this story of the early days of the Russian Revolution, Stalin's real last name of Jugashvili (as in Ioseb Besarionis dze Jugashvili) was mentioned a few times.

So were such historically accurate names as Alliluyev, Bakunin, Bogdanov, Chiedze, Chugurin, Eugeyevna, Kharkov, Kornilov, Krupskaya, Kshesinskaya, Lvov, Mdivani, Menshiviki, Milyukov, Nadezhda, Olinka, Orjonikidze, Plekhanov, Poltava, Rusikov, Sergeyevna, Smolensk, Sverdlov, Ulanov, Zasulich, and Zinoviev.

There were a few sons of a -vich, too: Borisovich, Efimovich, Isopovich, Nikolayevich, and Visaryonovich. Add to these such terms as Right Socialist and Left Menshevik—not to be confused with Left Trudovik—and such SAT-worthy words as "ineluctable," "simulacrum," "schismatisms," and "cacique."

Can average theatergoers take in all that? Isn't life hard enough? By the time they reached Scene Five and met Molotov, they must have needed cocktails.

Perhaps Chayefsky should have done what Henry Denker did in *A Case of Libel:* change the names to protect the theatergoers. But Chayefsky apparently wanted to be as historically accurate as possible; each scene was named for the date on which the actual events took place, from March 11, 1917, to January 26, 1924.

Frankly, even if Chayefsky had named his characters Tom, Dick, and Harry or O'Brien, Ryan, and Goldberg, *The Passion of Josef D.* might not have run longer than its fifteen performances. Chayefsky simply didn't do a good job of dramatizing history.

Beginning the play with a conflict between soldiers and peasants one day before the revolution was solid enough. But why not show what happened on the day itself? Omitting those events was less than good playwriting.

Instead, Chayefsky's Scene Two was in Siberia, where a barefoot and disheveled Stalin had been imprisoned but was now freed. Oddly, however, he seemed to be in no hurry to leave. He was content to deliver exposition to Kentinov, his now-former captor.

By scene's end, Stalin did take some action: He stabbed Kentinov in the back, which dramatically presaged the dictator's eventual reign of terror. Then Stalin broke the fourth wall and told the audience, "When a barefoot fellow tells you he is revolting against tyranny, watch out: he's only after your boots."

Instead of dramatizing, Chayefsky often chose to have a character speak to the audience. One offered theatergoers "a brief history of the Marxist movement in Russia. Otherwise our American comrades may find our ways curious if not entirely grotesque."

Stalin was described by one party member as "a mediocrity" but by another as "a very capable fellow." The latter remark came courtesy of Vladimir Ilyich Ulyanov, who changed his surname to Lenin. Stalin was thrilled by the compliment: Lenin, he said, "has this gift of making one feel significant."

Perhaps Lenin admired what audiences didn't: that Stalin, after his wife died, abandoned his child to work in the underground movement. Now audiences could see him matter-of-factly grab the breasts and buttocks of Nadya, who was a mere sixteen.

Imagine that scene today, when few find any aspect of sexual harassment amusing or excusable. Back then, however, there was virtually no outrage; "boys will be boys" was an accepted explanation.

And yet, Nadya came to love Stalin. On the first night that she expected to have sex with him, he turned down the chance because Lenin summoned him. "A man," he explained, "would rather have a god than a woman any time."

Once again: love vs. career.

Although Stalin became more and more immersed in his work, Nadya stayed interested. "Then let's get married," he told her. "That's the proper thing for a man to do when he's lost all feeling for his girl."

As for that widely held dramatic theory that a villain doesn't know he's a bad person, Stalin admitted that he was "violent, cruel, greedy and durable. I'm a brute. I lack all purpose other than to protect myself."

Perhaps Chayefsky knew he wasn't providing enough entertainment, for he started Act Two with a Gallagher-and-Shean-like vaudeville routine in which two Soviet businessmen sang "Nothing Has Changed." They weren't waiting for a five-year plan to fail; they started complaining after four months.

Matters were so bad that one of the singers took out a knife and slashed his wrists and throat. Not content to leave it at that, he then endeavored to hang himself, but before he could finish himself off that way, he took out a gun, stuck it in his mouth, and pulled the trigger. All in (supposed) good fun, of course; he didn't really die.

Chayefsky started Act Three in a similar fashion. His stage directions described Lev Davidovich Bronshtein, better known as Trotsky, as "a great actor." Actor Alvin Epstein was given a genuine routine to do in describing his participation in the historical events: "I not only played the leading role, I also costumed and choreographed the entire revolution. I simply staged every minute of it, really."

Trotsky told his minions that "I don't expect you to grasp the complexities of expressionistic theater." Now *that's* a line that should have been delivered directly to the audience.

Lenin had told Stalin in Act Two, "You'll be running the party while I'm in hiding," which certainly was enough for Stalin to proclaim, "I commend my soul to thee!" When Act Three started, they weren't speaking. Stalin resented that Lenin "came on the balcony like a Pope, commended the vast assembly for their revolutionary fervor and cautioned them against violence."

Why didn't Chayefsky know enough to have Lenin deliver this speech? Why have Lenin say that Stalin "has already murdered a thousand men" and not show an example or two of this? No one would expect a cast of thousands on a Broadway stage, but seeing a few examples of how Stalin treated the average Russian could have been harrowing.

The production had the manpower to do it. *The Passion of Josef D.* required a cast of thirty-four—a larger number of actors than was found in some of the season's musicals.

Arthur Cantor, who had a forty-year producing career dominated by such popular hits as *A Thousand Clowns* and *Beau Jest,* may have believed in the play.

A better guess is that he'd been the producer on Chayefsky's most recent hits, *The Tenth Man* and *Gideon,* and had to be loyal. He must have blanched, however, when he started counting the needed "Soldiers, Exiles, Workers, Peasants, Delegates and Masses."

To call their number a chorus wouldn't be inappropriate, for the group did occasionally sing to music composed by the distinguished David Amram.

One song had everyone sing:

> *It was an agrarian-proletarian-bourgeois revolution!*
> *It was a feudal-agrarian-socialist-proletarian, capitalist-bourgeois revolution!*
> *It was a feudal-agrarian-peasant-socialist-proletarian-working class, capitalist-bourgeois-democratic revolution!*

This was followed by three "Hallelujahs!" And while there clearly was a good deal of passion in the song, there was precious little passion in Josef D. himself. When Nadya, wanting to stop her husband from becoming a workaholic, said, "I want his passion for the Socialist order destroyed," those theatergoers left in their seats must have wondered "*What* passion?" Not until the play's final moments—after Lenin unexpectedly died and an already banished Stalin got his second chance—did audiences see even a smidgen of emotion.

Exacerbating this was the casting of Peter Falk as Stalin. Granted, actors of his caliber have range, but when one thinks of Falk, one remembers his low-key Columbo. (To those who might say that Falk seemed too diminutive for Stalin, be apprised that the real man was a mere five foot four.)

Chayefsky can't blame the director for casting Falk, for Chayefsky *was* the play's director, ignoring the theatrical dictum that Arthur Laurents would also disregard later in the season. Note, however, that Chayefsky was for the first time in his four Broadway outings staging what he wrote. His previous three plays averaged 445 performances—430 more than *The Passion of Josef D.*

Chayefsky never got another play to Broadway.

The question of what happened to Ibsen's Nora after she left Torvald and her doll house prompted Larry Grossman, Betty Comden, and Adolph Green to write a 1982 musical on the subject.

But what happened to June Hovick immediately following her disappearance from *Gypsy* following Act One, Scene Nine? The vaudevillian and sister of Gypsy Rose Lee who reinvented herself as June Havoc first told her story in a 1959 memoir, *Early Havoc:* She had danced in seven marathons. In 1963–64, Havoc turned the book into a play called *Marathon '33* that she also directed.

Havoc would eventually have thirteen Broadway credits as an actress, from *Forbidden Melody* in 1936 to Miss Hannigan in *Annie* in 1982. But *Marathon*, of course, took place in '33, a thousand or so long days before her Broadway debut, when any success was far from certain.

At the time, Havoc was twenty or perhaps twenty-one. (Louise wasn't the only Hovick to wonder how old she was.) To play her at that age, Havoc cast an actress who was already thirty-eight.

But nobody would miss the chance to work with the already legendary Julie Harris. Besides, Harris always passed for being many years younger—and she passed muster here. While Taubman said that Harris had "rarely given a more convincing performance," Chapman unflinchingly said it was "her finest performance to date"—quite a statement, considering Harris's Tony-winning stints as Sally Bowles in *I Am a Camera* and Saint Joan in *The Lark*. *Marathon '33* would mark her first Tony loss, but she did secure a nomination.

Havoc retained the name June for the waif "in a child's pleated skirt" who walked into the euphemistically named Golden Slipper, a dingy dance hall where endurance contests took place: The couple who could dance the longest and stay standing while others collapsed would win some cash.

"Bring the kiddies!" the emcee told his customers. A sign suspended from above hardly told the truth: "This is a place of refined amusement." June had naively expected that it would be, but was soon advised, "Don't sit down on the toilet seat. A louse can jump in any direction fifty feet."

She was there to perform her act while the marathon dancers had their fifteen-minute breaks each hour. Her payment? Five dollars. The men who ran the show, however, tried to entice June into marathoning. "You don't need more than a thousand, maybe fifteen hundred hours to get rich," she was told. "A thousand hours goes real fast."

June instead insisted, "I belong in a real theater.... I've been on a real stage," a statement that any *Gypsy* fan could verify.

And yet, she had to admit through that famous show business euphemism that she was "between bookings." Later she admitted, "There's no place for me to work." The vaudeville that had disappeared for Rose and Louise had vanished for June as well. How humiliated she was, too, when one of the dancers remembered seeing her perform in vaudeville to great audience acclaim.

So when the impoverished June saw that still-solvent spectators occasionally threw loose change at the dancers, she reluctantly agreed to join the marathon.

"This is temporary," she told her partner, Patsy.

"So's a ride in a hearse," said Patsy, played by Lee Allen, who would be Tony nominated, too, en route to playing Fanny Brice's friend Eddie first onstage in *Funny Girl* and then in the film.

"Buy a picture postcard of your favorite dancer," said the emcee; "they may be gone tomorrow." Said one dancer, "Sadism is sexy; masochism is talent."

Another dancer wondered if June could manage a marathon because she looked "dainty." Theatergoers who knew *Gypsy* must have felt ice-cold chills invade their spines, as they recalled that June in the musical was known as "Dainty June" when she performed with her "farmboys." But chills dozens of degrees colder arrived when June was told that because she couldn't verify her age, she would have to get a parent's signature. June, they knew, couldn't ask Rose for any favors. As for her father: "Mother removed him when I was two."

June could avoid the signature requirement if she changed her name, so "Jean Reed" she became. Indeed, even in the script, Havoc ceased calling the character June and made her Jean for the rest of the play.

Onto the dance floor Jean went, surrounded by, as the stage direction stated, "bleachers that look as high as prison walls." As she danced with the empathetic Patsy, she was disgusted by what she witnessed immediately off the dance floor: the surreptitious sex acts under blankets, the pathetic attempts at hygiene, the scraps of food that passed for meals, and the complaints from men who suspected that whatever meals they were given had been laced with saltpeter.

Patsy told her that some marathoners took Holy Communion to fill a bit of their bellies. He said of one dancer, "I seen her eat cheese sandwiches which was thirty percent mold, twenty percent worms, and she didn't even belch."

"Walk away from the losers," Jean was advised. "They'd walk away from you." If that had only been the worst of it. Many dancers attempted to get others disqualified, squealing when they saw the slightest infraction of a rule. "She's dead!" said one man of a rival dancer. "Bury her!" Such a comment often led to fighting, which was against the rules, too, and resulted in dismissal.

"Let the arches fall where they may," crowed the emcee. After hundreds of hours on the dance floor, Rose Hovick suddenly didn't look all that bad. Jean gave her side of the story to Patsy: "I tried half my life trying not to grow, to stay a baby for her.... I was a freak. I'm still a freak and now I'll never make her proud of me again...because I'll never be cute anymore."

Gypsy aficionados may be asking, "And where was Tulsa?"—meaning the young man who'd been planning a song-and-dance act with his new bride, June. Here came some unexpected news: Jean admitted that "I just wasn't good enough" to remain as his dance partner. This was the first we'd heard that June's talents weren't adequate.

So she on went dancing, if that verb can be used. More accurately, men and women were hanging on to each other in hopes of keeping them both vertical. As a publicity stunt, a couple would often be married on the dance floor to suggest that love could bloom even in these conditions. An annulment immediately followed, but not until the ceremony had pleased the spectators. Jean was "married" under these conditions, too, while her hastily assigned "bridesmaids" struggled not to fall asleep on their feet.

But this was the era when most everyone was suffering. The emcee called Roosevelt "a madman" because he was "throwing the bootleg hoodlums out of work, so now they muscle into honest business."

And while Jean did emerge from the contest with some money—after Patsy had almost died on the floor—she was offered the chance to become a prostitute. She was told that a madam would "get the lice out of your muff," in one of the season's most shocking lines.

Such realism may be why Havoc didn't originally have Broadway in mind. She had her eye on the Riviera Terrace, a ballroom at 1686 Broadway, which belonged to Columbia University. When the school suddenly sold the building, she took her show to the ANTA under the sponsorship of the Actors Studio.

Said Nadel, "It is neither play, musical, carnival, comedy, tragedy, side show, contest, melodrama, documentary, grotesque, social commentary, torture session, sentimental journey, romance, circus nor vaudeville," perhaps setting a record for the number of words used between the correlative conjunctions "neither" and "nor."

"It frequently seems as if the play is taking longer than an actual dance marathon," complained Watts, who wasn't above admitting that he used to attend such functions when he was younger, unable to "deny that they held a shameless interest." McClain and Chapman may not have attended, but they had no compassion for the entrants; each referred to marathoners as "idiots."

"You don't feel you have seen a play. You feel as if you dialed Information," Kerr said, using the then-current term for Directory Assistance. That he and Taubman ("thin in dramatic content") disapproved helped seal its fate, of course, but as Chapman pointed out, the cast was "big enough for two musicals." With a payroll of thirty-seven, forty-eight performances was the best *Marathon* could muster.

Havoc had to be assuaged that she was the first American woman to be Tony nominated for Best Director. (Joan Littlewood had been the first woman, regardless of nationality, three years earlier with *The Hostage*.) And yet, the heartbreak of commercial failure obviously haunted her. She couldn't bear to see the sets and costumes destroyed, so she appropriated them and kept them in her garage in Cannon Crossing, Connecticut.

"And," says longtime press agent Joshua Ellis, "she never stopped hoping for a Broadway revival." Alas, Havoc died in 2010 without having the chance to see one.

In 1969, a film about dance marathons that was far more dour than *Marathon '33—They Shoot Horses, Don't They?*—was the sixteenth-highest-grossing film of the year. Perhaps watching dancers suffer on film is easier than seeing them agonize in real life.

Actually, *Marathon '33* might fare better today, considering the ever-increasing interest that *Gypsy* has acquired over the years through its four revivals (making for 2,081 total performances) and a 1993 TV movie. If Broadway can't afford the show, some enterprising well-heeled regional theater (if there is such a thing) might consider doing *Gypsy* and *Marathon '33* in rep.

Fifty years ago, plays about the military showed up with regularity. They had many potential customers thanks to the men who'd been drafted or had volunteered for the Korean Conflict or either of the World Wars. As 1963–64 began, *Mister Roberts, The Teahouse of the August Moon,* and *No Time for Sergeants* were among the top twenty-five longest-running plays—and *South Pacific* was then the third-longest-running musical.

So why did Arnold Wesker's *Chips with Everything,* at 149 performances, only make it to 778th place?

For one thing, all those hits dealt with life in our own armed forces; *Chips* was set in England and concerned the Royal Air Force. So when Corporal Hill told his raw recruits, "I will tear and mercilessly scratch the scorching day-lights out of anyone who smarts the alec with me," U.S. veterans recalled their commanding officers delivering this message in a less effete way.

"American audiences are less likely to feel themselves immediately in-volved," Kerr admitted.

Chips did show recruits from all walks of life: the boulevards, the streets, and the gutter. While both World War I doughboys and subsequent wars' GIs could recall pretentious types in their units, the aptly named Pip Thompson was awfully pip-pip, tally-ho—one of the men, as Kerr wrote, "who are priv-ileged to have two jowls and one mustache apiece."

Pip, the son of a retired general, told of the time his car broke down in London's East End, where—horrors!—he was forced to eat in a run-down café that actually boasted "Chips with Everything."

That's french fries to the rest of us. Perhaps the play would have done better on Broadway if it had been called *French Fries with Everything*—although that would have suggested a more farcical play than Wesker had intended. His theme was that no matter how lofty or intelligent a man may be, the military always overwhelms him and makes him conform.

The British have always had more of an interest in class distinction, and that was certainly in the *Chips* script. Andrew, one of the airmen, noted that Pip's kind would occasionally "come drinking in the pub and talk to us as though we were the salt of the earth. And then one day, for no reason any of us can see, they go off, drop us, as though that was another game they were tired of."

Andrew had a point. At that moment, the officers were actually playing a game in which they pointed to a man and decided whether he was a "gentle-man or scum."

Pip's getting his comeuppance would seem to have pleased most audiences.

But *Chips* had a scene that must have been a factor in keeping it from succeeding. After one rookie accidentally dropped his gun, Hill snarled, "You're like an old Jew."

No one keeps statistics on how many people walk out of a show (and wouldn't it be interesting if someone did?). While Coleman reported that the play "kept Plymouth first-nighters on the edge of their seats," one wonders how many leapt out of them—if not then, after Hill's next lines: "You know what happens to Jews? They go to gas chambers." At a time when New York had more Jews than Israel and the wounds from "the camps" were still raw, many must have opted to leave.

Under these circumstances, how could Chapman predict that *Chips* would have "quite a stay"? Miraculously, not one of the seven critics alerted readers to this anti-Semitic remark. Instead came "a drama of striking power" (Watts), "a lively evening" (McClain), and "a dynamic, throbbing evening" (Taubman). As for Nadel, his stating that "*Chips with Everything* has everything" wouldn't be enough to tip off readers that an ethnic slur and a reference to the Holocaust were included in the "everything."

When John Osborne researched Martin Luther, he undoubtedly came across the man's vitriolic anti-Semitism. Luther had said that Jews were "miserable and accursed people … a brood of vipers " who were involved in "poisonous activities" in "their synagogues, where nothing was found but a den of devils in which sheer self-glory, conceit, lies, blasphemy, and defaming of God and men are practiced most maliciously."

Osborne spared his audience these lines, settling instead for Martin's contention that "there are blasphemies flourishing that make the Jews no worse than giggling children." Note, however, that he was stressing that Catholics were more to blame.

Wesker brought out heavier artillery. Considering these slurs, John Dexter, making his Broadway debut, would seem to have been the ideal director for *Chips*. In the next quarter century, in which he staged eleven more shows, Dexter would time and time again be regarded notoriously as Broadway's most insensitive and tyrannical director.

To be fair, one reason he held the title is because Jerome Robbins would only do two more Broadway shows in his career.

* * *

If Ellen Gordon in *Any Wednesday* felt old as her thirtieth birthday approached, how did the heroine of *The Chinese Prime Minister* feel?

"She," as she was solely known throughout the three-act drama, was a fine actress approaching seventy and about to close the play that would mark her retirement. Thus, She was simultaneously experiencing old age and a type of death.

Although She was regal and elegant—hence Margaret Leighton, although she was only forty-two—one reason she was retiring was simply for lack of work. "Why," she asked, "does not one write real plays about the fascination and disaster of being old?"

That's what Enid Bagnold endeavored to do. By the time her play opened on January 2, she was in her seventy-fifth year. While Bagnold had had great successes with *National Velvet* and *Serena Blandish,* she'd written those novels decades earlier. Now the world wasn't paying as much attention to her, and nine seasons had passed since her last Broadway outing—the acclaimed but commercially unsuccessful *The Chalk Garden.*

She envied "a Chinese Prime Minister who makes a triumph of his retirement." Oh, for that earlier era "when age was near paradise and not a prison." Give She credit, however, for looking at the bright side when she looked into a mirror. "It was charming of God that as beauty vanishes, the eyes grow dimmer."

Nevertheless, She still had "extra vitality and extra expectations" and missed her work the way so many retirees do: "Without the theater I feel diminished."

So She decided to invite her two warring sons, Oliver and Tarver, and their wives, Roxane and Alice, to celebrate her next birthday. As is the case with so many parties that involve only the immediate family, the evening was disappointing and contentious. Roxane was on her way to extricating herself from Oliver because "women grow downhill, and if I can't get respect now, when do I get it?" Alice felt much the same after only a few months of marriage.

All this caused She to note that "there are many pleasant things about age, but listening to the young is not one of them."

As many parents have learned, when you have children, you are giving birth to your future judges and juries. As the accusations flew, She pleaded, "Can't I get out of being a parent? Can't you just listen to a woman?"

Alice's observation on the matter didn't help: "It seems shocking, doesn't it, that someone should be old … and yet have slept with someone."

That might have made She amenable to seeing the husband She once discarded, one that Oliver never knew. Sir Gregory, described by She as "the only man to whom I seem young," entered. He encouraged her to find happiness outside her children: "Women who outstay their motherhood become damn boring," he ruefully observed.

Sir Gregory had been enduring his own unhappiness, for his employers had decided he was too old to continue with the firm. "Just as a man is at the top of his life, off they want to tip him," he said, although "it's only the old who are on top of things."

So, with no other obligations, She and he decided to leave on an extended trip. No sooner was she out the door than she returned—because she forgot her gloves. (Hmmm, maybe *Here's Love* had a point, after all.)

Were her gloves calling her back to tell her that she shouldn't leave with Sir Gregory? The final scene had her return to report that She and he "quarreled in the back of the taxi that took us to the plane and all over the mountains of Arabia." The problem? "It was I who was told to change." She admitted that she resumed her relationship with him simply because she wanted her "femininity confirmed."

Although *The Chinese Prime Minister* received approvals from four of the critics (including the coveted Taubman and Kerr), it could only run 108 performances. Theatergoers might well have been pulled in by the bigger stars that played that season, but older theatergoers—and there were plenty of them then—may have found the message of aging and dying as bitter a pill to swallow as the ones they were taking for low thyroid and high blood pressure.

Even having a butler for comic relief wasn't enough to push the play into the winner's circle. Although Bent was as old as or even older than She, he wasn't devastated when a younger woman on whom he'd pinned his hopes stood him up. Eventually he did find one who was willing to share his life, causing She to remark, "You should have never married so young a woman. It always brings a loss of dignity."

The extra activity apparently wore him out, too, although he saw it differently: "Most people are murdered by some disease or accident. I'm merely withdrawing." His last words are "Put a screen around me so you can go on talking." Ever the servant!

To be sure, the Broadway audience could relate to such lines as "Marriage—the beginning and end are wonderful, but the middle part is hell."

Quite often, theatergoers heard references to "in my day" both from She and Sir Gregory, as well as Alice's referring to the here-and-now as "in *our* day." But who says that "in my day" must only mean one's youth?

In the end, Sir Gregory got an equally wonderful job, while She—and Roxane—decided that a man wasn't a necessity. That members of two different generations came to the same conclusion might have been too forward-thinking for both the younger and older wives who came to see *The Chinese Prime Minister*. Still, considering how increasingly difficult it is for middle-aged people today to find new jobs, the play is another 1963–64 entry that was ahead of its time.

There was another factor that may have kept it from succeeding: Bagnold and director Joseph Anthony didn't see eye to eye. If they had, Anthony wouldn't have given Bagnold an opening-night present with a note that said she was "a monster as well as magnificent."

As much of a surprise success as *Any Wednesday* was, 1963–64 offered an even bigger astonishment.

On March 12, 1964, Frank D. Gilroy was desperately looking for a new producer for his play *The Subject Was Roses*. Two unknowns, Richard Altman and Leonard Soloway, had held the option for years. Raising money wasn't easy on the playwright, whose *Who'll Save the Plowboy?* received a 1961–62 Obie Award but only lasted seven weeks.

Producer David Black was interested, but he had another 1963–64 offering on his plate: a London import called *Semi-Detached*. It was akin to a British and nonmusical version of *How to Succeed*.

Fred Midway wanted to go all the way to the top of the insurance game. He figured that his goal would be more easily realized if he married off his daughter, April, to a wealthy man. Fred got the two to the altar, but April's husband turned out to be chronically unfaithful. As the play ended, Fred deeply questioned his own motives and values.

Black promised Gilroy that he'd option *Roses* if *Semi-Detached* was a hit—and it might have been had it come over with Laurence Olivier, who'd played it in London. When it opened here, Leonard Rossiter had the lead and two weeks of employment. Gilroy had his answer.

That was the situation on March 12, 1964. But seventy-four *days* later, *The Subject Was Roses* opened on Broadway. Yes, it only had a $165 advance sale, which translated to about two dozen tickets to a stalwart number of theatergoers who must have had a policy of seeing *every* Broadway show.

Believing that is easier than imagining twenty-five people saying, "Gee, I gotta see that new play by that failed off-Broadway playwright that's directed, produced, and acted by people I've barely heard of."

Many more were interested once the reviews were published. Taubman: "An honest and touching work." Kerr: "Quite the most interesting play to be offered on Broadway this season." Watts: "It is realism of a high order." McClain: "It justified the prediction that he has extraordinary gifts as a dramatist." Nadel: "From this day forth, Frank D. Gilroy is a major playwright."

While every one of them had an objection or three, Chapman was the only one totally unimpressed: "He has chosen three uninteresting characters to write about."

The Clearys were indeed small people, although paterfamilias John never expected to be. He was once a rising businessman, who, as his wife, Nettie, told their grown son, Timmy, "expected to be a millionaire by the time he was forty. Nineteen-twenty-nine took care of that."

Now it was 1946, when John was doing only a little better than Willy Loman. Like Miller's character, he'd cheated on his wife. In this play, however, Nettie had learned the truth. She stayed in the marriage, for where was a woman in that era going to go?

The play began the morning after a party that celebrated Timmy's coming home from World War II. Because John and Nettie expected him to be precisely the person he was when he left, the family would now experience its own World War III.

That Timmy no longer wanted to visit his developmentally disabled cousin disappointed Nettie; that he refused to attend Sunday mass infuriated John. That he wanted to leave home and room with a friend made both parents aghast; the conventions of the time demanded that a man, no matter how old he was, stay home until he married. Many playgoers identified with the situation, for their young baby boomers were starting to leave home without benefit of marriage, whether or not they were going to college.

Gilroy saved his ace trump for the last few pages of his script. Timmy told his father that he was always haunted by the fact that John had never said he loved him. But the previous night, he said, "something occurred to me that I'd never thought of before. It's true you never said you love me. But it's also true that I've never said those words to you. I say them now. I love you, Pop. *I love you.*"

No one can say for sure that there wasn't a dry eye in the house, but there certainly were plenty of wet ones. And yet, with such a small advance, could the play hang on? As Taubman wryly concluded, "Don't these people know that it's flying in the face of tradition to bring in an honest work this late in May?"

"These people" included first-time director Ulu Grosbard and rookie producer Edgar Lansbury (Angela's brother). The latter even designed the set to save a few bucks.

He needed to, for before Lansbury committed himself to the project on March 13, Gilroy was raising money himself in a way that anticipated Kickstarter: He simply asked friends to put in a few bucks here and there. Perhaps this way he could get the $40,000—not the usual $85,000 to $100,000—that he estimated as the absolute minimum to get the show on.

Of course, there would be no out-of-town tryout; previews would have to suffice. Yes, *Who's Afraid of Virginia Woolf?* had tried that nineteen months earlier and got away with it, but wasn't that the exception to the rule?

The budget certainly would allow no stars. Jack Albertson, cast as John, was a journeyman actor who got the part after Art Carney, Dan Dailey, Van Heflin, Walter Matthau, Edmund O'Brien, Robert Preston, Jason Robards Jr., and David Wayne refused it. Gilroy was so grateful that he even volunteered to type Albertson's bio for the *Playbill*.

Dan Dailey's sister, Irene, however, didn't turn down the chance to play Nettie. She'd only landed it after Colleen Dewhurst, Geraldine Fitzgerald, Lee Grant, Judy Holliday, Vivian Nathan, Geraldine Page, Maureen Stapleton, and Teresa Wright said no.

The Tonys take a great deal of (justifiable) heat for putting nominees in the wrong categories. This was especially true in the first quarter century of the awards, when leading performers were placed in the Featured-or-Supporting category (as it was then called) simply because they were billed under the show's title. Hence, Jack Albertson would "only" get a Best Featured Actor Tony for his role in the Gilroy hit. But Hollywood didn't view Albertson any differently after he'd filmed the movie; he received a Best Supporting Actor Oscar.

Everyone apparently saw it as the son's play. It probably was. And yet, Timmy, played by newcomer Martin Sheen, was paid $37.50 for each show.

Since then, Sheen has made substantially more per performance.

Roses didn't sell out until Saturday night, September 19, at its 136th performance. Despite *four* moves from theater to theater, it lasted 832 performances—then making it the seventh-longest-running serious play in Broadway history, right behind *A Streetcar Named Desire.*

Kerr wrote in his opening-night review, "Too bad, really, that the prize-giving season is just over." And yet, *The Subject Was Roses* bucked the odds there, too. The following year—although such worthy works as Arthur Miller's *Incident at Vichy,* Edward Albee's *Tiny Alice,* Friedrich Duerrenmatt's *The Physicists,* and even such popular hits as *The Odd Couple* and *Luv* were in contention—and more fresh in the voters' minds—*The Subject Was Roses* was remembered enough to win the Best Play Tony Award, the Pulitzer Prize, and the New York Drama Critics' Circle Award.

It was also named a Best Play in the annual Best Play series. And there's a story behind that, too.

After the 1919–20 season, *New York Evening Mail* theater critic Burns Mantle decided to publish a book that contained cast lists, opening dates, and other information about each of the season's works. He called the book *The Best Plays* because he included summaries of what he considered to be the season's ten most worthy entries.

Mantle was followed by John Chapman, Louis Kronenberger, and Henry Hewes, all of whom continued the practice of annually choosing the ten scripts they deemed the most worthy. In 1963–64, Hewes's final year as editor, he chose *After the Fall, Barefoot in the Park, Chips with Everything, The Deputy, Dylan, Luther, The Passion of Josef D., The Rehearsal,* and *Hello, Dolly!,* as well as *Next Time I'll Sing to You,* an off-Broadway play.

What—no *The Subject Was Roses?*

Perhaps Hewes had made his selections before Gilroy's play had opened; after all, when it was set to debut, only a week remained in the season, and an eight-performance flop looked likely.

On the other hand, Hewes, when reviewing the play for *Saturday Review,* said of Gilroy, "One is tempted to call him 'slice-of-life,' for indeed his latest play is full of ordinariness, small talk, and a reluctance to explore the larger significance of his subject." So Hewes may not have chosen *The Subject Was Roses* simply because he didn't like it.

The following year, Otis Guernsey Jr. succeeded Hewes. He thought enough of *The Subject Was Roses* to include it as one of *his* ten Best Plays, and never mind that he was chronicling 1964-65.

"Statistically speaking," he wrote, "*The Subject Was Roses* is registered forever as a 1963–64 production. Yet all of its glass-slipper success story happened in 1964–65. It opened too late for consideration for the major 1964 awards but won *both* [italics his] of them in 1965: the Pulitzer Prize and the New York Drama Critics Circle for the best play of the year."

(Notice that Guernsey doesn't include the Tony as one of the "major awards." This was more proof that it needed a nationally televised broadcast to leapfrog over the other prizes.)

"*Roses,*" Guernsey continued, "was the year's Cinderella play, and in those eight 1963–64 performances it had never even *heard* about the ball. For all of these reasons (and making an exception, not setting a precedent), we hereby declare *The Subject Was Roses* an honorary member of the season of 1964–65."

The upshot? Here's more proof that the 1963–64 season was extraordinary; it's the only one for which the *Best Play* series celebrated eleven plays.

A six-foot-one man gets into a genuine, slug-it-out boxing match with a six-foot-two woman?

Now *that's* theatrical—and Edward Albee knew it once he read that scene in Carson McCullers's *The Ballad of the Sad Café.* He decided to adapt the novella into his play that would follow *Who's Afraid of Virginia Woolf?*

What's fascinating from a twenty-first-century standpoint is that the production offered no credit for "Fight Direction." Apparently director Alan Schneider oversaw the battle between Lou Antonio and Colleen Dewhurst, or the two performers were left to duke it out on their own.

We know from Albee's first stage direction that although Miss Amelia Evans lives in Georgia, she is no southern belle. "Dressed in Levis and a cotton work shirt," she "kicks the door shut with a foot."

But she'd open it wide for her Cousin Lymon, a hunchbacked dwarf. Miss Amelia was quite lovely to him, which surprised the townspeople, who'd only seen her as nonstop ornery. Exhibit A: Her marriage to Marvin Macy had lasted all of ten days.

Miss Amelia threw out Marvin when he wanted to consummate the marriage. He was so despondent that he began a crime spree that led to his being incarcerated.

When Lymon wasn't seen after his first few days, one townie assumed that Miss Amelia had murdered him for the contents of his suitcase. Word soon spread and was believed. (In small towns where there's little entertainment, rumor spreading must take its place.)

Some hoped that Miss Amelia *had* murdered Lymon, for they would have enjoyed seeing this (literally) high and mighty woman incarcerated or executed. But Lymon reappeared and actually improved both Miss Amelia's life and the town's well-being. After Lymon helped and encouraged her, she opened a café where liquor was "clean and sharp on the tongue, but once down a man, it glows inside him for a long, long time."

Was Lymon the son Miss Amelia never had? Did she accept him because he, unlike Marvin, could not possibly be a threat or exude sexuality? Or was the theme a variation of Robert Frost's assertion "Home is the place where, when you have to go there, they have to take you in"?

As Miss Amelia went, so went the town. The citizens accepted Lymon, although they regarded him as "a Martian; a friendly Martian, but still a Martian." Who else would have dared to call the proprietress Amelia without the honorific "Miss"? That was as shocking as if someone on Broadway in 1963–64 called "Mr. Abbott" George.

Lymon may have criticized Amelia's cooking, but he did say, "I do love you." She wasn't far enough along to do better than "I'm fond of you." Events would eventually prove precisely the opposite.

The returning Marvin Macy inspired the chaos. Audiences knew trouble was coming, for in the middle of Albee's otherwise straightforward adaptation, he had the spurned Marvin dictate a letter to his cousin Henry.

"Dear Miss Amelia, my wife. I hate you," it began; it ended with "And when I come back, I gonna fix you. I gonna kill you."

When Lymon heard that Marvin was returning, he gushed, "He's been to Atlanta, he's had to deal with the law, and has spent time in the penitentiary!" Like Caitlin and Doreen, he was attracted to a bad boy.

Marvin was indeed bad to Lymon, calling him "a brokeback" and "a runt" before slugging him. The slights rolled right off Lymon's hunchback because he'd never been insulted by someone whom he admired as much.

Amelia and Marvin were Martha and George from *Virginia Woolf* all over again, although here she was emotionally even stronger and he even weaker. Is there another story where a man says "I love you" only to hear "You come one step closer and I'll blast your head off"? Martha told how she inadvertently once sucker-punched George; here Amelia took a premeditated action when she broke one of Marvin's teeth.

And so they continued their knock-down, drag-out fight. Amelia was battling for more than her life; she wanted to regain the love of the Marvin-mesmerized Lymon.

She might have won, too, if Lymon hadn't joined the fight and caused her to lose. His interference emotionally devastated her. After Marvin and Lymon went off together, she closed the café.

What may surprise some is that Albee kept to McCullers's implication that the relationship would be platonic. On the other hand, as Mart Crowley wrote a few years later in *The Boys in the Band*, "With the right wine and the right music, there are damn few that aren't curious."

Albee did contribute a Narrator. Robert Brustein in *The New Republic* stated that his "single function is to provide the information which the author has been too lazy to dramatize." He certainly had a point in a passage where the Narrator stated that Marvin brought gifts to Amelia, which she promptly sold. How much more effective a genuine scene showing that would have been.

McClain was pleased by "an engrossing evening, a salutary success." So was Chapman: "Magnificent theater. It is beautiful, absorbing, exciting, touching and absolutely enthralling." Nadel's opinion: "*Here* is a play." (Italics his.)

Kerr didn't use italics when calling it "a shell of a play." Nor did Taubman when stating that some of the time Albee's adaptation was "uncomfortable on the stage." Watts chided the playwright for not "moving straight ahead in the unfolding of his own qualities as a distinguished creative writer."

Who's Afraid of Virginia Woolf? ran nineteen months; twenty-five months after it closed, it was on movie screens. *The Ballad of the Sad Café* ran four months and saw its movie version filmed twenty-seven *years* after the closing.

Oh, well. At least six weeks after the February 15 closing, *The Ballad of the Sad Café* was again in the avid theatergoer's consciousness when *The Salad of the Mad Café* opened off-Broadway. Danny Logan starred in this revue by Danny Logan that was directed by Danny Logan. Considering that one of the producers was Danorm Productions, here's betting that Danny Logan was the Dan and Norman Foster, also in the cast, was the Norm. The show opened on March 31 and closed on April 11—the same night that marked the uptown closing of *Anyone Can Whistle*, which could just as easily been called *The Salad of the Mad Café.*

The quick closing of Albee's play might have been predicted. History proves that after a playwright wins a Best Play Tony, his next play suffers from critical and box office disappointment.

Out of the sixty-plus playwrights who have won the big prize, Joseph Hayes once (*The Desperate Hours/Calculated Risk*) and Tom Stoppard twice (*Travesties/ Dirty Linen* and *New-Found Land; The Coast of Utopia/Rock 'n' Roll*) saw longer runs with their next works, but only respectively by nine, three, and two performances. The only true exception to the apparent rule involves Terrence McNally. His 1994–95 Tony winner *Love! Valour! Compassion!* amassed 248 performances, but his 1995–96 Tony winner *Master Class* more than doubled it to 598. That *Love!* dealt with gay love may have limited its audience; *Master Class,* although examining gay icon Maria Callas, was more universal because she was shown not as an opera diva in her prime but as a ferocious and unforgiving teacher. Haven't we all had a teacher or two who has scared the bejesus out of us?

As for 1963–64, *Luther* only outran *Inadmissible Evidence,* Osborne's next play in 1965 by a margin of one month, six to five. But Frank D. Gilroy of *The Subject Was Roses* fame saw his next play, *That Summer—That Fall,* last nine days.

The flop that follows the Tony-winning play sometimes doesn't even warrant a Best Play nomination. Albee at least got that for *Ballad,* but not much else. As he would later write, "It is dangerous to have a huge commercial success early on, for more often than not, your next plays will be judged not by how you're proceeding in your growth as a playwright, but by how similar your new work will be to the blockbuster."

He deserves credit, too, for providing McCullers's characters with much of their dialogue; in her descriptive story, seldom is heard any kind of a word from their mouths.

Historians should also note that Albee and Schneider were early adherents of nontraditional casting. While McCullers provided the voice in her own story, the stage production had the Narrator played by the black Roscoe Lee Browne. That choice was pretty maverick for a story set in the Deep South. Even Northerners must have been as surprised by that as by the no-holds-barred fight between a strong man and a stronger woman.

And then there were those three aforementioned dramas that closed after one night.

Of Robert Thom's *Bicycle Ride to Nevada* (September 24), McClain wrote, "Having devoted a large part of my adult life to avoiding windy and drunken bores, I was less than enchanted last evening to be trapped by one."

Thom should have done better, considering that his character was based on Nobel Prize–winning author Sinclair Lewis.

Based on, but not precisely. Here he was Winston "Brick" Sawyer, as he was in Barnaby Conrad's novel *Dangerfield*. The danger came from a party in which Sawyer's friends had to admit that his latest book wasn't much good. He so railed against all of them that his mistress (in the old-fashioned sense of the word) hoped that his twenty-two-year-old son might be able to raise his spirits.

What would bring her to that conclusion, given that the two men have been estranged? Nothing good comes from the visit, although the son learns that his father is into physical fitness. Brick has pedaled his stationary bicycle for so long that he could have traveled from his Santa Barbara home to Nevada. That would be a substantially longer run than *Bicycle Ride to Nevada* would have.

John Sherry's *Abraham Cochrane* (February 17) had its title character pay a visit to his ol' friends the Hallidays. That Myra and her daughter, Helen, each had a husband didn't stop Dishonest Abe from romancing each of them. Helen became pregnant, and Myra died of a coronary. The end!

Neither woman was played by newcomer Olympia Dukakis, who had a small part. Yet Kerr praised her "for treading that very fine line between playing into laughs that aren't there and trying to pretend they should be." She probably did much of it on her own, given that *Abraham Cochrane* didn't have a director credited when it opened (and closed). When no director is listed on a *Playbill*'s title page, that isn't a kiss of death; it's a Mack truck of death.

Chapman's opinion—"If the characters can't get excited about it, why should I?"—was exacerbated by Nadel: "I shall suggest to the editors of the *World Almanac* that they include it in that fascinating section that catalogues the year's catastrophes."

One of these one-night flops seemed to have deserved a better fate. Yves Jamiaque's *A Murderer Among Us* (March 25) sounded intriguing. Lahutte had ten years earlier been accused of homicide. In those pre-DNA days, he couldn't convince a jury that he was innocent and was convicted. Now, ten years later, the real killer gave a deathbed confession that exonerated Lahutte, who was released. Considering that he'd already paid the price for the crime, Lahutte felt he would now be entitled to a murder.

In actuality, Lahutte wasn't serious—although no one in town gleaned that he was making a macabre joke. When Lahutte said that he wanted to do a public service by killing the town's most horrible human being, virtually every guilt-ridden citizen became paranoid and assumed that he'd be Lahutte's victim.

In union there was strength enough in town for everyone to frame Lahutte for another crime. Back to prison he went.

Taubman, Kerr, and Nadel couldn't help noticing the parallels with Friedrich Duerrenmatt's *The Visit,* in which hell had no fury like Claire Zachanassian, who was now wealthy enough to offer a fortune to each townsperson if one of them would kill her former beau who'd once done her very wrong.

The Visit had the Lunts; *Murderer* had Pierre Olaf, George S. Irving, Edith King, Loring Smith, and Tom Bosley, whose *Happy Days* were years away. They were solid pros all, but not legends.

With these journeymen on the window cards, first-time producer Jeff Britton probably wouldn't have had the resources to continue, even if Taubman hadn't concluded, "If DeGaulle is looking for reasons to get back at us, he has a prime one here."

The half-dozen one-night stands had one commonality: Each was a three-act play. But we can't put the blame on that structure. Even as late as 1963–64, a playwright's apportioning three acts per play was still more common than his dispensing two. Of the thirty-seven new plays in 1963–64, twenty-one were in the tried-and-true three-act structure, leaving thirteen to do their business in two acts. (That, of course, included the double bill of *The Private Ear and The Public Eye*.)

Oh Dad, Poor Dad, Mamma's Hung You in the Closet and I'm Feelin' So Sad and *Ballad of the Sad Café* were especially forward-looking; each played without an intermission, a policy that many playwrights of the late twentieth and early twenty-first centuries would adopt.

That plays were written in three acts is more surprising when one considers that shows in 1963–64 routinely started at 8:30 P.M. and not at 8 P.M. or even 7 P.M. as some performances now do. Didn't people have to get up in the morning and go to work?

Those who worked for the producers of *Abraham Cochrane, Bicycle Ride to Nevada,* and *A Murderer Among Us* did not.

One reason that two intermissions were the norm then and non-intermissionless shows reign today? That can be gleaned from what Thornton Wilder's Stage Manager in *Our Town* says as Act One comes to an end: "You can go and smoke now, those that smoke." And how pervasive was smoking in 1963–64? Meredith Willson offered love from "L & M to Lucky Strike." Anyone writing this song today wouldn't think to mention cigarettes, because they aren't nearly as much in the public consciousness.

Back then, however, cigarettes were—pun intended—on everyone's lips. *Smoking and Health: Report of the Advisory Committee to the Surgeon General of the United States* wouldn't be released until January 1964, not long before a press photo of John Gielgud showed him directing *Hamlet* while a cigarette dangled from his scowling mouth. Photos from the recording session of *What Makes Sammy Run?* reveal that in between takes, Steve Lawrence smoked, too.

For one week in October, Howard Teichmann's *A Rainy Day in Newark* had two union leaders (Eddie Mayehoff, John McMartin), locked into an office by angry employees, show tremendous anxiety when one must share his last cigarette. *Have I Got a Girl for You!* introduced a woman who had a cigarette lighter attached to her charm bracelet in order to save time in lighting up. There was no surprise in *A Case of Libel* when the plaintiff said, while enduring the interminable wait for the verdict, "I'm going out to grab another smoke." As for *Playbill,* virtually every one in 1963–64 had full-page ads for Lark on the back cover and Kent cigarettes inside.

Say what you will about Communism, at least Lenin demanded, "There will be no smoking!" in *The Passion of Josef D.* And there wasn't.

Theater first and foremost involves collaboration. So the night before *After the Fall* was to begin previews at the ANTA Washington Square Theatre, producer Robert Whitehead, director Elia Kazan, and playwright Arthur Miller were all working feverishly.

They weren't, however, making last-minute changes to the play or the production. Because all the seats hadn't yet been installed in this brand-new, $525,000 theater at 40 West Fourth Street, everyone—including these three luminaries—had to pitch in and wield screwdrivers.

Whitehead and Kazan were building more than that. They would be the first co-producers of the Repertory Theater of Lincoln Center, a new company that would be the closest America would have to a national theater. At least three productions would be offered a season; in 1963–64, two new plays and one revival would inaugurate the endeavor.

Everyone was so anxious to begin that the Repertory Theater of Lincoln Center would debut before it had its permanent home: the then-under-construction Vivian Beaumont Theater, one of five imposing buildings in the new Lincoln Center for the Performing Arts complex on Broadway in the West '60s. Until the Beaumont was ready, Whitehead and Kazan would use this temporary space, which had the same thrust stage and a number of seats (1,158) similar to what the Beaumont (1,105) would have.

All 1,158 had to be in place for the full house the following night. That this was New York's first new legitimate theater in thirty-six years wouldn't be the reason for the SRO sign. *After the Fall* was Miller's first new play in nine years. Until this drought, since 1944 he had never gone even three years without bringing something new to Broadway.

Of course, his June 1956–January 1960 marriage to Marilyn Monroe did get in the way. That Miller wrote the screenplay for *The Misfits* for her wasn't the only reason for the absence; tending to the troubled actress was another.

That would be the subject of *After the Fall.*

Miller must have known that the theater wouldn't necessarily be packed for the loftiest reasons. Broadway's sophistication level may have been loftier a half century ago, but let's face it: If Miller's new play hadn't centered on Monroe, public interest wouldn't have been as high. After Miller's *Death of a Salesman* had become an instant classic and the twentieth-longest-running play in Broadway history, where were Miller's full houses for his next three plays, all of which flopped?

Some sensed that Miller wrote about Monroe because he desperately needed a hit. The playwright could have rebutted that he wasn't in a hit-or-flop situation, for the Repertory Theater of Lincoln Center was a not-for-profit enterprise. Still, even if the tried-and-true definition of "hit = money-maker" was irrelevant, the secondary definitions—"hit = well-reviewed play" and "hit = long run"—would still apply.

That Miller was writing for a thrust stage—the first of its kind in New York—might explain his stage direction: "There are no walls or substantial boundaries." *After the Fall* took "place in the mind, thought, and memory of Quentin," who would reassess his relationship and marriage to a character named Maggie.

So considering the nine-year dry spell, Miller had a nice way to start the play. His lead character, Quentin (Jason Robards Jr.), looked into the audience and said, "Hello! God, it's good to see you again!"

Theatergoers might have answered, "It's good to see you again, too, Art," but Quentin wasn't actually speaking to them. As Miller's stage direction said, he was greeting "the Listener, who, if he could be seen, would be sitting just beyond the edge of the stage itself."

To obfuscate that he wasn't writing about himself, Miller made Quentin a lawyer who "quit the firm a few weeks after Maggie died" because he "couldn't concentrate on a case anymore." At least he'd found someone new: a foreign-born archaeologist named Holga. Theatergoers found her not so far removed from Miller's third wife, Austrian-born photographer Ingeborg Morath.

Yet the memory of Maggie wouldn't leave him. "You never stop loving who you loved," Quentin insisted. And just as many theatergoers were thinking, "Not necessarily," Quentin added, "Why do I make such stupid statements?"

Ears perked up when Quentin said, "When two women are whispering and they stop abruptly when you appear, the subject must have been sex. And if one of those is your wife, she must have been talking about you." What, theatergoers wondered, had Miller overheard Monroe say about his sexual ability?

The playwright didn't tell. Quentin instead chatted about his first wife, Louise. She may have been based on Mary Grace Slattery, Miller's wife from August 5, 1940, until they were officially divorced on June 11, 1956—a mere eighteen days before he married Monroe.

When Louise complained that Quentin didn't talk to her, he rebutted, "Last night I read you my whole brief." She certainly had a point when she responded, "You think reading a brief to a woman is talking to her?"

Was Miller so unsure of himself, as Quentin was, that he routinely read his plays to Slattery? What we do know is that he didn't read *After the Fall* to Monroe.

Quentin did much complaining. "Why is the world so treacherous?" he asked the Listener, without, of course, waiting for an answer. By this point in the play, theatergoers might have suspected that Miller chose the name Quentin because it was close to "question"—and *After the Fall* was full of questions to which theatergoers were asked to provide many of the answers when Miller chose not to respond.

There had to be one question that occurred to them: What was Kazan's reaction to Miller's line "A man's got to take the rap for what he's done"? Kazan, after all, had played ball with the House Un-American Activities Committee to avoid being blacklisted; Miller had not. We had to wait until 2009 to learn Kazan's opinion when he published his memoir; *After the Fall*'s turncoat, he wrote "was not unsympathetically portrayed."

However, many were surprised that Miller would even work with one of the committee's most cooperative witnesses. Ah, but Kazan was still considered one of America's great directors, and he'd helmed both of Miller's hits (*All My Sons* and *Salesman*) and none of his flops. This brought to mind Samuel Goldwyn's often-cited if oxymoronic sentiment about never using a person again unless he was needed.

After the Fall dealt with some blacklist issues as Quentin's marriage to Louise fell apart. Finally, after Quentin had ruminated for a full half hour about his first wife, mother, father, brother, and girlfriends, too, the audience was introduced to Maggie, looking very un-Monroe-like. At this point, some had to think that Barbara Loden, whom Kazan had discovered in 1960 and cast in his films *Wild River* and *Splendor in the Grass*, was miscast.

Maggie and Quentin met at a bus stop. She shyly expressed her ambition to become a singer and wished she had the money to buy records of the entertainers she most admired. Not much time passed before Quentin found himself saying, "I wish you knew how to take care of yourself."

When he offhandedly told his wife about this young woman he'd met, Louise became suspicious. That made him quickly dismiss Maggie as "quite stupid, silly kid.... She was just there, like a tree or a cat." Louise wasn't fooled any more than the theatergoers—or perhaps the Listener.

After Miller returned to more blacklist issues, he asked the Listener, "You don't mind my staying? I'd like to get this finished—although, actually," he soft-pedaled, "I just dropped by to say hello."

Was that the end of the first act? No, Miller was enough of a showman to give the audience a glimpse of Maggie, who was now made to look very Monroe-like. The audience gasped in recognition as Loden said in the former screen queen's soft voice, "Quentin? Quentin?"

"I'll get to it, honey. I'll get to it" were Quentin's last words before intermission.

So theatergoers still had to wait fifteen minutes more before meeting the character they came to see. Now the young woman who had struggled to buy phonograph records was a singing star who sold plenty of them. She credited Quentin and "the way [he] talked to me" for giving her the courage to find an agent, which in turn led to her success.

Lest that seem simplistic, Quentin said to the Listener, "All I can see now is the power she offered me."

The audience's voyeuristic goals were met when Maggie said, "I'm a joke to most people," and revealed that she'd check into hotels as "Miss None" because "I just have to think of nothing and that's me."

Maggie's fans were shown as carnal: "Take off your sweater, Maggie. It's hot out!" Quentin noted that he often heard "her name floating in the stench of locker rooms and parlor-car cigar smoke." Maggie admitted that she "was with two men the same day," and that Miller didn't name names here must have disappointed some.

When Quentin proposed to her, she warned, "There are people who are going to laugh at you." Quentin saw it differently, if not very nobly: "You're a victory. You're like a flag to me."

And so they were wed, and that's when their troubles began. All Maggie had to do was see him with an admirer and she was asking, "Why'd you let her rub her body against you?" Later, it was "When I walked into the party, you didn't even put your arms around me." When Miller had her say "*Hold* me," he indeed put the verb in italics. Then he succumbed to giving Quentin one of the most commonplace lines imaginable: "I never knew what love was."

Even Miller and Monroe apparently had money problems. There was much talk of back taxes and Maggie being penalized for not showing up for work, which sent Quentin into his lawyer mode; he got a $100,000 fine reduced to $20,000. "I'm putting 40 percent of my time on your problems," he said tersely. That he wasn't giving 100 percent to his law firm resulted in his termination.

Miller created—or simply re-created—a woman who would have been a handful for an octopus. Maggie forbade Quentin's mother the house because the woman told her that she'd gained weight. "Slap her down," she demanded of Quentin.

Quentin's insisting, "She adores you. She's proud of you," made Maggie roar, "Are you trying to make me think I'm crazy? I'm not crazy!" and resulted in "Don't shit me!" And when Quentin demanded she not use "that language with me," she angrily showed that she didn't care when yelling, "Call me vulgar, that I talk like a truck driver. Well, that's where I come from. I'm for Negroes and Puerto Ricans and truck drivers!"

Now some voyeurs felt that they were seeing too much, especially when two suicide attempts were mentioned and another was shown. "A suicide kills two people," Quentin said. He later railed that he did "hate women, hate men, hate all who would not grovel at my feet."

By this point in the three-hour play, the audience may have taken that last outburst personally and lost sympathy for Quentin, even as he yelled, "You won't kill me!" to Maggie three times in a row. The title of the play was revealed seconds before the final curtain: "Is the knowing all? To know, and even happily, that we meet unblessed; not in some garden of wax fruit and painted trees that lie in Eden, but after, after the Fall, after many, many deaths." Then Miller ended the play with hope, as Quentin walked toward Holga.

Anna Hill Johnstone put Maggie in a gold dress that complemented Loden's golden performance, which was "stunning" (Taubman) and "an astonishing reminder of the late Marilyn" (Chapman). The term "channeling" wasn't yet in popular use, but had it been, Kerr might have employed it when mentioning that Loden's blond wig and pajama tops were evidence that Monroe was on Miller's mind. And yet, while Kerr described what Loden did onstage, he never once offered an opinion on whether she was good, bad, or indifferent. Perhaps his having to make a tight deadline after seeing a three-hour play was responsible for this major omission.

Kerr didn't like *After the Fall*, finding it sensational in the first meaning the dictionary gives the word ("arousing by lurid details a quick, intense, and usually superficial interest") and not the second ("exceedingly or unexpectedly excellent"). He felt that "we do not watch the scenes as if we're following characters in a play."

McClain not only thought *After the Fall* was "pretentiously and intolerably long," but he was also "offended by its lack of taste. The girl must be permitted to rest in peace." Watts saw it as "a disappointing and self-indulgent kind of personal apologia.... It might have been entitled 'Whatever Became of Arthur Miller?' "

While the headline on Chapman's review said *"After the Fall* Overpowering," nothing in the review said anything of the kind. Critics don't write their own headlines, so the person on the copy desk who'd been assigned the task may also have been facing an all-too-quick deadline, read in Chapman's first paragraph that the company was off to "an impressive start" and didn't read in paragraph two that Chapman felt it was "a long, long, do-it-yourself psychoanalysis."

Nadel was far more enthusiastic: "We have come into a treasure ... a powerful and portentous drama, one to arouse an audience and enrich a season."

The all-important Taubman wrote a rave—and I mean "rave." Too often those connected with shows mistakenly or optimistically use that word to describe what is merely a positive review or even a qualified approval. In this case, however, "rave" is the only appropriate description for a review that began "Which to celebrate first? The return of Arthur Miller to the theater with a new play after too long an absence? Or the arrival of the new Repertory

Theater of Lincoln Center with its high promise for a consecration to drama of aspiration and significance?"

Those who don't read an entire review but just skip to the final paragraph found "Rejoice that Arthur Miller is back with a play worthy of his mettle. Rejoice also that a new company has been born committed to theater of consequence."

Theatergoers who do trouble themselves to read every word of a review found that Taubman considered *After the Fall* "Miller's maturest" and that Quentin "represents any and all courageous enough to hunt for order in the painful and joyous chaos of living. How can one commend Jason Robards, Jr. adequately?"

Taubman then provided his own answer, saying that Robards was "beyond praise." As for his leading lady, Taubman said that "Loden all but enkindles the stage."

Never mind not-for-profit. This was a money review. And yet, interest in the play soon waned and full houses were rare. What might have hurt was location, location, location; some theatergoers don't like to leave the theater district (which was then defined as Forty-first through Fifty-fourth Streets). Word of mouth may well have warned about the three-hour length. Miller's fans might have also been unnerved by a play that didn't resemble his previous seven linear and naturalistic ones. Even the thrust stage might have hindered their enjoyment. "*After the Fall* does not require such a stage," Kerr said.

And perhaps, just perhaps, theatergoers wanted two acts of Monroe and not one. Miller made a rookie writer's mistake: He tried to cover a lifetime rather than a telescoped period of time. Had Miller eliminated his first marriage, the Red Scare, and the blacklist, and only dealt with his relationship with Monroe, he could have dug even deeper and thus made a more powerful play.

Nevertheless, at 208 performances, *After the Fall* would, aside from *The Price* in 1968, be Miller's longest-running play of the remaining six that he'd bring to Broadway. Henry Hewes reported in that year's *Burns Mantle Yearbook*, "Miller calmly predicted that in time *After the Fall* would be regarded as his best play."

Salesman and *Crucible* have enjoyed four Broadway revivals, while *Bridge* has had three. *After the Fall* has had one. "In time" has not yet arrived.

* * *

Five weeks after *After the Fall* opened, The Repertory Theater of Lincoln Center made good on its name by adding a second play to accompany it: S. N. Behrman's *But for Whom Charlie.*

Behrman certainly had Broadway experience—twenty shows, albeit only five real hits: *The Second Man* in 1927, *Biography* in 1932, *No Time for Comedy* in 1939, *Jacobowsky and the Colonel* in 1944, and the book for *Fanny* in 1954. Approximately one hit a decade seemed to be Behrman's speed; Whitehead and Kazan had to hope this new one with the impossible title would be the one for the '60s.

It wasn't. While the play wasn't as bad as the title, it held little appeal for audiences. The long-held theory that theatergoers aren't interested in the troubles of artists reached an apotheosis here. Should biographer Willard Prosper get a grant from the Seymour Rosenthal Foundation? How about memoirist Brock Dunnaway? And what of poet Sheila Maloney? Whether applicants should or should not get free money couldn't be of interest to those theatergoers who'd just come from a hard day at work.

Although it's Seymour's foundation, Charles Taney calls the shots. As he expositionarily explains to Gillian, who gets her grants from rich husbands, he's known Seymour since their days at Yale. Charlie had been accepted into a fraternity, but once he heard that it wouldn't accept Jews—even the phenomenally wealthy Seymour—he quit.

After Gillian asked, "Did you perhaps have an intuition that someday Seymour might come in handy for you?" Charlie baldly admitted, "It was more than intuition, darling. It was a plan."

Hating Charlie was easy even before he turned out to be corrupt, denying grants to people he simply didn't like rather than considering their merit alone. Clearly he would get his comeuppance; clearly he did, in not any surprising fashion.

How were the reviews? Put it this way: When Random House published the play, on the inside dust jacket flap it give capsule reviews of four of Behrman's *previous* plays.

Behrman blamed Kazan. In calling the production "a mutilation," the playwright may have had a point. Kazan, who was opening a new theater, planning three productions for this season, and considering three for the following one—not to mention directing *After the Fall*—must have been exhausted by the time he had to stage *Charlie.*

"A beaut of a mistake" was what Behrman eventually called the production when he was ready to move on. And he was: to writing prose, and never again to try another play in the nine years he had left.

CHAPTER SIX

*

The Revivals

A theater that was meant to be quintessentially American had to do a play by the country's greatest playwright. Then, as now, that was considered to be Eugene O'Neill, so the third 1963–64 offering of the Repertory Theater of Lincoln Center would be one of his plays.

Whitehead and Kazan must be commended for not playing it safe with any of the acknowledged masterpieces. When they announced that their choice would be *Marco Millions,* though, the second-guessing began.

For it was perceived to be second-rate O'Neill. He'd written the play in 1923 but couldn't get a production until 1928. Broadway's producers didn't seem to care that he'd won one Pulitzer Prize in 1920 (*Beyond the Horizon*), another in 1922 (*Anna Christie*), and had had three hits that had run longer than each of those: *All God's Chillun Got Wings, Desire Under the Elms,* and *The Emperor Jones.* They simply didn't think that it was good enough.

Neither did the critics or public when it finally debuted: ninety-two performances. A revival in 1930 could muster only eight. So Whitehead and Kazan were definitely taking a chance.

One doesn't associate O'Neill with such exotic locales as Venice, Syria, Persia, India, Mongolia, and China, but that's where Marco Polo went to make his millions. Indeed he did, in literally introducing paper money to the Orient, raping land and businesses, and showing Kublai Khan what he believed to be some good ol' Italian know-how.

These were the days when Asians didn't play Asians. David Wayne was summoned to portray Kublai Khan, probably from his experience as the wily Sakini in *The Teahouse of the August Moon.*

Just as Brecht had masked Hitler with his Arturo Ui, O'Neill made Marco a stand-in for the voracious American businessmen who were profiteering after the war. Kerr, McClain, Nadel, and Watts all mentioned Sinclair Lewis's *Babbitt* in their reviews.

Marco kept quiet about his girl back home when dealing with Princess Kukachin (Zohra Lampert). She fell in love with him and summarily got her heart broken. Nadel didn't much like her performance, but did admit that she "was distracted by her left eye makeup which kept coming unstuck so that she appeared to have three nostrils."

(That's what Lampert got for turning down *Any Wednesday.*)

Nadel went on to say that *Marco* was "not an important play," which was echoed by Watts ("among his least successful works"), Taubman ("does not belong with O'Neill's finest plays"), McClain ("certainly not one of Mr. O'Neill's finest efforts"), Kerr ("the play is not and never has been one of O'Neill's more successful assaults"), and Chapman ("wasn't very good O'Neill in the first place").

Neither *Marco Millions* nor *But for Whom Charlie* could crack the fifty-performance mark; *Marco* was gone by mid-June, and *Charlie* disappeared in early July. *After the Fall* continued to play in repertory until May 29, 1965, along with Miller's next play, *Incident at Vichy,* and revivals of *Tartuffe* and *The Changeling.*

Kazan, who directed *Charlie* and *Changeling,* too, mentioned in his memoir that *After the Fall* "was the only one that was worth a damn" before revealing that "I found the first act very dull" and that "Quentin, who could pass for Miller, talked to the audience endlessly, and, I thought, without much interest."

How, then, could it be "the only one that was worth a damn"? Kazan explained, "Then came the second act and on stage came the character based on Marilyn Monroe...played brilliantly by Loden"; here, he said, Miller was "amazingly honest."

In addition to Kerr's remark about the incompatibility between play and theater, other comments about the new house ranged from "functional" (Nadel) to "impressively utilitarian" (Taubman) to "quite fabulous" (McClain). Chapman and Watts might have felt no need to comment because the playhouse would soon be disassembled. (As it turned out, it was sold and shipped to Rhode

Island's Trinity Square Repertory Company, which planned to resurrect it somewhere in Providence. That never happened.)

When the Vivian Beaumont Theater opened on October 12, 1965, Whitehead and Kazan weren't in attendance. Bad reviews and subscriptions dropping from 46,500 to 27,000 caused the board to fire Whitehead before Christmas 1964; Kazan then resigned in protest. New directors Herbert Blau and Jules Irving, who immediately abandoned the practice of repertory, didn't fare substantially better and the still-named Repertory Theater of Lincoln Center died in 1973 after, ironically, a production of *A Streetcar Named Desire*, which Kazan had originally guided into his longest-running hit. Taubman's hope of a "high promise for a consecration to drama of aspiration and significance" wasn't realized.

However, one Lincoln Center collaboration lasted thirteen years, for Kazan and Loden married in 1967. It might have continued had Loden not died of breast cancer at forty-eight. One reason that her scenes in *After the Fall* caught fire may have been that she and Kazan were discovering love both on and off stage.

Marco Millions was one of ten Broadway revivals—eight plays, two musicals—out of 1963–64's seventy-five productions. That computes to 13.33 percent.

Fifty years later, the 2013–14 season offered fifteen revivals: three musicals and twelve plays. Fifteen out of forty-three makes for 34.88 percent—meaning that the percentage had almost trebled.

One could argue that revivals are now more plentiful because fifty more years have passed and there are that many more shows that *can* be revived; indeed, four of the 2013–14 batch couldn't have been remounted in 1963–64 because they hadn't yet been written.

But revival-itis is with us because the names of the shows are somewhere between recognizable and famous, and with theater tickets as expensive as they are, theatergoers prefer to take as few chances as possible. At these prices, missing a play during its original run is very easy; a Broadway revival gives people a chance to catch up.

Another component: Plays that have met with success off-Broadway now rely on the cachet of their name value to sell at Broadway prices.

And that brings us to the first production of 1963–64.

* * *

The season was officially christened on August 27, 1963, with a revival whose title undoubtedly sounded familiar to Broadway audiences: *Oh Dad, Poor Dad, Mamma's Hung You in the Closet and I'm Feelin' So Sad.*

Today, that title would never be used, for it would take up half a tweet. Even then, the sign on the Morosco, on which electric letters hung, literally left it at *Oh Dad Poor Dad, Etc.*

Arthur Kopit's absurdist comedy had been an off-Broadway hit the previous season, so now two producers decided to try something new and mount a new production for Broadway.

While a few shows had dared to move to Broadway *during* an off-Broadway run (such as *The Golden Apple*), this was the first time an off-Broadway play started a new production from scratch, albeit with the same director: Jerome Robbins. The better-known Hermione Gingold would replace Jo Van Fleet in the lead.

And who got top billing? You'd expect Gingold, of course, but the actual credits stated, "Roger L. Stevens and T. Edward Hambleton by arrangement with Phoenix Theatre present"—and then "JEROME ROBBINS' PRODUCTION" and in equally large letters on the next line "HERMIONE GINGOLD," followed by the unwieldy title.

It failed after forty-seven performances. In those days, off-Broadway was the place a theatergoer went to see revivals, while Broadway was reserved for new work.

But now producers follow the pattern established by *Oh Dad.* They give a long-closed off-Broadway success a brand-new Broadway production—but only after the show has made a brand name for itself: *Little Shop of Horrors, Oleanna, Three Days of Rain*—in fact, as of this writing, every season of this new century had at least one erstwhile off-Broadway entry make it to the Main Stem in a fresh production.

Not only did Eva Le Gallienne translate Chekhov's *The Seagull* for her National Repertory Theatre, she also directed it . Who else would cast a sixty-four-year-old—herself—as Madame Arkadina, the mother to a twenty-something Constantin?

Le Gallienne tried to solve the age issue by hiring thirty-five-year-old

Farley Granger as her son and, as Nina, Anne Meacham, who was—as *Little Me*'s Belle Poitrine described herself after she'd hit her sixtieth birthday— "frankly forty."

Oh, well; esteemed classical actresses were famous—nay, notorious—for this type of, shall we say, nontraditional casting. In 1913, Julia Marlowe was forty-seven when she brought her Juliet Capulet to Broadway; Sarah Bernhardt was fifty-six when she played Roxane in a 1900 Broadway revival of *Cyrano de Bergerac*. Still, "Miss Le G," as she was chummily known, was wise to choose a theater (the Belasco) with a second balcony.

So would she dare play Elizabeth Proctor in *The Crucible*? No, perhaps because she wasn't directing this one; Jack Sydow, in his first staging job since *Sophie* the year before, chose Meacham instead. Or was Le Gallienne bucking to play Abigail Williams?

The 1963–64 season was still a time when a troupe could come from France, present two plays that were nearly three hundred years old—in French, yet— and do business.

Marie Bell, then artistic director of the venerable, 143-year-old Théâtre du Gymnase in Paris, played the title roles in Racine's *Phèdre* and *Bérénice* for a week each.

How highly regarded was Bell? Today, Théâtre du Gymnase is known as Théâtre du Gymnase Marie Bell. That says even more than Taubman's "She commands the kind of grandeur that Charles de Gaulle invokes for France."

However fluent the Broadway audience was in French, it was probably better versed in Hebrew. So the National Theatre of Israel, originally called Habimah (the Stage), dared to bring over three foreign-language entries for a seven-week run.

Two were new plays: Ben-Zio Tomer's *Children of the Shadows* and Hanoch Bartov's *Each Had Six Wings*. Both dealt with postwar Jews who were adjusting to their new homes in Israel while attempting to put the Holocaust out of their minds.

The centerpiece was the fortieth-anniversary production of *The Dybbuk*, S. Ansky's classic. It concerned a father who wanted his daughter, Leah'le, to marry a wealthy man instead of Hannan, the Talmudic scholar whom she loved. Hannan was so distraught that he dropped dead, but he returned as a spirit that invaded Leah'le's body. All the rabbis couldn't separate the lovers, who were soon reunited in death.

The subject matter would be on everyone's lips when William Peter Blatty's *The Exorcist* reached No. 1 on the *New York Times* bestseller list in 1971; in 1973, it became the first horror film nominated for an Academy Award. Both have since faded, while *The Dybbuk* is still often performed in Israel.

Precisely one month after *Café Crown* offered its final "*King Lear* Ballet," Shakespeare's actual *King Lear* appeared in a more faithful version, courtesy of the Royal Shakespeare Company of Stratford-on-Avon. With Lear being played by Paul Scofield—the esteemed British actor who'd created a Tony-winning sensation as St. Thomas More in *A Man for All Seasons* in 1961—management anticipated an even greater ticket demand than Alexander H. Cohen expected for Richard Burton's *Hamlet,* which he'd placed in a musical-sized house.

Another reason for management's optimism was that the production was a radical one; director Peter Brook turned it into a cautionary tale in which Lear imagined what *could* happen if he split up his kingdom in unwise fashion.

Washington Post critic Richard Coe, when seeing the pre-Broadway engagement, reported that Scofield &Co. had received "a ten-minute standing ovation" at the opening—and this in a time when theatergoers stood at the end of a performance only to put on their coats.

So *Lear* was looking for the biggest possible house. The Broadway wasn't available; *Folies Bergère* would begin previews two days after *Lear* was to open. But the Majestic, with upwards of 1,600 seats, had been available since *Anyone Can Whistle* had closed.

And yet, management decided it required something larger still. So it was off to Lincoln Center and the 2,500-seat-plus State Theater.

One reason this theater had more seats than usual was the absence of left and right aisles. "Continental seating" meant one long row after another. Cartoonist Alan Dunn soon commented by showing a full house of seated patrons with one disgruntled row's worth where two people are shuffling their way to the middle: "Excuse me, excuse me, excuse me, excuse me, excuse me," went the caption.

Theatergoers were turning to their seatmates during the play and saying "Excuse me" followed by "What he did he just say?," for the $17 million five-ring theater was quickly found to have terrible acoustics. That wasn't a problem when the New York City Ballet christened the house, but now it was; acoustic panels to right the wrong had to be hastily installed.

The unknown Julie Christie was part of the company. As Goneril? No, that was Irene Worth. Cordelia? No, that was a just-starting-out Diana Rigg. Regan? No, that was Pauline Jameson, who would not become as famous as the other two in these United States, but in England became just as highly regarded.

Christie, as it turned out, wasn't in *Lear* at all. She portrayed Luciana in *The Comedy of Errors,* which the company played in rep with *Lear,* giving twelve performances of each. Little did the twenty-three-year-old Christie know that she was only twenty-three months away from winning an Oscar for *Darling.*

IBDB.com doesn't include *King Lear* and *The Comedy of Errors* in its season round-up, on the technicality that they weren't housed in sanctioned Broadway theaters. Hewes in *The Best Plays* and Blum in *Theatre World* felt differently: When Paul Scofield plays King Lear, and when Alec McCowen and Ian Richardson play the Antipholi, attention must be paid.

In the not-quite-Broadway category were the New York City Center Light Opera Company revivals. Director Jean Dalrymple would buy the sets and costumes of just-closed long-running shows, store many of them in the basement of City Center (where Manhattan Theatre Club now resides), and bring them out to furnish two-to-four-week engagements.

These productions suddenly qualified as Broadway if the Tony committee decided to include them. That happened sometimes from admiration, and at other times from a need to fill a category so that the season would appear to have been more successful than it actually was.

Even here 1963–64 proved extraordinary, for this season represented the greatest Tony success for Dalrymple's organization. Granted, Bob Fosse's nomination as Best Actor in a Musical for *Pal Joey* was a holdover that had opened the previous May. But this season's *West Side Story* got a Best Conductor nod for Charles Jaffe and Best Producer of a Musical citation for the company—which is why it's included in IBDB.com's listing while Dalrymple's other entry—the unnominated *My Fair Lady*—is not.

And yet, Dalrymple did her smartest producing here. As her Eliza Doolittle, she chose Marni Nixon, who was then experiencing her greatest fame.

Nixon had already played the role, in a manner of speaking—no, in a manner of *singing*. During the 1963 filming of *My Fair Lady*, star Audrey Hepburn's singing voice was found wanting, and Nixon was called in to provide more mellifluous sounds.

Truly, this was an enormous news story all year long, one that Nixon told with relish in her 2006 memoir *I Could Have Sung All Night*. Too bad that her editor didn't approve the title that she and co-author Stephen Cole preferred: *Audrey Hepburn Dubbed My Face*.

We'll include all four productions. *King Lear* and *The Comedy of Errors could* have played a genuine Broadway theater, had management gone that route. And while City Center was never meant to be a Broadway house, those Tony nominations allow us to include its offerings.

Finally, 1963–64's most-heralded revival, which owed its existence to the most anticipated film of 1963. And yet, once *Cleopatra* was released in June, it became an immediate critical and financial disaster. Only Rex Harrison, who'd played Julius Caesar, received good reviews.

But Harrison's co-star who'd played Marc Antony received the life-changing career boost.

Richard Burton was mentioned in newspapers and on television virtually every day of 1962 and 1963—and 1964 would prove to be no exception. This was the result of Burton's discarding his wife, Sybil, in favor of Mrs. Eddie Fisher, better known as mega-star and Oscar winner Elizabeth Taylor. Liz and Dick suddenly became the world's most scandalous couple, which naturally made him almost as big a name as she.

In the decade before hooking up with Taylor, Burton had appeared in ten films; in the decade after, he would star in twenty-four, most of them stinkers. Still, he doubled his $250,000 *Cleopatra* salary when he did his next film, *The Night of the Iguana*.

But in 1964, Burton still had his eye on Broadway and proved it by daring to do *Hamlet*.

What a natural project for so-called prestige producer Alexander H. Cohen. Truth to tell, Cohen was most famous for producing flops while somehow convincing the public and investors that he was extraordinarily successful. He kept that fiction alive when signing as *Hamlet*'s director no less than John

Gielgud. It would seem to be a natural fit; in 1950, Gielgud had guided Burton to an acclaimed Broadway debut in *The Lady's Not for Burning*.

And just as Gielgud had acted in that production, he did so again here—in (literally) a manner of speaking. Gielgud would provide the voice of Hamlet's father's Ghost as a twenty-foot image was represented by a shadow projected against the back wall.

(*Hamlet* is one play where the deux ex machina comes in early.)

Although Shakespeare's most famous work would be caviar to the general, Cohen knew that people would flock to see the new inamorato of Elizabeth Taylor Hilton Wilding Todd Fisher TBA in the flesh. Many theatergoers purposely bought orchestra seats on the extreme left or right side in hopes of spying a violet-eyed attendee standing in the wings and cheering on her man at the curtain calls.

During the tryouts, some wouldn't get too good a look at Burton, for Cohen brought the production to Toronto's O'Keefe Centre (3,000 seats) and the Shubert in Boston (nearly 1,800). He then transported it to one of Broadway's biggest theaters: the Lunt-Fontanne, with over 1,500 seats.

Earlier in the season, a show featuring Shakespeare—granted, an Elizabethan Drama 101–level anthology called *The Golden Age*—chose the Lyceum, which had less than two-thirds the Lunt-Fontanne's seating capacity. Chapman liked the show more than he would this *Hamlet;* Taubman and McClain had nice things to say about it, too.

But it closed in a week, while this *Hamlet* would become the longest running of sixty Broadway productions dating back to 1761. *The Golden Age*'s "stars" Douglas Campbell, Gordon Myers, Lester Rawlins, Douglas Rains, James Stover, Nancy Wickwire, and Betty Wilson all rolled into one didn't have a percentage point of Burton's sudden fame.

The Golden Age offered so few costumes and so negligible a set that no designers were credited. But the stage for this *Hamlet* wasn't much more ornate. Said Gielgud, "This is a *Hamlet* acted in rehearsal clothes, stripped of all extraneous trappings, unencumbered by a reconstruction of any particular historical period. This performance is conceived as a final run-through, as actors call it. When a play has been thoroughly prepared, there is always a full final rehearsal of the text and action played straight through without interruption from the director."

Is *this* where the much-overused term "trappings" started as a description of scenery and costumes that range from nice to elaborate? Why are genuine and realistic sets and costumes—or fanciful and imaginative ones—an attention-destroying detriment?

Let's face it: Nine times out of nine-point-nine, when perfunctory costumes and the absence of scenery are trumpeted as the avoidance of "trappings," the sole motivation is to save money.

Hamlet's stage deck with a few steps here and there appeared to have cost around $1.50. That arras behind which Polonius hid wasn't much more than a shower curtain. And if this was said to be a production's "final run-through," then this production clearly wasn't going to have any more of a set when it opened the following night.

"Will there be lighting? If so—why? There would never be any but the most minimal lighting during a run-through." So said William Redfield, who played Guildenstern, in a letter he sent to a friend. (From the day he was cast through the start of the New York run, Redfield took meticulous notes, all of which became a book called *Letters from an Actor.*)

That he and Clement Fowler (Rosencrantz) were dressed in both jacket and tie suggested that these would be their costumes, and that the production would be modern dress—which often means saving the production some money as well. Gertrude, however, wore a ring so large that it could pass for the 68-carat diamond that Burton would eventually buy for Elizabeth Taylor Hilton Wilding Todd Fisher Burton.

The production, of course, saved on royalties to the playwright, whose copyright had long expired. Some of this unspent money went to Burton, who got 15 percent of what would be a $6 million gross, not to mention Cohen, who lived like a Midas and a Medici combined whenever he produced a show.

As usual, Wittenberg student Hamlet would be portrayed by a long-in-the-tooth actor; Burton was thirty-eight. Well, we *were* in an era where kids were starting to take some time off after they were graduated from high school and started their college education. But why were Eileen Herlie and Alfred Drake, playing his parents, respectively only five and eleven years older? (In Herlie's case, maybe she was grandmother-claused-in, for in the 1948 film of *Hamlet,* she was Gertrude to Laurence Olivier's Hamlet, although she was eleven years *younger* than he.)

Their backgrounds in musicals may have helped: Herlie in *Take Me Along*, Drake for his Tony-winning performances in *Kiss Me, Kate* and *Kismet*. Any actor who's appeared in a Bard play as well as a Broadway musical will note that Shakespeare's lines and rhythms inherently sing.

Drake, by the way, had already been involved with two musicals earlier this season. First, he was the dashing leading man who did double duty in *Zenda* (as in *The Prisoner of*). But that show, set to open at the Mark Hellinger Theatre on November 26, closed in Pasadena.

That freed the theater for the February opening of *Rugantino*. Strangely enough, it had Drake's name on it, albeit not as star. Drake, born Alfred Capurro, translated the Italian book and lyrics.

Drake had finished his *Rugantino* duties long before *Hamlet* went into rehearsal on January 30. That day, he met other performers who would make their mark in musicals. Two Tonys each would eventually go to John Cullum (Laertes) and George Rose (First Gravedigger) as Best Actor in a Musical. Robert Burr (Bernardo) would find soon after *Hamlet* closed that his next Broadway job would be in the musical *Bajour*.

As for ensemble member and Horatio understudy Gerome Ragni, perhaps his hearing dozens of times "The rest is silence" and "What a piece of work is a man" influenced him to include the words in the musical he co-wrote three years later: *Hair*.

Don't forget, too, that Burton had won a Tony for singing and dancing in *Camelot*. His versatility, however, wasn't always a boon to Gielgud. He said that Burton "could play Hamlet fifteen different ways—almost in the same rehearsal. I will give him notes before he went on, propping them on his dressing room table, and he will act on every note at that same performance without even rehearsing at all. He is enormously skilled in that way, but he is also apt to be rather undisciplined."

Redfield mused that Burton was "in many respects wrong for this particular part. He is far too strong and far too well put together. The very notion of Burton not killing a man who stands in his way strains credulity." And yet, he admitted, "Who else could draw in the box-office gelt to make such a production feasible?"

The reviews in Toronto were dreadful, which didn't keep the show from grossing in the $100,000 sellout range for each of the four weeks. Three acts turned into two, thanks in part to some editing. Yes, like every other playwright with a show out of town, Shakespeare lost some material.

When the company flew into Boston, Redfield reported that approximately five hundred screaming fans met the plane (which was possible in those pre-security-screening days when one could saunter right up to the gate). They weren't there for Shakespeare, and their appearance must have rankled Gielgud. Redfield reported him saying, "I'm weary of Richard and these endless peccadillos. It's all too fearfully immoral. Immoral, I say! Disgraces the English theatre! We're all grouped with him when he does those things."

As Mart Crowley would later say in *The Boys in the Band*, "Well, that's the pot calling the kettle beige." It's an odd statement coming from a man who had been convicted of "persistently importuning for immoral purposes" in 1953. The incident even spurred Terence Rattigan to write about it in his 1954 play *Separate Tables*.

Burton kept fine-tuning his performance. He didn't mince a word when he branded Queen Gertrude's remarrying so quickly as "common." He didn't pull back when she asked, "Why seems it so particular with thee?" for he roared when repeating "Seems!" When she tried to touch his cheek in a gesture of peace, he warded it off with disgust.

After Burton made the famous joke to Horatio of how the meals served at the funeral were all too quickly recycled for the wedding banquet, the actor suddenly turned serious. No, this situation was no laughing matter. "There are more things in heaven and earth, Horatio," he said before distinctly pausing, as if deliberating whether or not he should continue the criticism. Of course he did add "than are dreamt of in your philosophy."

Before he started his "To be, or not to be" soliloquy, he looked around, as if to make certain that no one would be able to overhear his suicidal thoughts. Midway through, however, he sat down and took on the demeanor of a college professor delivering a lecture. En route, the audience saw him change his mind.

The strife between the two lovers seemed fresh. Hamlet casually leaned on a chair when he instructed Ophelia, "Get thee to a nunnery." (While actress Linda Marsh didn't take that advice, she didn't get herself to Broadway ever again, either.)

Gielgud sharply put Ophelia's mad scene in front of the throne, underlining that had all gone well, she would have one day occupied it. Herlie had an innate regality; when she sat on a mere chair, she somehow immediately elevated it into a throne. Sad to say, when Burton took a seat, he, too, suggested a nobility that would never be realized.

In his final words about the play-within-a-play, Burton said, "To catch the conscience," paused, and then hissed out "of the King" with a you'd-better-watch-out warning and a definite finger point.

Based on the advice that Hamlet gives the players, he would have been a good director. Shakespeare was telling future directors how to handle his plays: speak naturally, modulate your voice, don't overuse gestures, but don't be overly demure, either. The Bard also had Hamlet damn the cheap laugh, upstaging, and hamming it up. "Suit the action to the word, the word to the action" deserved to become as famous as "to hold, as 'twere, the mirror up to nature."

Burton spoke the forty-odd lines with the experience of one who'd long dealt with actors and directors who were guilty of such infractions. And yet, during *The Murder of Gonzago* (or, if you will, its revisal title, *The Mousetrap*), Gielgud didn't have the players take Hamlet's advice; they overacted in arch fashion. Was Gielgud implying that actors never listen?

The mannered presentation of the play was not, of course, the reason that Claudius walked out. Herlie had tried to steady him by putting her hand on his knee—only to have Burton immediately and roughly remove it. Hesitation was over; he was planning to take action.

Or so it seemed. Would he really worry that if he killed Claudius while praying, the usurper would go to heaven? Does God forgive fratricide that easily? Burton's Hamlet fully believed that He wouldn't.

Drake offered an unusually long pause before he started praying, which made effective sense. After what he'd done, what could he say to God? Later, when he continually minimized Gertrude's grief, he proved that her husband's crown and not his love for her was his motivation.

Herlie's Gertrude seemed to be a woman who required extra love and attention, and realized that this needlessly got her involved in this murder and remarriage. She and Gielgud didn't neglect the famous Oedipal theory; Gertrude and Hamlet came close to kissing on the mouth after he told her of Rosencrantz and Guildenstern's fate.

Burton roared out, "YOU have my father much offended," and didn't worry about killing Polonius. He took it for granted that it was collateral damage; violence does beget violence. When his father's Ghost reappeared, Burton made Hamlet seem to be in denial, or even hallucinating. He became increasingly unhinged and emitted an unexpectedly giddy laugh before "Alas, poor Yorick." Meanwhile, Rose played First Gravedigger with a Cockney accent, dropping *h*'s everywhere.

Drake engaged in some fast talk to spur Laertes to revenge his father by killing Hamlet. And if anyone had a doubt that Shakespeare still had something to say to contemporary audiences, that notion would have been dispelled when Claudius spoke to Gertrude about "your son" and not "our son."

In the final scene, Drake yelled, "Gertrude!" with such alarm that she would not have possibly continued drinking, especially with all that had gone on. After Hamlet forced Claudius's death, he pushed the dead king off the throne as if he were throwing out the garbage. When the time came for Hamlet to die, he atypically stood tall when stating "The rest is silence."

Of course, the critics were hardly silent. Taubman: "Burton dominates the drama as Hamlet should, for his is a performance of electrical power and sweeping virility." McClain: "A most dominant and distinctive Hamlet." Watts called Burton "forceful, direct, unpretentiously eloquent, more thoughtfully introspective than darkly melancholy with the glint of ironic humor and decidedly a man of action and feeling."

If that sounds expansive, what of Nadel, who spent his first nine paragraphs on the actor? "Burton," he said, "swept mind and memory clear of all other Hamlets in a performance so lucid and sensible that people will speak of it for years."

Kerr wouldn't be one of them. He felt that the star had "all the qualities that Hamlet requires except one: Mr. Burton is without emotion." Still, Kerr did duly note that "he can convey better than I have seen anyone do the kind of savage glee that sometimes comes of horrifying knowledge."

Least impressed was Chapman: "His voice, whether loud or soft, has surprisingly little color." Chapman wasn't above concluding his review with information that none of his brother wizards imparted: "Mrs. Burton sat quietly in the sixth row four off the aisle." He knew what his *Daily News* readers wanted to know.

Chapman followed suit, however, in his appreciation of Hume Cronyn's

Polonius—"perhaps the best performance" of the production. Kerr was more definite: "the one wholly successful performance." McClain found Cronyn "particularly effective," while Nadel said he was "not only valid but fascinating." Watts and Taubman used the same word, although the former chose to use it as an adjective—"superb"—while the latter chose to employ it as an adverb: "superbly managed and richly fatuous."

What made Cronyn's Polonius special was best expressed by Watts: "He realizes that the old man is a bore and a nuisance who irritates everyone around him, but he also knows that there is a residue of humor and even wisdom somewhere beneath the senility, and he makes the role both comic and touching without sacrificing the credibility of the nuisance value."

(My, journalists wrote long sentences back then.)

Cronyn and Burton would be the only two Tony nominated. Cronyn had no trouble winning, first and foremost from his reviews. But his august reputation certainly helped; this was Cronyn's seventeenth performance on Broadway, while his three competitors—Lee Allen in *Marathon '33*, Michael Dunn in *The Ballad of the Sad Café*, and Larry Gates in *A Case of Libel*—had nine combined. Their shows had all closed, too.

Would Burton win for his Hamlet? Donald Wolfit in 1947, John Neville in 1958, and Donald Madden in 1961 hadn't received as much as a nomination—but none of them had careers that could have matched Burton's, headed by two Oscar nominations and that *Camelot* Tony.

However, none of the three was as notorious, either (although we'd learn more about Wolfit's dark side sixteen years later when his not-so-loyal employee Ronald Harwood wrote *The Dresser*). Would Burton's offstage life make voters snub him?

Thought to be the Welsh actor's main competition was a British actor playing a Welshman: Guinness as Dylan. He didn't have a Tony, and he'd only been eligible once before, when he made his second-ever Broadway appearance in *The Cocktail Party* in 1950. Guinness did, however, have an Oscar for *The Bridge on the River Kwai*.

Still, Hamlet is a more challenging role than the one Sidney Michaels fashioned for Guinness. It's Shakespeare's longest role at 1,495 lines, representing 37 percent of the entire play.

And yet, Guinness won—letting producers George and Granat enjoy an unprecedented achievement in 1963–64. Since the Tony Awards began, no management had ever sponsored the winners of Best Actress and Best Actor in two different plays. These men did just that via Guinness and Sandy Dennis in *Any Wednesday.*

Did Burton's scandalous personal life with that woman in the sixth row four seats off the aisle influence the voters? We may forever speculate about their motivations, much as scholars hypothesize about Hamlet's. Meanwhile, we can assess Burton's Hamlet for ourselves, for it was recorded in Electronovision.

Electronovision! What then sounded state-of-the-art (before people were actually using the term "state-of-the-art") sounds woefully retro now.

Entrepreneur Bill Sargent had cameramen record a performance on a then-new high-resolution videotape, which was later transferred to film and then to kinescope. He even had his eye on *Fade Out—Fade In,* but *Hamlet* was the only one brought to fruition. It was given only a limited theatrical release in late 1964, but in 1999 it became available on DVD.

That's more than *The Advocate* can say.

CHAPTER SEVEN

*

The Minorities

I t was such a novelty that *Time* made a point of remarking on it.

Here's Love, it said, had "a cast that is 10% Negro. They are Macy's shoppers, spectators, secretaries—everything but Santa Claus—and do not play the roles of Negroes as such."

The practice was revolutionary for its time. We were still in an era in which *Baby Want a Kiss* and Chapman's review of *Bicycle Ride to Nevada* used the word "colored" to respectively describe a nanny and a servant.

McClain's lede for *Tambourines to Glory* was "The American Negro can sing and move better than anybody, and he has an original and exuberant sense of humor about himself and the world at large which has nothing to do with Civil Rights. In this climate he is endearing as it is possible for any human being to be."

In his next paragraph, McClain seemed a little less clueless: "There is no condescension suggested in such a statement; he has exhibited his ability at serious drama, at which he is as good, but no better, than anyone else."

A qualified approval followed of this musical by Langston Hughes (1902–67), one of America's most distinguished black writers. Were it not for Hughes, Lorraine Hansberry would have had to find a different title for her landmark play, for Hughes had coined the phrase "a raisin in the sun" in his 1926 poem *Harlem.*

Hughes never had a success commensurate with Hansberry's, although his *Street Scene* with Kurt Weill in 1947 was a prestigious project. Now, after four attempts on Broadway, he'd try again with *Tambourines to Glory,* which employed both an occasional spiritual ("When the Saints Go Marching In") and a few original songs that he wrote with Jobe Huntley in the latter's sole Broadway outing.

Quite often, the first character theatergoers meet is the one they'll root for all night. Hughes wouldn't want us to do that here, for he first brought in the devil—the real Mr. Applegate, here known as Big-Eyed Buddy Lomax, although he did admit to using Brutus, Henry VIII, Catherine the Great ("I put on drag sometimes"), Hitler, and Khrushchev.

"In Harlem, I'm cool; in Spain, I'm hot," he said. "In Katanga, I'm Tshombe."

Now he'd be Buddy, as he insinuated himself into the life of Essie Belle Johnson (Rosetta LeNoire), who'd been dispossessed and was now on the street. "I reckon God'll provide," she said.

Not quite. As Laura Wright Reed observed, "The Lord is no respecter of persons." She was the one who took in and saved Essie.

There are no statistics on how hard the audience laughed after Laura said to Essie, "Why don't you and me start a church?" But ten years earlier, L. Ron Hubbard had done just that, and he didn't do badly at all.

Laura's converts would be those who "drink without gettin' sick, gamble away the rent, cheat the welfare department—more'n I do. Lay with each other without gettin' disgusted, no matter how many unwanted kids they produce. Support the dope trade. Hustle."

No one can accuse Hughes of sugarcoating his perceptions.

Although Essie was content to believe that "I was born to bad luck," Laura wouldn't let that be an excuse. "Raise your fat disgusted self up off that suitcase you're setting on and let's go make our fortune saving souls."

Essie was "converted" as quickly as those passersby Laura had collared on the street corner. They believed that she indeed "saw a flash, heard a roll of thunder, felt a breeze and seen a light and voice exploding over heaven." She added, "You can't get saved for nothing," and for each coin, "The Lord thanks you."

The police weren't as gracious. Laura thought nothing of bribing an inquiring officer and didn't flinch when he asked for some monies for the cops downtown. Essie, a true believer, got her first taste of disillusionment.

Laura was easily seduced by Buddy, who told her to leave the streets, move into a storefront, call it a church, and sell water for a dollar a bottle—not like today's water, but allegedly Holy Water. He predicted "a Cadillac by Christmas."

Perhaps the play's most telling line—one that still says the most about those times—occurred after Buddy told Laura that his friend Marty could get her anything she wanted. That spurred her to ask, "Is he colored?" and for him to dryly refer to the man's power and affluence by answering, "You know he can't be colored."

A church is a natural location for spirituals, so Hughes and Huntley peppered their show with traditional ones. Afterward, Laura and Buddy sang "Love Is on the Way," around the time the church was on its way to success. It sported a mural in which Adam was made to resemble boxing champion Joe Louis, Eve was a dead ringer for singer Sarah Vaughan, and the devil was Caucasian.

"The devil should be named Buddy," said an ever more suspicious Essie, unaware of how right she was. Laura's rebuttal was an enigmatic "Some snakes have diamonds in their heads."

And the money kept rolling in from every side. Laura wanted a mink, while Essie preferred to "make a playground for the neighborhood kids, establish an employment office, set up a day nursery for children of mothers what's working. I'll get me some new clothes in due time."

Once Laura saw that Essie was losing faith in her, she said they'd spend money to bring to town her sixteen-year-old daughter, Marietta (future Broadway songwriter Micki Grant). She knew that that was Essie's Achilles' heel.

There was not only enough money to get Marietta on the premises but also enough to move the church from its storefront to a genuine theater. Laura was thrilled that the marquee that once stated "Lana Turner" now said "Laura Wright Reed." Buddy confided in the audience: "The church racket's got show business beat to hell, but some churches don't have sense enough to be crooked." After all, "the government can't tax church money."

So when Buddy suggested that they announce "lucky numbers from the pulpit," Laura thought it was a splendid idea. She was less thrilled when he began calling Marietta by a term of endearment. "Her name's Marietta, not 'Baby,' " she snarled.

Soon Laura suggested that Marietta's stay become "a little visit." Essie, now experiencing mother-daughter love for the first time in years, wished that Marietta could stay and that Laura would drink less.

"I ain't no saint," Laura admitted. "How good do you want to be? So good you ain't got a dime? You got a daughter to educate."

"I," said Essie, "want other people's daughters to get through school, too."

Marietta was taken with C.J., a church member who was more age-appropriate than Buddy. The devil wouldn't relent, however, and forced himself upon her just as—here's that all-too-convenient device again—Laura walked in. She struggled mightily to deny what she saw.

Act Two began with Buddy giving the audience tips on how to be a good devil: "Just be yourself. Don't pretend to be good." He offered his own résumé as evidence of success: "I wrote *The Carpetbaggers*. I rigged the TV quiz shows."

Marietta denied C. J. sex—until he wrote a beautiful song for her. His success with the young girl incensed Buddy, which brought out C. J.'s wrath, too: "You've turned the temple into a gambling den and that's bad for Harlem. Harlem is the dream of black folks down in the Deep South. And then they come here and sometimes find it's a nightmare. Harlem is full of good people and people trying to be good. Some are already up in the world. Ralph Ellison! Margaret Bonds!"

(What a song this could have been—and should have been.)

Buddy's response was a knockout punch to C. J.'s face in order to impress Marietta. This finally made Laura see how terrible he was.

In a monologue (which should have been a song, too) she imagined a conversation with her mother: "Silk sofa. French chairs. The best drapes money can buy. Ten dollar Scotch! A toast to your daughter Laura! A toast to Miss Bitch!"

Buddy turned out to be more critical. "You been a good ol' wagon, but you done broke down." When he began hitting her, she stabbed him to death and received life imprisonment.

Kerr said that it "has just the wrong number of songs: enough to declare itself as a light entertainment and to keep you from taking its story-line seriously and not enough to make you forget the story-line altogether."

Taubman: "It shifts carelessly from comedy to satire to melodrama to piety." Chapman: "The story is pretty scattery—but this is all right because it does serve to give the singers their cues." Nadel: "Hughes' story-with-song is especially distressing in that the ingredients for a much better play are there."

The most courageous critic was Watts, for Langston Hughes was then a syndicated columnist who was carried by the *Post*. That didn't deter the critic from saying that *Tambourines to Glory* "misses its opportunities to be a fresh and stimulating entertainment with melancholy" and "succeeds only too rarely in catching fire."

The only fire that *Tambourines to Glory* experienced was metaphorical. After a week, it went down in flames.

Four months later came *Sponono*, a collaboration between a white South African playwright and an Indian writer-director. The former was Alan Paton, the noted antiapartheid writer whose 1948 novel *Cry the Beloved Country* became Kurt Weill's final musical, *Lost in the Stars*.

Krishna Shah, twenty-five at the time, would go on to direct films as disparate as *The River Niger* and *Hard Rock Zombies*.

Paton had served as a principal at a prison school in South Africa. As his *Playbill* bio stated, "In ten years Alan Paton transformed the place. The barbed wire vanished and gardens took its place."

That might have been a better story about the reformatory than the one he and Shah decided to tell. Sponono was a young man who was literally holding court and about to pass judgment on Joseph, who'd escaped from the reformatory after stealing a gold watch. Said Sponono, "You know that every time someone runs away, it is harder for the rest of us."

The Principal recommended prison, while a tribal councilor wanted Joseph to stick his arm in a pot of boiling water to retrieve pebbles. The councilor truly believed that if the lad was innocent, he wouldn't be burned; if he was guilty, he would be.

Sponono was inclined to mercy, but his opinion counted for far less, for he'd been an inmate at the school; now that he was about to be released, he'd been given some limited authority by the Principal, who simply wanted to see how he'd handle it.

Sponono's sudden power rankled Walter, another inmate, who called him "the bumsucker" for his reformed ways. Walter said that he needed authority "like shit on my bread."

(Six days after *Sponono* opened, that City Center *West Side Story* revival still had the Jets saying "buggin' " and "Where the devil are they?" as opposed to the words their counterparts on the street would really say. At least *Sponono* used language more appropriate to juvenile delinquents.)

After the trial, Sponono asked the Principal—begged him, really—if he could work full-time in his garden. "If I could stay with you my whole life," he implored, "then I would be safe my whole life."

He wasn't kidding. Just as the audience came to care about Sponono and was impressed with his role as "the protector of the small kids," they learned that he'd been guilty of two counts each of theft and assault, and one count of robbery. "The boy with the silver tongue," as he was described, once had feet of clay.

He still did when dealing with a local girl named Elizabeth. "You're pretty," he said, to which she responded with a realistic "All girls are pretty to you." His rejoinder was that she was special enough for him to want to marry her. "The Principal is begging me to come work for him," he lied.

Elizabeth couldn't overlook his police record and refused. Sponono was furious when he learned that she'd planned to marry Spike, not merely because he was his best friend; Spike was a convicted felon, too.

This led to a downward spiral in which Sponono stole, assaulted, and lied. Spike did all that and more; he tried to rape Elizabeth when she started asking some very level-headed questions about their future.

Twenty performances. If an up-and-coming black actor such as Billy Dee Williams, Paul Winfield, or Louis Gossett Jr. had played Sponono, a run might have been achieved. There simply weren't enough Cocky Tlhotlhalemaje fans out there.

Even when the characters weren't saying words from various African dialects, American audiences might well have been flummoxed. Take one teacher's statement: "Some colored people regard themselves as superior to African people to compensate themselves for being regarded as inferior to white people." Unless theatergoers knew that in South Africa, "colored" (more often, "coloured") was a label for people of mixed ethnic origin, they'd be confused.

McClain bluntly maintained that the problems of South Africa might not interest a Broadway audience because "we have enough troubles on our own."

Only three weeks after he wrote that, Broadway dramatically agreed when James Baldwin's *Blues for Mister Charlie* debuted.

The date was April 23, 1964—the four hundredth anniversary of the day historians accept as Shakespeare's birthday. And *Mister Charlie* had a Bard-sized cast: twenty-five actors, about as many as are needed for *King Lear*.

But Shakespeare, unlike Baldwin, never used the word "motherfucker."

No other Broadway playwright had, either. And while one congregant in *Tambourines to Glory* had referred to Buddy as a "mother fouler" and another in *Sponono* referred to "mofoking," Baldwin dared to eliminate any possible euphemism.

Four years later, "motherfucker" could be heard on the No. 1 record album in the country: *Hair.* Things change quickly.

Some things. Racism hasn't. Compassion seemed to take a giant step forward when the nation heard Martin Luther King's "I Have a Dream" speech on August 28, 1963. But only eighteen days later, on September 15, 1963, there was a larger step backward when the Ku Klux Klan bombed a Birmingham church where four black teenage girls died.

The latter was the reality that Baldwin stressed in his play, which he loosely based on the notorious Emmett Till murder in Mississippi in 1955. The fourteen-year-old black lad may or may not have whistled at a white woman. Nevertheless, three days later when the woman's husband returned home, she told him that Till had, which motivated him and his friends to find the young man and murder him.

Elia Kazan wanted to stage *Charlie* at Lincoln Center, until Baldwin complained that its board had no blacks. He later admitted that Kazan's still-august reputation had cowed him.

Meanwhile, the board at the Actors Studio had approved a workshop, but Lee Strasberg, its artistic director, thought the play so important that he demanded a genuine production. Strasberg made it the fourth of five that the organization would bring to Broadway in a fifteen-month span (after *Strange Interlude, Marathon'33,* and *Baby Want a Kiss* and before *The Three Sisters*). One hit out of five—and a lucky hit at that—made the Actors Studio retreat forever to its converted church on Forty-fourth Street.

Mister Charlie didn't resemble the other four. Theater critic Tom F. Driver of *The Reporter,* a publication that had run many an editorial in favor of civil rights, endorsed the play, but his editor found his review too incendiary and refused to publish it. Driver resigned but received offers to have his review published, both by *The Village Voice* and—here's a surprise—*Christianity and Crisis.*

Baldwin separated the stage into Whitetown and Blacktown, although, he wrote, "the audience should always be aware of the American flag as well as the steeple of the church."

The blacks wouldn't get much protection from either country or church. Baldwin upped the ante on Chekhov's famous belief that a gun introduced early in a play should eventually be used. The first sound heard was a gun-shot, followed by the lights coming up on Lyle Britten, a middle-aged white man with a smoking gun in his hand, and the body of Richard Henry, the young black man he'd just killed.

The first line was equally shocking: Lyle said, "And may every nigger like this nigger end like this nigger—face down in the weeds."

Baldwin was just getting started. Of the play's first thirty-eight words, seven were "nigger." The word would be used repeatedly in the three-act drama.

Richard's father was the Reverend Meridian Henry, who was devastated by his son's murder but feared retaliatory violence. Richard's friend Lorenzo couldn't understand how the pastor and his wife could "sit in this house of this damn almighty God who don't care what happens to nobody unless they're white." He railed against "that damn white God that's been lynching us and burning us and castrating us . . . If I could get my hands on Him, I'd pull Him out of heaven and drag Him through town at the end of a rope."

(Under these circumstances, Baldwin's use of a capital *H* when referring to God was a surprising choice.)

Richard's friend Juanita rebutted, "And then you'd be no better than they are"—a common rationalization from those who have no power. Lorenzo noted that "we've been demonstrating—*non-violently*—for more than a year now," and he hadn't seen any tangible results.

Meridian believed that Parnell James, the editor of the local newspaper, although white, would be brave enough to demand in print that Richard's killer be brought to justice.

Lorenzo: "I don't trust as many people as you trust."

Meridian: "We can't afford to become too distrustful, Lorenzo."

Lorenzo: "We can't afford to become too trusting, either."

All this occurred in fewer than five minutes of stage time.

Parnell—"the editor of a newspaper nobody reads," as he acknowledged—arrived and said that he'd heard a warrant would be issued for Lyle's arrest. But the following scene took the audience to Lyle's house, where the unruffled murderer was shown playing with his infant son. Once his wife, Jo, heard about Richard's fate—and recalled that Lyle hadn't arrived home until four in the morning—she became suspicious that he'd been involved. After all, for the last few weeks, blacks had been boycotting their convenience store, which had made Lyle resentful.

Jo's repeated questions finally made Lyle state that he'd killed Richard in self-defense. "I swear, I don't know what's come over the folks in this town," he complained. "Raising so much fuss about a nigger."

So he felt compelled to add that Richard "went north and got ruined and come back here to make trouble—and they tell me he was a dope fiend, too." He later told friends that "I don't want no big buck nigger lying next to Jo, and that's what this will lead to."

Baldwin dared to talk about the black man's superior-sized organ in quite a few instances, something that had seldom if ever been mentioned on or outside of Broadway. We were about to enter an era when women would finally become less concerned about the size of their breasts but—now that the birth control pill was allowing them to see a man's private parts early and often—men would begin troubling themselves about the size of their penises.

A flashback showed that Richard had been an on-the-rise star at Harlem's Apollo Theater and had come home for a visit. He didn't make his grandmother happy when saying that he didn't believe in God—not since his mother died from a fall down a flight of stairs. Richard believed that she'd been pushed, and was angry that his father never troubled to investigate.

"Whites," Richard said, "are responsible for all the misery I've ever seen. The only way the black man's going to get any power is to drive all the white men into the sea." When his father rebutted, "Son, you're going to make yourself sick with hatred," Richard insisted that his bitter feelings were going to make him *well*. Lyle, he said, "expects us to step off the sidewalk when he comes along."

At a local nightspot, Richard admitted to using drugs, which substantiated some of Lyle's story. As Nadel would notice, Baldwin "no more made the blacks a group of heroes than he has made the whites."

But then Juanita disclosed that Lyle had earlier murdered "Old Bill," another black man, and hadn't even been prosecuted. This happened after Lyle had been consorting with Old Bill's wife, Willa Mae; after her husband discovered their affair, Lyle killed him.

Muttered Richard, "They can rape and kill our women and we can't do nothing. But if we touch one of their dried-up, pale-assed women, we get our nuts cut off."

Richard disclosed that up north he was constantly besieged by white women. "You say black people ain't got no dignity?" he said to his friends. "Man, you ought to watch a white woman when she wants you." He then showed pictures of these women, which made Joel, the roadhouse owner, quite nervous.

Joel's nickname was Papa D., but it could just as easily have been Uncle Tom. He was deferential when Lyle entered, and didn't say a word when Lyle accidentally-on-purpose jostled Juanita when she and Richard were dancing. The tense moment between the two men didn't escalate—not then.

Meanwhile, Meridian was telling Parnell how a black man could embrace what many presumed to be a white God. "Maybe I had to become a Christian to have any dignity at all," he told Parnell. "Since I wasn't a man in men's eyes, I could be a man in the eyes of the Lord."

Even Parnell, the most compassionate white man in town, responded with "The poor whites have been just as victimized in this part of the world as blacks have ever been. We must forget all the past injustice."

Far easier said than done. Such statements made Meridian question if he and Parnell were really friends "or if I'm just your favorite Uncle Tom."

Act Two began with Lyle and Jo's friends dropping by to give the couple an impromptu first-anniversary party. It had been slated for the following night, but the friends feared that Lyle could be taken into custody at any moment.

Lyle was asleep, and Jo urged that they let him rest. Conversation replaced revelry. Lillian said she preferred the era "when things were the way God intended," followed by Susan's insistence that "niggers can't learn like white folks." Reverend Phelps claimed that "blacks have turned away from God." But Baldwin balanced this by having Hazel speak with great affection of her black nanny: "She knew more about me than my own mother and father did."

Susan changed the subject by asking about Parnell: "I wonder if he's sober this morning?" This was the first mention that the man might have a drinking problem, of which the audience had seen no physical evidence. When Parnell arrived—sober—Ellis demanded to "know where you stand."

Parnell fielded the question by telling them to read his newspaper, and they let loose their feelings. Lillian called it a "Communist newspaper," which made Parnell point out that "the father of your faith was a Communist" and that "we know he did some drinking."

Susan bluntly responded by saying that Parnell was "worse than a nigger." George insisted, "White men come before niggers! They *got* to." When Parnell asked "Why?" Baldwin strangely tabled the question by having Lyle suddenly enter from his nap.

"I ain't worried," he said. "I know the people in this town is with me." Ellis was concerned, however, because "they're trying to force us to put niggers on the jury."

A hasty change of subject only brought them to an equally incendiary topic: sex between whites and blacks. Lyle said he was repulsed by the thought of a white woman with a black man. If what Juanita had said earlier was true, however, Lyle certainly was guilty of a double standard.

After the party ended, Jo asked Parnell point-blank if Lyle had had a relationship with Willa Mae. Parnell avoided the question by admitting to his own relationship with a young black woman. Although they'd both appreciated and could discuss Stendahl's *The Red and the Black,* they couldn't sit together when they went to a movie. "And I loved her!" he admitted.

Despite this conversational detour, Jo said she'd always suspected that Lyle had feelings for Willa Mae that he'd never had for her. Lyle later admitted it—albeit to Parnell. And, oh, wasn't he the altruist—for when referring to Old Bill, he said, "I was doing his work for him." Soon came the disclosure that Papa D. was the one who had informed Old Bill—but that certainly wasn't out of altruism; he'd wanted Willa Mae for himself.

Lyle was more concerned with the here-and-now and "that crazy boy who got himself killed." He put his hand on Parnell's shoulder and said, "I know you ain't gonna let nothin' happen to me," before telling his side of the story. Richard had come into the store at a busy time and flashed a twenty-dollar bill when buying two twenty-cent Cokes. Lyle and Jo said they didn't have change, and Richard taunted them for not having very much money. "You get your black ass out of here," Lyle demanded, spurring Richard to taunt, "You white motherfucker, you don't even own twenty dollars."

Lyle brought out a hammer, but the lad wrestled it out of his hands. "Now who you think is the better man?" he demanded to know. "Ha-ha! The master race! You let me in that tired white chick's drawers," he said, pointing to Jo, "she'll know who's the master."

"Niggers was laughing at me for days," Lyle muttered, implying that he had to avenge himself.

Parnell left to attend the funeral, where Meridian delivered an impassioned speech to God ("What shall I tell the children?"). Kerr wrote that "for all the vehemence the actor pours into it, he states nothing that we have not clearly deduced from the action preceding it."

But it was what a father and minister would say at a funeral. Kerr complained that Baldwin "overwrites.... Having lifted his angry, candid, declaiming voice, he cannot cut off its sound when the point has been made."

Or did Baldwin feel that didacticism was the only way to get across his message of how American whites had victimized American blacks for over three hundred years?

Act Three took place at the trial, where Jo testified in her husband's defense, saying that Richard "wasn't one of our colored people. He said all kinds of things, dirty things, like—well—just like I might have been a colored girl." Imagine!

A flashback showed Lyle preparing Papa D. for the trial: "You don't say the right thing, nigger, I'll blow your brains out, too."

And yet, Papa D. found the courage to tell the truth. Lorenzo and Juanita had their day in court, with the latter eloquently telling of Richard's last moments with her. Even Kerr, who had problems with the play, did acknowledge that Diana Sands, the original Beneatha in *A Raisin in the Sun,* made the most of her opportunity: "I know of no other single sequence as powerful in New York today."

The white jury found Lyle not guilty.

Watts said that "few plays have a deeper core of furious resentment and completely unrelenting resentment and contempt." McClain preferred to say, "It proves very little that all of us aren't aware of—and ashamed of."

Taubman sympathized the most. His review began: "James Baldwin has written a play with fires of fury in its belly, tears of anguish in its eyes, and a roar of protest in its throat." The play, he said, "throbs with fierce energy and passion. It is like a thunderous battle cry" and "brings eloquence to one of the most monstrous themes of our era." Baldwin, he wrote, "seeks to express the outraged thoughts and emotions that blazed within seemingly placid Negroes for so many deceptive years."

Shouldn't such an endorsement from the town's most powerful critic result in a run longer than 148 performances? But if many whites in 1964 didn't want blacks living next door to them, they certainly didn't want to sit next to them at a play that, frankly, told the truth.

As Chapman reported, "Last night's integrated audience was, judging from its cheers, not on the side of Mister Charlie." Early in the run, many white attendees must have squirmed as the accusations and proof poured from the stage while the blacks around them nodded or shouted their agreement. Late in the run, fewer white attendees chose to have the experience.

"Never before had I seen a Broadway theater half-full of Negroes," Kenneth Tynan noted in his review. Later on, estimates had blacks making up 80 percent of the audience.

Why didn't the blacks attend *Tambourines to Glory* or *Sponono*? To say that the former was too trivial and the latter too remote may only be part of the explanation; so might the amount of money each had to spend on advertising. *Blues for Mister Charlie* opened the debate on the issues that blacks most wanted to see addressed. When the play opened, the Civil Rights Act wasn't yet the law of the land; by the time it closed in August, however, the bill had passed.

After Cheryl Crawford, the Actors Studio executive producer, announced that she was closing the play, Baldwin threatened to sue. He never did. Crawford insisted that she'd done what she could, including getting an endorsement from Roy Wilkins, the executive director of the NAACP, and enticing Nelson Rockefeller's daughters, Mary and Ann, to donate $10,000.

All was not in vain. The interest blacks showed in attending a play that was relevant to their lives encouraged Douglas Turner Ward, Robert Hooks, and Gerald S. Krone to start the Negro Ensemble Company three years later. The troupe, like so many other not-for-profit theaters, has endured some hard times, but unlike so many others, it is still with us.

How much *Blues for Mister Charlie* helped in terms of eliminating racial violence is another matter. On July 13, 2013—fifty years to the day since Strasberg made the decision to mount *Mister Charlie*—George Zimmerman, a white Southerner who'd claimed self-defense in his murder of unarmed black teenager Trayvon Martin, was acquitted of all charges. Lyle Britten again emerged victorious.

There was another minority that was still years away from liberation, let alone acceptance.

    1. Joyous and lively; merry; happy; light-hearted
    2. Bright, brilliant
    3. Given to social life and pleasures
    4. Wanton, licentious

Such were the definitions for the word "gay" in the 1964 edition of *Webster's New Twentieth Century Dictionary*.

Notice that no mention was made of "homosexual."

The 1963–64 critics agreed with definition 1. Taubman's review of *Any Wednesday* stated that the cast performed "with gay, dry lightness." Chapman's plot synopsis of *The Rehearsal* told of a count and countess who have a mistress and a lover—"and are ever so gay and French about it." Watts mentioned that *Rugantino* contained "a gay little jest."

Of course, in *Luther,* a sixteenth-century cardinal was implying nothing sexual about young Martin when he called him "as gay and sprightly as a young bull." Even in *The Passion of Josef D.,* when Nadya noticed that there were "huge crowds on the Nevsky, curiously gay," she was using an apt term for 1923. Osborne and Chayefsky didn't worry that audiences would misconstrue the word or greet it with snickers.

Likewise, in the 1963–64 shows set in "Time: Now," we had the father in *Semi-Detached* knock his daughter's beau as "a gay Lothario." In *The Public Eye,* when Belinda told Julian about her husband and said that he was "really gay," she was not referencing his secret other life; she meant how joyous-and-lively he'd been before they'd settled into the doldrums of marriage.

Were Broadway's playwrights unaware of a more sexually charged meaning for "gay"? Of course not. But they knew what the word still meant to much of the theatergoing public.

Some playwrights would acknowledge homosexuality with a passing nod, never making it the main event of their works.

In *Marathon '33,* June Havoc had Jean speak of a former colleague whom she regarded as "the best female impersonator on the boards," only to hear from one marathon dancer, "He's a swish" and "a faggot."

Havoc was replicating a long-passed era, but 1963–64 plays set in the here-and-now weren't above using the term. In *Nobody Loves an Albatross,* after Nat made many remarks about a female comedy writer's overly masculine qualities, he blatantly called her "a fag." Arthur Miller wasn't above having his Maggie note that "they gave me a fag" as a director, one who made "faggy jokes." Lest that seem to be an isolated comment, Maggie was soon criticizing Quentin's wardrobe: "Fags wear pants like that."

"You calling me a fag now?" Quentin said, barely controlling his voice.

Maggie's rejoinder: "I've known fags and some of them didn't even know themselves that they were."

Sidney Michaels could have addressed the many gay encounters that scholars of Dylan Thomas allege that he had, but he didn't mention any such incident in *Dylan.* What he wrote instead was a scene in which an intoxicated Dylan told a group of party attendees, "I'm a Communist! I'm a Puritan! I'm a drunk! And I'm heterosexual!"

Did the poet protest too much? "I love Caitlin, but I love Annabelle," he said to his fellow poet Brinnin, referring to a woman he'd just met. "I love them all. I love women. I love men. I love you. I love my shipmate." By stressing everyone, Dylan was simultaneously saying everything and nothing about his sexuality.

Once for the Asking had the line "I'm the first fairy ever to live on Long Island." This offense was more benign, for it was said by that "Good Fairy" who'd magically appeared in the house next door. However, Kerr reported that actress Dorothy Sands stood there "beaming, waiting for that big ghostly laugh" that never arrived. It was another miscalculation from playwright Owen G. Arno.

In *Baby Want a Kiss,* Emil urged Edward to feel his muscles. When Edward abstained courteously, Emil groused, "Come on, I'm not going to grab you. I'm no fairy. I hate fairies." But he continued to make so many vague overtures to Edward ("I could kiss you on the mouth but it wouldn't mean anything") that audiences could see what was on his mind.

Meanwhile, in *But for Whom Charlie,* a woman assumed that the foundation head was "a pansy," but executive director Charlie pooh-poohed the notion. A novelist who said of a colleague "He was perhaps the gayest member of the international homosexual set" had just come from the man's funeral. Four years later, Mart Crowley would say in his *The Boys in the Band,* "Not all faggots bump themselves off at the end of the play," but in this era, playwrights were still fond of doing it for them.

Although this season isn't that far away from June 28, 1969, when the police raid at the Stonewall Inn in Greenwich Village led to riots and the gay rights movement, most homosexuals still had to be closeted on Broadway in 1963–64.

Jonathan in *Oh Dad, Poor Dad* was never established as gay, but many would assume that his dead father wasn't the only one in the closet. Whether or not his domineering mother was responsible would be best answered by psychoanalysts; however, that he killed the attractive young woman who desperately wanted to bed him suggested that he wasn't inclined toward heterosexual lovemaking.

In *The Student Gypsy,* the character named Muffin, played by Dom DeLuise, provided comic relief. But as in all operettas, the fey man's sexual identity went politely unmentioned. No one else onstage was either rude enough or brave enough to ask about it.

In *The Ballad of the Sad Café,* if Cousin Lymon expressed anything more than hero worship for the big butch Marvin, Edward Albee didn't tell his audience about it. That didn't stop Taubman from inferring that the two experienced "unnatural love."

In recent years, although President James Buchanan—the nation's only unmarried chief executive—has often been alleged to be homosexual, that wasn't mentioned in *The White House.* You think that Helen Hayes would have had anything to do with the show if our nation's fifteenth president had been outed?

For the first couple of months of the season, *No Strings,* a still-playing 1961-1962 hit, had a Richard Rodgers lyric that proclaimed that romantically speaking, "women are stuck with men" for they "just have Hobson's Choice"—that is, no choice at all.

Well, no, Dick; women do have another option. You just didn't want to think about it, that's all.

Still, the love that dared not speak its name was occasionally spoken. In the case of *A Case of Libel,* stony silence followed the mention that Robert Sloane had once been engaged in "a desperate battle to prove his client wasn't homosexual."

More often than not, however, the references were oblique. In *Barefoot in the Park,* an aghast Paul told Corie about their neighbors: "Mr. and Mrs. J. Bosco are a lovely young couple who just happen to be of the same sex and no one knows which one that is."

Imagine!

Laurette Harrington, who made Sammy run after he showed up at her bungalow to have sex, was vague on why she was breaking the date.

But she did say she was meeting a woman.

An aviatrix.

Named Babe.

There were some daring moments. The executive director of *But for Whom Charlie* did say, "What are the most successful marriages you know? . . . Between homosexuals. Absolutely happy." In *Sponono,* the title character was accused by school bully Walter of having sex with a younger boy. Sponono hotly denied it. Was it a case of projection? The stage directions stated that Walter was "a seducer of small children" and that he "had his eye on Ha'penny." Did *Sponono*'s two playwrights mean that he was a nonsexual Pied Piper or a pedophile? That he later approached Ha'penny and said, "I've got sweets for you," would suggest the latter.

In *Chips with Everything,* an officer put his hand on an enlisted man's knee. The private softly but courageously pleaded, "Don't do that, please, sir." The officer pulled rank and sternly told his subordinate not to mention this conversation to anyone. Playwright Wesker didn't mention it again, either. This truly was the era of "Don't ask, don't tell."

The most blatant scene came from Terence Rattigan's *Man and Boy.* Charles

Boyer played Gregor Anontescu, a character loosely based on Ivar Kreuger, who began his first company when he was twenty-eight, unaware that his life was more than half over.

For after building an empire of more than four hundred companies, Kreuger was accused of financial irregularities that had cost investors millions, and committed suicide at fifty-two. Kreuger, then, was the Bernie Madoff of his day (which is one reason *Man and Boy* was revived on Broadway in 2011).

Whether Kreuger or Madoff ever attempted what Gregor did has never been alleged. Rattigan's plot stated that Gregor would be saved if a merger could be arranged. When it appeared it would fail, Gregor noted that one company's head was a "silly, pale-faced fairy." To get him to make the merger, he would offer him his handsome grown son in return.

Although neither son nor executive agreed, the situation had to unnerve some of the 1963 audience, which kept *Man and Boy* from making it into 1964. At fifty-four performances, it was Rattigan's shortest-running play of his last eight Broadway productions, dating back more than nineteen years.

By the time that it was revived in 2011, the landscape had greatly changed. In 1983, Harvey Fierstein's *Torch Song Trilogy* surprised Broadway with its long-run success and its Best Play Tony. Since then, eight other plays with at least one prominent gay character have won the Tony for Best Play. As for Best Musical, a great step forward was taken by Lee Roy Reams in *Applause*, playing Margo Channing's assistant as a human being first and foremost who just happened to be homosexual. Since *Applause*'s 1970 victory, nine Best Musicals have had characters who were out or damn close to it.

Finally, there was a sketch in the 1962–63 revue *Beyond the Fringe* that was retained for the updated *Beyond the Fringe 1964*. Four fey and effeminate actors were seen talking about fashions while they were preparing to film a TV commercial; once they were in their costumes, in front of the cameras, and playing seamen, they suddenly were so butch that each could have been called a Quinn Martin Production.

What's most interesting from a twenty-first-century perspective is that none of the four fops said a word about musicals. The erroneous belief that musicals were the exclusive province of gays wouldn't take hold for some years. In 1963–64, musicals were still considered the domain of the upper middle class (and higher) with decidedly heterosexual inclinations.

CHAPTER EIGHT

✳

The Recordings

Billboard, the bible of the recording field, was published every Saturday. And given that June 1, 1963, was a Saturday, it certainly got the 1963–64 Broadway season off to a great start.

The front-page lead story said that Jule Styne and Lester Osterman had signed a $1 million deal with ABC-Paramount Records to record the three upcoming musicals that these two would produce:

A Girl to Remember, which we've already seen as *Fade Out—Fade In.*

The Ghost Goes West, with music by Styne, lyrics by his son Stanley—but no mention of a bookwriter (or Christopher Plummer in the lead).

Mrs. A., an adaptation of the Gertrude Lawrence biography of the same name by Richard Aldrich, her second husband, which would reunite the *Kiss Me, Kate* team: book by Sam and Bella Spewack and score by Cole Porter.

One out of three isn't bad. *Ghost* never happened, and *Mrs. A.* turned out to be wishful thinking, since Porter was only seventeen months away from death and the Spewacks were never to complete another show.

But ABC-Paramount did record *Fade Out—Fade In,* and at the time was mighty glad to have it. Back then, recording companies often engaged in fierce bidding wars to land the rights to issue a show's original cast album.

(Tell that to *Café Crown.*)

To be fair, *Double Dublin,* a low-profile, four-person Irish revue with traditional songs, didn't get a cast album, either. No surprise; you could count the number of performances that *Double Dublin* played on one of Mickey Mouse's hands: four.

But every other 1963–64 musical got an album—and far more often than not, an investment from a record company hot to do it. *Rugantino*'s Italian cast album was released here by Warner Bros., which had invested $100,000. The recording included a handsome 12" x 12", 36-page booklet with Alfred Drake's entire English translation.

As we've seen, Columbia didn't disclose how much it put into *Anyone Can Whistle*, but it did make public that it invested $150,000 in *What Makes Sammy Run?*, $297,000 in *The Girl Who Came to Supper*, and for *Here's Love* a whopping $375,000—the most it ponied up for any show that season.

(Some may wonder how *Here's Love* producer Stuart Ostrow even had the nerve to go to Columbia, given that the company had given him $400,000 for his last project, *We Take the Town*, which certainly didn't take Broadway, because it closed in Philadelphia. But such chutzpah is what makes a good producer.)

The big surprise is that Columbia didn't record *Funny Girl*; after all, it starred the label's most prominent up-and-coming artist. But before Streisand was signed, Capitol Records was already negotiating to invest $200,000 in the show.

Luckily for Capitol, Streisand had a contract that allowed her to record a cast album for another label. This wasn't the case in 1950 when RCA Victor had invested in *Call Me Madam*, which allowed the company to record the show but not its star; Ethel Merman had a contract with Decca. So Merman made her own album of the songs, and RCA brought in Dinah Shore to play Merman's role with the rest of the cast in place. Such a situation happened with the recordings of the *Pal Joey* revival, the *Porgy and Bess* soundtrack, and even *Oh, Captain!*

Luckily, this bureaucratic problem was solved by 1963–64. If it hadn't been, we shudder to think which female recording artist in Capitol's stable would have been Fanny Brice on the near-original cast album.

June Christy?

Nancy Wilson?

Cilla Black?

(It was a little early for Mrs. Miller.)

Funny Girl with Streisand became Capitol's biggest-selling original cast album. That must have taken some of the sting out of its having invested in *Zenda*.

RCA Victor executives must have wished they had invested more than a mere $70,000 in *Dolly*. On the other hand, they had to be satisfied that they received $67,000 on their $50,000 investment in *110 in the Shade*.

But RCA Victor lost all $49,000 in *Foxy* and made no album. Collectors had to wait more than a dozen years for a *Foxy* recording, after record producer Bruce Yeko secured a tape recording that had been surreptitiously made during a performance. He transferred it to vinyl, making an "original cast album" with woeful sound that was obstructed by audience applause, laughter, comments, and burps (and worse). "I made three hundred copies," Yeko said, "and it took me thirty years to sell them."

As for *Jennie*, Richard Halliday, ever protective of his wife, Mary Martin, wouldn't disclose whether RCA had put up everything, nothing, or something in between.

Even some plays received original cast albums. Caedmon recorded *After the Fall* on four long-playing records; Columbia issued *Dylan* and *The Subject Was Roses* each on three discs and Burton's *Hamlet* on four, and signed a contract to record *The Deputy*, although it didn't get around to that one. As a result, 1963–64 saw not only three of its musicals' Tony winners captured for all time—Channing, Cassidy, and O'Shea—but three of its play winners as well: Guinness, Cronyn, and Loden.

For those who didn't have four hours for *Hamlet,* one disc that featured the play's greatest hits was also made available; remarkably, it stayed on the charts for fourteen weeks. Columbia even released Burton's take on the "To be, or not to be" soliloquy on a 45 rpm single that made its way into some of the city's jukeboxes.

Musicals weren't solely represented by original cast recordings. The Living Strings did an album that shared songs from *Here's Love, 110 in the Shade,* and even *The Student Gypsy.* Frank Chacksfield's orchestra devoted an entire LP to *Here's Love,* which included the song "Dear Mr. Santa Claus" that was subsequently cut from the show. In 1963–64, the excitement over a Broadway musical was so palpable that many artists recorded the scores during the show's out-of-town tryout, sometimes resulting in songs that would only be heard in Philly, Boston, or Baltimo'. When pop artists included show songs on their albums, they proudly followed the name of each selection with "from the musical [name]" on both the record jacket and the label.

RCA had Jesse Pearson, whom they signed after he'd appeared as Conrad on their *Bye Bye Birdie* soundtrack album, record *Foxy*'s "Talk to Me, Baby." Frank Sinatra did the same on his Reprise label, too, proving that even if the show's cast album belonged to a rival company, a singer would record one of its songs if he liked it or its writer(s) enough. And Johnny Mercer had been awfully good to Sinatra via "Too Marvelous for Words," "Blues in the Night," and "That Old Black Magic." Sinatra was probably most grateful for "One for My Baby (and One More for the Road)"; that alone would be enough for him to do one more Mercer.

Sinatra's "Talk to Me, Baby" would reach No. 81 on the charts—because the song on the *other* side, "Stay with Me" from the film *The Cardinal*, was the one that people requested and bought. "Talk to Me, Baby" just went along for the ride.

Similarly, Petula Clark on Warner Bros. recorded "You'd Better Love Me" from ABC-Paramount's *High Spirits* and saw the record sell over three million copies—because the megahit "Downtown" was on the other side. We'll never know how many even turned over the 45 and listened to the Martin-Gray song.

Martin Denny on Liberty did "Everything Beautiful Happens at Night" from *110 in the Shade;* Kaye Ballard on Roulette recorded "Here and Now" and "I Remember Him" from *The Girl Who Came to Supper.* But for the most part, singles of show songs were recorded by pop singers who were under contract to the record company that had the cast album rights. Hence, Ed Ames covered "My Love Is Yours" and "Somewhere" from *The Student Gypsy.*

An edited version of Carol Burnett and Tiger Haynes's rendition of "You Mustn't Be Discouraged" from the actual *Fade Out—Fade In* cast album was released by ABC Paramount as a single, too. All this, even as "rock 'n' roll"—as rock was then called—dominated the singles market. Record company brass had to be surprised when kids pushed Barbra Streisand's "People" to No. 4. They had to be absolutely astonished when teens helped Louis Armstrong's *Hello, Dolly!* to reach No. 1.

It wasn't *Dolly*'s only No. 1 showing; it hit the top of the bestselling long-playing records, too. For a few of the weeks that it reigned, *Funny Girl* was No. 2.

This would be, however, the last time that recordings of two Broadway musicals would occupy the top spots.

Let's move ahead almost twenty years to the January 29, 1983, *Billboard.* That issue reflected on "The Top 20 Original Cast Albums of the Last 20 Years," starting in January 1962. It ranked each record according to the highest position that each reached on the charts, and how many weeks it stayed on the Top 200.

> *Hair* (1968) reached No. 1, stayed for 151 weeks.
> *Hello, Dolly!* (1964) reached No. 1, stayed 90 weeks.
> *Funny Girl* (1964) reached No. 2, stayed 51 weeks.
> *Stop the World—I Want to Get Off* (1962) reached No. 3, stayed 76 weeks.
> *Oliver!* (1963) reached No. 4, stayed 99 weeks.
> *No Strings* (1962) reached No. 5, stayed 62 weeks.
> *Fiddler on the Roof* (1964) reached No. 7, stayed 206 weeks.
> *Dreamgirls* (1981) reached No. 11, stayed 29 weeks.
> *Mr. President* (1962) reached No. 14, stayed 24 weeks.
> *She Loves Me* (1963) reached No. 15, stayed 17 weeks.
> *All American* (1962) reached No. 21, stayed 16 weeks.
> *Mame* (1966) reached No. 23, stayed 66 weeks.
> *What Makes Sammy Run?* (1964) reached No. 28, stayed 14 weeks.
> *Man of La Mancha* (1965) reached No. 31, stayed 167 weeks.
> *Jesus Christ Superstar* (1971) reached No. 31, stayed 10 weeks.
> *The Girl Who Came to Supper* (1963) reached No. 33, stayed 14 weeks.
> *Godspell* (1971) reached No. 34, stayed 61 weeks.
> *Golden Boy* (1964); reached No. 36, stayed 16 weeks.
> *Cabaret* (1966) reached No. 37, stayed 39 weeks.
> *110 in the Shade* (1963) reached No. 37, stayed 15 weeks.

Of the Top 20, more than half—eleven—opened in little more than a two-year span—from *No Strings* (March 15, 1962) through *Funny Girl* (March 26, 1964).

Of those eleven, five were onstage money-losers: *What Makes Sammy Run?, She Loves Me, Mr. President, The Girl Who Came to Supper,* and *All American.* A sixth, *110 in the Shade,* as we've seen, barely broke even.

And yet, the record-buying public was interested enough in seeing what was happening on Broadway that these also-rans did better on record than on stage.

Golden Boy and *Fiddler on the Roof,* both 1964–65 entries, saw the latter poised to pass eventual musical long-run champ *Dolly.* But *Fiddler*'s best week was still six places lower than *Dolly*'s peak, although it did stay on the charts more than twice as long.

In 1965–66, *Man of La Mancha* saw a similar fate: Thirty-first place was the best it could do, but it stayed around for a longer period of time than the big sellers used to—167 weeks—so there was some consolation there. *Mame* peaked a little higher at No. 23, but sixty-six weeks was substantially lower than *La Mancha*'s achievement. The following season's *Cabaret* didn't fare as well as *Mame* and *La Mancha.*

The implication is that people were still buying cast albums, but they were taking their sweet time in doing it. Longer runs but fewer sales suggested that people purchased a recording of a musical after they'd seen the show and not until, while in previous times they'd bought the latest original cast album just to see what Broadway was offering now.

True, *Hair* in 1967–68 eclipsed them all, but it wasn't show music as the world had known it—which was also true of *Godspell* and *Jesus Christ Superstar.* Both of those opened in 1971, and would represent the final albums of the decade to reach the Top 20. That means that such big hits as *Grease, Annie, Pippin, The Wiz, The Magic Show, Ain't Misbehavin', The Best Little Whorehouse in Texas, Evita,* and, yes, *A Chorus Line* didn't make the cut. Thus, the appearance of *Dreamgirls,* a 1981 show, is all the more impressive.

One reason for the shift was, of course, the baby boomers. In the '50s, the postwar generation had relied on allowances from their parents to buy records. Singles at eighty-nine cents each were all the kids could afford in their tween and high school years.

By the middle of 1964, however, many boomer teens had reached working age; those still living at home suddenly had disposable income. A few had enough to buy the new Ford Mustang, but most could only afford to buy monaural $3.98 long-playing records or $4.98 stereo ones.

Original cast albums usually went for $4.98 in mono and $5.98 in stereo. Some with elaborate packaging listed for $5.98 mono and $6.98 stereo— such as *Here's Love* with its gatefold cover and extra page inside replete with color photos.

Kids weren't counting the days until *Rugantino* was in the stores. They bought the style of music that in 1954 was thought to be a passing fad when "Rock Around the Clock" debuted. No, that sound was still very much alive and very well as 1963–64 started. Needless to say, it still is.

A small piece of that shift was the result of an event that occurred during the 1963–64 season.

CHAPTER NINE

*

The Great Parade Pauses

The saddest parade of the season took place on Monday, November 25, 1963, some 250 miles away from Broadway.

It was more of a procession, of course, for it was the funeral of John Fitzgerald Kennedy. The thirty-fifth president of the United States had been assassinated the previous Friday, and now his body would be taken from the United States Capitol in Washington to Arlington National Cemetery in Virginia.

The headline writer at *Variety* might have been more delicate and not chosen "All Show Biz Dims in Grief." This was not the time for *Varietese* slang.

And what of its reporter who wrote, "Show business closing down Friday night as it did of its own volition was doing what comes naturally"? He could have been more judicious, too; considering what had happened, a line from a show whose title sported the word "gun" was inappropriate.

Still, the reporter's choosing a line from a Broadway musical was apt. Kennedy's interest in the art form was public knowledge. When he went to see *How to Succeed,* his picture made the cover of the *Daily News* above a caption that read "He needs a lesson?"

The president so desperately wanted to see *Here's Love* during its Washington tryout that he told producer-director Stuart Ostrow's wife that he'd allow her to sit in his much-photographed rocking chair if she'd provide him with tickets. Both parties got what they wanted.

When *Mr. President* was choosing cities in which to try out, one reason it chose Washington was because of Kennedy. All right, he didn't show up on opening night until the second act, but instead watched the heavyweight championship fight between Floyd Patterson and Sonny Liston. That fact may make Kennedy appear to be a parvenu, but it could also suggest what an in-touch theatergoer he was; he had undoubtedly heard word from the Boston tryout that the show stank.

And then there was *Camelot*—and not merely because Kennedy loved it so much that he invited Richard Burton to the White House. That Kennedy's administration came to be associated with a musical is one of the greatest honors to be bestowed on Broadway.

A week after the assassination, Jacqueline Kennedy gave an interview to noted historian Theodore H. White. While musing about the human side of the president, she said, "The song he loved most came at the very end of this record, the last side of *Camelot*, sad *Camelot*: 'Don't let it be forgot, that once there was a spot, for one brief shining moment that was known as Camelot.'"

Since then, of course, "Camelot" has been the unofficial name of the Kennedy administration.

That all Broadway shows resumed performances literally twenty-four hours after the president had been declared dead now seems terribly insensitive. Television's regular programming came to a standstill in order to cover any possibility of breaking news, and NBC's plan to give the television premiere of *Singin' in the Rain* in its *Saturday Night at the Movies* series was obviously preempted. The film had to wait until December 7—another ominous date in American history.

Until Carol Burnett's pregnancy had forced a postponement, *Fade Out—Fade In* had scheduled an opening date of Saturday, November 23, 1963. Had she not been with child, would the show have debuted that night given the events of the previous day? While Broadway did resume performances on that Saturday, the pageantry of an opening night would have seemed too celebratory; the opening surely would have been postponed.

That Saturday afternoon, before the matinee of *Jennie*, Mary Martin came out in front of the curtain and confessed that the company was reluctant to do the show, but they felt they had to carry on so that the audience would have a temporary distraction.

Perhaps the crowd did—until the second act's snazzy cheer-up song "High Is Better than Low."

At any given performance, the dull *Jennie* might well have lost its audience by Act Two, but imagine what the first postassassination attendees felt when hearing the perky advice "Joy is better than woe, glad is better than sad...up is better than down, smile is better than frown." And to think this was followed by a veritable hymn called "The Night May Be Dark" that included the lyric "Oh Lord, there's so much to be thankful for"— sung more than once.

June Havoc, about to start previews of *Marathon '33,* had a line in her script that referred to Giuseppe Zangara's assassination attempt on Franklin Delano Roosevelt. She cut it, although she reinserted it when Dramatists Play Service published the script in 1969.

Some shows that were already running had to make some adjustments. The title song of *Here's Love,* which as we've seen urged peaceful coexistence between antagonists, originally suggested that love be dispensed from "JFK to U.S. Steel." It referenced the 1962 war that Kennedy had waged with the steel companies. He'd hoped that they'd give their employees a raise, which they did—2.5 percent—before raising the cost of steel by 3.5 percent. Willson changed the lyric to "C.I.A. to U.S. Steel," which didn't make much sense, but he had to come up with three syllables in a hurry.

The still-running 1962–63 hit *Stop the World—I Want to Get Off* had Ginnie Romaine, a woefully uninformed "All-American," sing, "I think that Mr. Eisenhower is absolutely swell"—which was followed by the musical director's judgmentally tapping his baton on his podium. The audience wasn't to hear what he said to her, but they could hear her blithely say to him, "Oh, really? When?" She then unabashedly returned to the song and sang the same line of music with the lyric "I think that Mr. Kennedy is absolutely swell."

That Friday, Anthony Newley quickly changed the lyric to the apolitical "I think push-button telephones are absolutely swell." Newley then turned to memorializing Kennedy by writing "Lament for a Hero," not for a show, but from grief. The B-section went "The world was stunned and silent on that sad November day when a mad assassin's bullet took that gallant heart away."

Far more affected was Noël Coward, whose *The Girl Who Came to Supper* was then in Philadelphia. He had to spend all Friday afternoon and evening writing a new opening number. No longer could the show start with Grand Duke Charles singing "Long Live the King—If He Can"—especially because the third and fourth lines of the song had the Regent baldly state, "My loving people cultivate an impulse to assassinate."

Under pressure, Coward could do no better than to borrow the melody of his "Countess Mitzi," a song he'd written twenty-five years earlier for the London musical *Operette*. He turned it into "My Family Tree" while retaining verbatim thirty-three of its fifty-eight lines. The new lyric had the Duke admit that his family tree was "a little shady." Witty as that was, a song that has a character proclaim "This is who I am" is never as compelling as one that has him stress a stressful situation.

As we've seen, *The Girl Who Came to Supper* was doomed anyway. A story involving a British coronation of more than a halfcentury earlier turned out to be of less interest to the public than four new British singers.

On November 29, 1963—the same day of that Jacqueline Kennedy–Theodore H. White interview—the Beatles released a recording of "I Want to Hold Your Hand" in England. On January 18, 1964—two days after *Dolly* had opened—it was brought to the United States. On February 1, it reached No. 1, paving the way for the group's live television debut eight days later.

Musical theater enthusiasts would like to think that everyone who watched *The Ed Sullivan Show* on Sunday, February 9, 1964, tuned in to see the cast of *Oliver!* sing two songs or Tessie O'Shea do a medley (but not the one from *The Girl Who Came to Supper*; she'd already performed that on the show seven weeks earlier). Nevertheless, even the most militant Broadway fan had to admit that fifty-three million—some say as many as seventy-four million—turned in to see John, Paul, George, and Ringo.

"But," said theatrical agent Lionel Larner, who was in the theater that night, "the Beatles were very excited at the prospect of meeting Tessie O'Shea. They'd all grown up hearing her on the radio, and couldn't wait to shake hands with her. For the rest of her life, all her press kits contained a picture of the Beatles looking thrilled that Tessie was deigning to speak with them."

The "Fab Four" did have some knowledge of musicals, for on their first album and on the *Sullivan Show*, they performed the only show song that they would ever record: "Till There Was You" from *The Music Man*. While it received screams from the many teens in the house, the decibels were much higher for "I Want to Hold Your Hand."

How did a song with this lyric do so well in 1964? After all, male teenagers of the baby boomer generation were well past telling girls "I want to hold your hand." They'd *already* held hands and had long moved on to other parts of girls' bodies (or they'd at least attempted or implored to).

Of course, the teen girls were the group's biggest fans. Still, plenty of boys adopted Beatles haircuts in early 1964. Some didn't get haircuts at all, ushering in an important component of the hippie era.

Simply put, the young people of America needed something—*anything*—to pick up their spirits and to replace their youthful president. The guys who wore strange haircuts and lapel-less jackets might have had a harder time of it in America if the kids hadn't lost Kennedy.

One piece of evidence that the Beatles started out as a for-kids-only phenomenon can be supported by a film that debuted in late 1964: *Goldfinger.* James Bond, aghast at the way his latest female conquest settles for Dom Perignon at the incorrect serving temperature, says, "That's as bad as listening to the Beatles without earmuffs." And this from a super-cool dude who was British, yet!

Television helped rock music in another way. One reason that the guitar has had a sixty-year stranglehold on pop music is that it's a telegenic instrument. As a singer strums, he can look at his audience. With a piano—the previous champ—a player had to turn around on his bench to face the audience while keeping his hands on the keyboard. This didn't make nearly as much of a connection with the crowd.

In the days when radio reigned supreme, this wasn't an issue. When talkies came in, the camera could give us a close-up of the pianist at his keyboard. And while this was true of television, too, it still wasn't as immediate as a guitarist singing full-face *directly to you* while playing his instrument.

So while fans of Broadway musicals were hoping that Dorothy Fields would go on forever, the nation would become more interested in "Strawberry Fields Forever." The original cast album of *She Loves Me* had much less impact than the Beatles' "She Loves You." Broadway's Great Parade on the Hit Parade had been slowly waning through the early days of rock, but now its fate had been sealed. Every rock hit had been a nail in the coffin, but the Beatles provided the burial plot. How apt that the final song of the No. 1 album *Hello, Dolly!* was "So Long, Dearie": what Broadway was saying to the pop music charts.

Yes, *Man of La Mancha*'s "The Impossible Dream" in 1965 fit the template of the hit show tune that was full of optimism, but such songs weren't coming along as speedily as they once did. What's more, "The Impossible Dream" never had a recording associated with a single artist, unlike Johnny Mathis/"Small World," The Four Lads/"Standing on the Corner," and Anthony Newley/ "What Kind of Fool Am I?" And while Judy Collins would make "Send In the Clowns" into a well-known song—as Sammy Davis Jr. would do for "I've Got to Be Me"—both shows from which they sprang (*A Little Night Music* and *Golden Rainbow*) were long closed when the songs became hits. Critics of musicals love to say that Broadway is behind the times, but pop music was way behind in recognizing the hit-song potential of these numbers.

The film version of *Bye Bye Birdie* was released in April 1963. The "preview of coming attractions," as a trailer was known in those days, reveals that excerpts from eight of the dozen songs were shown. Nearly forty years later, when *Chicago* (finally) made it to the screen, the powers that be showed precious little singin' and dancin', obfuscating that the film was a musical and attempting to pass it off as a comedy.

True, *My Fair Lady, The Sound of Music,* and *Oliver!* were all Oscar-winning Best Pictures in the post-JFK era, but many more musical movies did terribly. Some, of course, were god-awful, but didn't the youth of America *want* them to be lousy, and weren't they happy to ignore them? The titles alone—*Man of La Mancha; Hello, Dolly!*—were punch lines to the baby boomers. These rickety vehicles contained old people's music.

Kids who'd complained that Rex Harrison couldn't sing when they overheard their parents' *My Fair Lady* album were now listening to Bob Dylan, who couldn't sing, either. But they, not their parents, had discovered him, so he was all theirs, and that's what was important. For the first time in American history, being old didn't mean venerable and wise but infirm and clueless. *The Chinese Prime Minister* had told the truth.

Adults had to have their escapism, too. To say that *Nobody Loves an Albatross* was another victim of the assassination, opening a scant twenty-seven days later, may seem to be an overstatement. And yet, it might have had an easier time of it a few years earlier—or a few years later. From November 23 through the remaining 191 days of the season, the shows that espoused escapism did the best business. Audiences at *Hello, Dolly!* wanted to believe Irene Molloy when she exclaimed, "Oh, Dolly! The world is full of wonderful things!"

And terrible ones as well. During *Dolly*'s run, Martin Luther King and

Robert F. Kennedy were assassinated within sixty-four days of each other. Later came the impact of the Vietnam War, the Watergate scandal, and a rash of serial killers. How could optimism stay in fashion?

So although we see that nine of the eleven Tony-winning musicals from the '60s had been filmed, we can count only five from the '70s, four from the '80s, and just one from the '90s: *Rent*.

Meanwhile, the countercultural and antiestablishment 1963–64 flop *One Flew over the Cuckoo's Nest*—which had debuted on Broadway only nine days before JFK's assassination—experienced a renaissance. In 1971, it had an off-Broadway revival that, despite twenty-six performers on the payroll, ran for 1,025 performances.

The 1975 film won a Best Picture Oscar. No play that had flopped on Broadway after this short a run had ever become an Academy Award winner. Granted, the film was most influenced by Ken Kesey's novel, but it cited the play during the end credits. *Cuckoo's Nest* was the highest grosser of the year, raking in $56.5 million, far ahead of second-place finisher *All the President's Men* at $29 million. Both pictures, you'll note, revealed authority as corrupt.

As much as young people admired Woodward and Bernstein for exposing Watergate, they embraced Randle P. McMurphy all the more for his antiestablishment stance. His willingness to fight the system at all costs literally cost him his brain power, but the kids loved his say-no spirit. They also related to the Native American chief who broke out of the hospital, as he provided their vicarious escape from authority. Young people came away from the film feeling that, like him, they wanted to change as much as they could of the system and make the difference that Randle could not.

Time had changed the perception that McClain had had of *Cuckoo's Nest*'s characters: "We don't care too much what happens to them." The youth of America didn't feel that the plot was "so unlikely that it borders on fantasy" (Nadel) or that it was "so preposterous a proposition" (Kerr).

David Merrick wasn't often cited as being ahead of his time, but his having produced *Cuckoo's Nest* was one instance when he turned out to be prescient, however inadvertently.

So summer was no longer, as Sheldon Harnick had written in his 1958 musical *The Body Beautiful*, "Sigmund Romberg in a music tent." Rock would spur profound changes in summer stock. Many who continued to produce musicals in tents and barns would soon go out of business. Others stayed around by hiring rock stars both current and faded.

The 1963 season at the Jones Beach Marine Theatre offered a musical version of *Around the World in 80 Days*; fifty years later, the renamed Nikon at Jones Beach played host to Pitbull, Alice in Chains, Jane's Addiction, and Middle Class Rut, among many others.

There were fewer headaches that way. Whatever demands Eminem might make of M&M's, he's only one person. A musical with a cast of two dozen can involve a drunk, a lecher, an illness, an accident, a performer who can't remember lines, and co-stars who don't get along. Plenty of musicals had staffs where there were too many chiefs and not enough Native Americans.

"A lot has happened to taste since we were young," said Sir Gregory in *The Chinese Prime Minister*. Little did we know what was to come. Only ten months after JFK's assassination, a musical opened in which a Russian milkman sadly told his wife, "It's a new world." Indeed it was. The assassination had as profound an impact on musical theater as it did in so many walks of American life. The Kennedy funeral was, to paraphrase a Tim Rice lyric that would be widely heard sixteen years later, the Broadway musical's funeral, too.

EPILOGUE

*

've purposely kept one 1963–64 Broadway production for last—*Never Live over a Pretzel Factory*—because I have a personal story to go along with it. I hope you'll bear with me.

Never Live over a Pretzel Factory opened on Saturday, March 28, and closed on Saturday, April 4, the same night *Anyone Can Whistle* opened. The two shows had one thing in common: a nine-performance run.

The sudden shuttering was a big break for one just-starting-out actor. Now that he was free, he could audition for *The Subject Was Roses*—although, as we saw, no one expected much from that low-profile play. But thanks to his getting the role, Martin Sheen saw his career truly begin.

Pretzel Factory's director, as well as its composer of incidental music, had to wait slightly more than nineteen months for their success. For in November 1965, Albert Marre and Mitch Leigh would respectively provide the direction and music for *Man of La Mancha*. For that matter, another writer who suffered during 1963–64—Dale Wasserman, who adapted *One Flew over the Cuckoo's Nest*—provided that musical's book.

Now for my part of the story. On Thursday, March 12, 1964, I came home from Arlington Catholic High School (in Massachusetts) and found a letter addressed to me from Merrimack College. I'd applied to the school, so now I'd know if its powers that be had deigned to accept me as a freshman starting in September.

Wonder of wonder, miracle of miracles, they had. The day that my parents swore would never happen—"You'll never get into college, not with you

258

always listening to show music when you could be studying!"—had actually arrived. I had to celebrate!

And while many of my friends marked their college acceptances with a six-pack, my idea of celebrating meant going to the theater.

The one show I hadn't seen in Boston was the tryout of *Never Live over a Pretzel Factory* at the Shubert. After a bus to Harvard Square, a subway to Park Street, a trolley to Boylston, and then a walk to the Tremont Street playhouse, I told the box office treasurer, "If you have a first-row seat, I'll take it."

A play by Jerry Devine with direction by Albert Marre starring Dennis O'Keefe and Robert Strauss? I got not only first row but first row center, right on the aisle.

I passed some of the hours to showtime at a coffee shop, where I bought a *Boston Traveler,* the town's premier afternoon paper. The theater section carried a story that Robert Strauss, best known as Animal in both the stage and screen versions of *Stalag 17,* was no longer with *Never Live over a Pretzel Factory.* For the first time (but hardly the last), I saw the term "artistic differences."

When I read that Sidney Armus, Strauss's understudy, would assume the role, I shuddered. In my previous twenty-seven trips to Broadway and Boston theaters, I'd never seen an understudy. This was going to be awful! He wouldn't know his lines! He probably hadn't learned where to walk, either! How could he? No one could learn a leading role so fast! If he had to wear a wig, I was sure that it would fall off, too.

I entered the Shubert and was given a *Playbill* that proved management had hard feelings toward their departed star. While Strauss had been pictured on the cover positioned back-to-back with O'Keefe, each of them smiling, now a little white piece of paper had been pasted over Strauss's face. Pity the poor production assistant who had to cut up pieces of paper into small rectangles and rubber-cement one on each program.

Granted, not that many *Playbills* were required. As the usher showed me to my front-row seat, I saw that the Shubert was certainly far less packed than it had been during my recent visit to the tryout of *Funny Girl.* Once the usher left, I turned around and saw that of the theater's 1,727 seats, about 200 people were in the orchestra, 50 in the first balcony, and 10 in the second.

I searched through the *Playbill,* found the cast list, and learned that of the eighteen (!) in the cast, Strauss would have been the tenth to enter. Frankly,

I wasn't paying much attention to the plot, which had something to do with young people trying to make a film against the insurmountable odds of a constantly drunk star. I was simply waiting for Sidney Armus.

Finally, he entered, and to this day, I swear that our eyes met and he saw this front-row teenager sitting there, wringing his hands, eyes ever-widening with fright. Perhaps my imagination told me that his look said, "Hey, kid. Don't worry. I'm fine. I know what I'm doing"—but I still believe he was reassuring me.

Armus gave as fine a performance as one can expect in a play called *Never Live over a Pretzel Factory*. That was the night I began to learn that understudies usually come through.

Three years later, while I was working my way through college as a desk clerk in a suburban hotel, I was dutifully checking to see who'd checked in and who'd checked out this morning. And whom did I find now occupying room 506?

Sidney Armus of *Never Live over a Pretzel Factory* fame!

I immediately phoned him in his room.

"Hello?"

"Is this Mr. Armus?"

"Yes."

"This is the front desk. We're going to have to move you to another room."

"Why?" he said, astonished. "There's nothing wrong with my room."

"There may not be, sir—but," I said, adding a dramatic pause, "room 406 is a pretzel factory."

APPENDIX 1

*

The Season's Facts and Figures

Shows in **boldface** *were money-making hits.*

1. *Oh Dad, Poor Dad, Mamma's Hung You in the Closet and I'm Feelin' So Sad*
Aug. 27–Oct. 5, 1963; 47 performances
Morosco Theatre

2. *The Irregular Verb to Love*
Sept. 18–Dec. 28, 1963; 115 performances
Ethel Barrymore Theatre

3. *The Rehearsal*
Sept. 23–Dec. 28, 1963; 110 performances
Royale Theatre

4. *Bicycle Ride to Nevada*
Sept. 24, 1963; 1 performance
Cort Theatre

5. **Luther**
Sept. 25, 1963–March 28, 1964; 211 performances
St. James and Lunt-Fontanne Theatres

6. **Spoon River Anthology**
Sept. 29, 1963–Jan. 4, 1964; 111 performances
Booth and Belasco Theatres

7. *The Student Gypsy*
Sept. 30–Oct. 12, 1963; 16 performances
54th Street Theatre

8. *Chips with Everything*
Oct. 1, 1963–Feb. 8, 1964; 149 performances
Plymouth and Booth Theatres

9. *Obratsov Russian Puppet Theatre*
    Aladdin and His Wonderful Lamp and *An Unusual Concert*
Oct. 2–Nov. 30, 1963; 76 performances
Broadway Theatre

10. *Here's Love*
Oct. 3, 1963–July 25, 1964; 334 performances
Shubert Theatre

11. *Semi-Detached*
Oct. 7–19, 1963; 16 performances
Music Box Theatre

12. *The Private Ear and The Public Eye*
Oct. 9, 1963–Feb. 29, 1964; 163 performances
Morosco Theatre

13. *A Case of Libel*
Oct. 10, 1963–May 9, 1964; 242 performances
Longacre Theatre

14. *Martha Graham*
Oct. 13–27, 1963; 6 performances
Lunt-Fontanne Theatre

15. *The Advocate*
Oct. 14–19, 1963; 8 performances
ANTA Theatre

16. *Jennie*
Oct. 17–Dec. 28, 1963; 82 performances
Majestic Theatre

17. *Phèdre*
Oct. 20–Nov. 3, 1963; 8 performances
Brooks Atkinson Theatre

18. *A Rainy Day in Newark*
Oct. 22–26, 1963; 7 performances
Belasco Theatre

19. Barefoot in the Park
Oct. 23, 1963–June 25, 1967; 1,530 performances
Biltmore Theatre

20. 110 in the Shade
Oct. 24, 1963–Aug. 8, 1964; 330 performances
Broadhurst Theatre

21. *Bérénice*
Oct. 29–Nov. 3, 1963; eight performances
Brooks Atkinson Theatre

22. *The Ballad of the Sad Café*
Oct. 30, 1963–Feb. 15, 1964; 123 performances
Martin Beck Theatre

23. *Tambourines to Glory*
Nov. 2–23, 1963; 24 performances
Little Theatre

24. *Arturo Ui*
Nov. 11–16, 1963; 8 performances
Lunt-Fontanne Theatre

25. *Man and Boy*
Nov. 12–Dec. 28, 1963; 54 performances
Brooks Atkinson Theatre

26. *One Flew over the Cuckoo's Nest*
Nov. 13, 1963–Jan. 25, 1964; 82 performances
Cort Theatre

27. *The Golden Age*
Nov. 18–23, 1963; 7 performances
Lyceum Theatre

28. *Once for the Asking*
Nov. 20, 1963; 1 performance
Booth Theatre

29. *Have I Got a Girl for You!*
Dec. 2, 1963; 1 performance
Music Box Theatre

30. *The Girl Who Came to Supper*
Dec. 8, 1963–March 14, 1964; 112 performances
Broadway Theatre

31. *Love and Kisses*
Dec. 18–28, 1963; 13 performances
Music Box Theatre

32. *Nobody Loves an Albatross*
Dec. 19, 1963–June 20, 1964; 212 performances
Lyceum Theatre

33. *Marathon '33*
Dec. 22, 1963–Feb. 1, 1964; 48 performances
ANTA Theatre

34. *The Beautiful Bait*
Dec. 24, 1963–Jan. 5, 1964; 8 performances
Morosco Theatre

35. *Double Dublin*
Dec. 26–28, 1963; 4 performances
Little Theatre

36. *The Milk Train Doesn't Stop Here Anymore*
Jan. 1–4, 1964; 5 performances
Brooks Atkinson Theatre

37. *The Chinese Prime Minister*
Jan. 2–April 4, 1964; 108 performances
Royale Theatre

38. *Hello, Dolly!*
Jan. 16, 1964–Dec. 27, 1970; 2,844 performances
St. James Theatre

39. *Dylan*
Jan. 18–Sept. 12, 1964; 273 performances
Plymouth Theatre

40. *After the Fall*
Jan. 23, 1964–May 29, 1965; 208 performances
ANTA Washington Square Theatre

41. *The Dybbuk*
Feb. 3–March 22, 1964; 24 performances
Little Theatre

42. *Josephine Baker*
Feb. 4–16, 1964; 16 performances
Brooks Atkinson Theatre
March 31–April 19, 1964; 24 performances
Henry Miller's Theatre

43. *Rugantino*
Feb. 6–29, 1964; 28 performances
Mark Hellinger Theatre

44. *Fair Game for Lovers*
Feb. 10–15, 1964; 8 performances
Cort Theatre

45. *The Passion of Josef D.*
Feb. 11–22, 1964; 15 performances
Ethel Barrymore Theatre

46. *Foxy*
Feb. 16–April 18, 1964; 72 performances
Ziegfeld Theatre

47. *Abraham Cochrane*
Feb. 17, 1964; 1 performance
Belasco Theatre

48. *Any Wednesday*
Feb. 18, 1964–June 26, 1966; 983 performances
Music Box and George Abbott Theatres

49. *Marco Millions*
Feb. 20–June 18, 1964; 49 performances
ANTA Washington Square Theatre

50. *The Deputy*
Feb. 26–Nov. 28, 1964; 316 performances
Brooks Atkinson Theatre

51. *Children of the Shadows*
Feb. 26–March 22, 1964; 17 performances
Little Theatre

52. *What Makes Sammy Run?*
Feb. 27, 1964–June 12, 1965; 540 performances
54th Street Theatre

53. *Each Had Six Wings*
March 11–22, 1964; 14 performances
Little Theatre

54. *But for Whom Charlie*
March 12–July 12, 1964; 47 performances
ANTA Washington Square Theatre

55. *A Murderer Among Us*
March 25, 1964; 1 performance
Morosco Theatre

56. *Funny Girl*
March 26, 1964–July 1, 1967; 1,348 performances
Winter Garden, Majestic, and Broadway Theatres

57. *Never Live over a Pretzel Factory*
March 28–April 4, 1964; 9 performances
Eugene O'Neill Theatre

58. *Sponono*
April 2–18, 1964; 20 performances
Cort Theatre

59. *Anyone Can Whistle*
April 4–11, 1964; 9 performances
Majestic Theatre

60. *The Seagull*
April 5–May 2, 1964; 16 performances
Belasco Theatre

61. *The Crucible*
April 6–May 2, 1964; 16 performances
Belasco Theatre

62. *High Spirits*
April 7, 1964–Feb. 27, 1965; 375 performances
Alvin Theatre

63. *West Side Story*
April 8–May 3, 1964; 31 performances
City Center

64. *Hamlet*
April 9–Aug. 8, 1964; 137 performances
Lunt-Fontanne Theatre

65. *Café Crown*
April 17–18, 1964; 3 performances
Martin Beck Theatre

66. *Baby Want a Kiss*
April 19–Aug. 22, 1964; 148 performances
Little Theatre

67. *Blues for Mister Charlie*
April 23–Aug. 29, 1964; 148 performances
ANTA Theatre

68. *The Sunday Man*
May 13, 1964; 1 performance
Morosco Theatre

69. *King Lear*
May 18–June 5, 1964; 12 performances
State Theatre

70. *The White House*
May 19–June 6, 1964; 23 performances
Henry Miller's Theatre

71. *My Fair Lady*
May 20–June 28, 1964; 47 performances
City Center

72. *The Comedy of Errors*
May 20–June 6, 1964; 12 performances
State Theatre

73. *Roar like a Dove*
May 21–June 6, 1964; 20 performances
Booth Theatre

74. *The Subject Was Roses*
May 25, 1964–May 21, 1966; 832 performances
Royale, Winthrop Ames, Helen Hayes, Henry Miller's, and Belasco Theatres

75. *Fade Out–Fade In*
May 26–Nov. 14, 1964; Feb. 15–April 17, 1965; 271 performances
Mark Hellinger Theatre

APPENDIX 2

The 1963–64
Tony Award Winners and Nominees

Winners are listed in **boldface.**

Best Play
***Luther* by John Osborne; Produced by David Merrick**
The Ballad of the Sad Café by Edward Albee; Produced by Lewis Allen, Ben Edwards
Barefoot in the Park by Neil Simon; Produced by Saint Subber
Dylan by Sidney Michaels; Produced by George W. George, Frank Granat

Best Actor in a Play
Alec Guinness (*Dylan*)
Jason Robards Jr. (*After the Fall*)
Richard Burton (*Hamlet*)
Albert Finney (*Luther*)

Best Actress in a Play
Sandy Dennis (*Any Wednesday*)
Elizabeth Ashley (*Barefoot in the Park*)
Julie Harris (*Marathon '33*)
Colleen Dewhurst (*The Ballad of the Sad Café*)

Best Featured Actor in a Play
Hume Cronyn (*Hamlet*)
Larry Gates (*A Case of Libel*)
Lee Allen (*Marathon '33*)
Michael Dunn (*The Ballad of the Sad Café*)

Best Featured Actress in a Play
Barbara Loden (*After the Fall*)
Rosemary Murphy (*Any Wednesday*)
Diana Sands (*Blues for Mister Charlie*)
Kate Reid (*Dylan*)

Best Actor in a Musical
Bert Lahr (*Foxy*)
Sydney Chaplin (*Funny Girl*)
Bob Fosse (*Pal Joey*)
Steve Lawrence (*What Makes Sammy Run?*)

Best Actress in a Musical
Carol Channing (*Hello, Dolly!*)
Inga Swenson (*110 in the Shade*)
Barbra Streisand (*Funny Girl*)
Beatrice Lillie (*High Spirits*)

Best Featured Actor in a Musical
Jack Cassidy (*She Loves Me*)
Will Geer (*110 in the Shade*)
Danny Meehan (*Funny Girl*)
Charles Nelson Reilly (*Hello, Dolly!*)

Best Featured Actress in a Musical
Tessie O'Shea (*The Girl Who Came to Supper*)
Julienne Marie (*Foxy*)
Kay Medford (*Funny Girl*)
Louise Troy (*High Spirits*)

Best Producer of a Play
Herman Shumlin (The Deputy)
Saint Subber (*Barefoot in the Park*)
George W. George and Frank Granat (*Dylan*)
Lewis Allen and Ben Edwards (*The Ballad of the Sad Café*)

Best Director of a Play
Mike Nichols (*Barefoot in the Park*)
June Havoc (*Marathon '33*)
Alan Schneider (*The Ballad of the Sad Café*)
Herman Shumlin (*The Deputy*)

Best Musical
Hello, Dolly! Book by Michael Stewart; Music and Lyrics by Jerry Herman; Produced
  by David Merrick
Funny Girl Book by Isobel Lennart; Music by Jule Styne; Lyrics by Bob Merrill; Produced by
  Ray Stark
High Spirits Book, Music, and Lyrics by Hugh Martin and Timothy Gray; Produced by Lester
  Osterman, Robert Fletcher, Richard Horner
She Loves Me Book by Joe Masteroff; Music by Jerry Bock; Lyrics by Sheldon Harnick; Pro-
  duced by Harold Prince in association with Lawrence N. Kasha and Philip C. McKenna

Best Book
Michael Stewart (*Hello, Dolly!*)
Timothy Gray and Hugh Martin (*High Spirits*)
Joe Masteroff (*She Loves Me*)
Harry Kurnitz (*The Girl Who Came to Supper*)

Best Producer of a Musical
David Merrick (*Hello, Dolly!*)
Ray Stark (*Funny Girl*)
Harold Prince (*She Loves Me*)
Jean Dalrymple and the New York City Center Light Opera Company (*West Side Story*)

Best Score
Jerry Herman (*Hello, Dolly!*)
Tom Jones, lyricist; Harvey Schmidt, composer (*110 in the Shade*)

Bob Merrill, lyricist; Jule Styne, composer (*Funny Girl*)
Timothy Gray and Hugh Martin, composers and lyricists (*High Spirits*)

Best Direction of a Musical
Gower Champion (*Hello, Dolly!*)
Joseph Anthony (*110 in the Shade*)
Noël Coward (*High Spirits*)
Harold Prince (*She Loves Me*)

Best Choreography
Gower Champion (*Hello, Dolly!*)
Herbert Ross (*Anyone Can Whistle*)
Carol Haney (*Funny Girl*)
Danny Daniels (*High Spirits*)

Best Conductor and Musical Director
Shepard Coleman (*Hello, Dolly!*)
Fred Werner (*High Spirits*)
Charles Jaffe (*West Side Story*)
Lehman Engel (*What Makes Sammy Run?*)

Best Scenic Design
Oliver Smith (*Hello, Dolly!*)
David Hays (*Marco Millions*)
Ben Edwards (*The Ballad of the Sad Café*)
Raoul Pène Du Bois (*The Student Gypsy*)

Best Costume Design
Freddy Wittop (*Hello, Dolly!*)
Rouben Ter-Arutunian (*Arturo Ui*)
Beni Montresor (*Marco Millions*)
Irene Sharaff (*The Girl Who Came to Supper*)

Special Award
Eva Le Gallienne, celebrating her 50th year as an actress and for producing, directing, and
   appearing with her National Repertory Theatre.

APPENDIX 3

*

The 1963–64 Performers the Tonys Spurned

Just for fun, let's take a look at those actors who didn't get Tony nominations.

1963–64 was such a great season that you could fill up each of the eight acting categories with a slate of *five*—that's right, not just four—consisting of those who weren't even nominated.

A few of these may not seem to be luminaries to some—time has dimmed a bit of their luster—but as you'll see, this list includes plenty of established names as well as potent up-and-comers who trod the boards during 1963–64. They had to be satisfied with their salaries and empty mantles.

And the nominees *weren't*:

Best Actor in a Play
Charles Boyer (*Man and Boy*)
Kirk Douglas (*One Flew over the Cuckoo's Nest*)
Paul Newman (*Baby Want a Kiss*)
Robert Redford (*Barefoot in the Park*)
Christopher Plummer (*Arturo Ui*)

Best Actress in a Play
Claudette Colbert (*The Irregular Verb to Love*)
Hermoine Gingold (*Oh Dad, Poor Dad...*)
Eva Le Gallienne (*The Seagull*)
Margaret Leighton (*The Chinese Prime Minister*)
Joanne Woodward (*Baby Want a Kiss*)

Best Featured Actor in a Play
Brian Bedford (*The Private Ear and The Public Eye*)
Gene Hackman (*Any Wednesday*)
Hal Holbrook (*After the Fall*)
Sam Waterston (*Oh Dad, Poor Dad...*)
Gene Wilder (*One Flew over the Cuckoo's Nest*)

Best Featured Actress in a Play
Coral Browne (*The Rehearsal*)
Betty Garrett (*Spoon River Anthology*)
Mildred Natwick (*Barefoot in the Park*)
Doris Roberts (*Marathon '33*)
Joan Tetzel (*One Flew over the Cuckoo's Nest*)

Best Actor in a Musical
Robert Alda (*What Makes Sammy Run?*)
Jose Ferrer (*The Girl Who Came to Supper*)
Harry Guardino (*Anyone Can Whistle*)
Louis Gossett (*Tambourines to Glory*)
Edward Woodward (*High Spirits*)

Best Actress in a Musical
Barbara Cook (*She Loves Me*)
Tammy Grimes (*High Spirits*)
Florence Henderson (*The Girl Who Came to Supper*)
Angela Lansbury (*Anyone Can Whistle*)
Mary Martin (*Jennie*)

Best Featured Actor in a Musical
Alan Alda (*Café Crown*)
Larry Blyden (*Foxy*)
David Burns (*Hello, Dolly!*)
Dom DeLuise (*The Student Gypsy*)
Laurence Naismith (*Here's Love*)

Best Featured Actress in a Musical
Eileen Brennan (*Hello, Dolly!*)
Rita Gardner (*Pal Joey*)
Sondra Lee (*Hello, Dolly!*)
Rosetta LeNoire (*Tambourines to Glory*)
Ethel Shutta (*Jennie*)

Before anyone starts railing that Barbara Cook was part of the 1962–63 season, yes, that's true—but not where the Tonys were concerned. Her show opened eight days after the previous Tony deadline, which is why her castmate Jack Cassidy was nominated in 1963–64 and even won as Best Featured Actor in a Musical. Ditto Rita Gardner, who played Linda to Bob Fosse's Pal Joey. Opening on May 29, 1963, it was clearly too late for the 1962–63 Tony deadline; indeed, the 1963–64 Tonys were given out three days earlier.

Even with those forty non-nominees, there were *still* some notables that didn't make the list: Oscar-winner Van Heflin, Tony winners Cyril Ritchard, Robert Preston, and Jason Robards Jr. (as Best Featured Actor in a Play for another Lincoln Center offering), as well as Barnard Hughes, Corin Redgrave, Emlyn Williams, Janis Paige, Lee Remick, Craig Stevens, Brenda Lewis, and, of course, bringing up the absolute rear, Tallulah Bankhead and Tab Hunter.

BIBLIOGRAPHY

Books

Albee, Edward. *The Collected Plays of Edward Albee*, vol. 1. Overlook Press, 2007.

Bagnold, Enid. *The Chinese Prime Minister*. Random House, 1964.

Bentley, Eric. *The Storm over "The Deputy."* Grove Press, 1964.

Bianculli, David. *Dangerously Funny: The Uncensored Story of The Smothers Brothers Comedy Hour.* Touchstone, 2009.

Blake, Betty, and Joan Marlowe, eds. *New York Theatre Critics' Reviews, 1964*. Critics' Theatre Reviews, 1965.

Blum, Daniel. *Theatre World, 1963–64*. Crown, 1964.

Bogar, Thomas A. *American Presidents Attend the Theatre*. McFarland, 2006.

Brustein, Robert. *Seasons of Discontent*. Simon & Schuster, 1965.

Burr, Eugene, ed. *The Billboard Index of the New York Legitimate Stage Season, 1933–1934 and 1934–1935*. Billboard, 1935.

Burrows, Abe. *Honest Abe*. Atlantic–Little Brown, 1980.

Crawford, Cheryl. *One Naked Individual*. Bobbs-Merrill, 1977.

Channing, Carol. *Just Lucky I Guess*. Simon & Schuster, 2002.

Coffin, Rachel W., ed. *New York Theatre Critics' Reviews, 1963*. Critics' Theatre Reviews, 1964.

Crawford, Cheryl. *One Naked Individual: My Fifty Years in the Theatre*. Bobbs-Merrill, 1977.

Crowley, Mart. *The Boys in the Band*. Farrar, Straus & Giroux, 1968.

Day, Barry, ed. *The Letters of Noël Coward*. AAK, 2007.

Dietz, Howard. *Dancing in the Dark*. Quadrangle, 1974.

Engel, Lehman. *The Critics*. Macmillan, 1976.

Gilroy, Frank D. *About Those Roses, or How Not to Do a Play and Succeed* and the text of *The Subject Was Roses*. Random House, 1965.

Gilvey, John Anthony. *Before the Parade Passes By*. St. Martin's Press, 2005.

Gottfried, Martin. *Opening Nights*. G. P. Putnam's Sons, 1970.

Gould, Jonathan. *Can't Buy Me Love—The Beatles, Britain, and America*. Three Rivers Press, 2007.

Guernsey, Otis, Jr. *The Best Plays of 1964–65*. Dodd, Mead, 1965.

Harris, Andrew B. *The Performing Set*. University of North Texas Press, 2006.

Havoc, June. *Marathon '33*. Dramatists Play Service, 1964.

Heilpern, John. *John Osborne*. Knopf, 2006.

Herman, Jerry, and Ken Bloom. *Jerry Herman: The Lyrics*. Routledge, 2003.

Hochhuth, Rolf. *The Deputy*. Dell, 1965.

Isaac, Joel, and Duncan Bell. *Uncertain Empire: American History and the Idea of the Cold War.* Oxford University Press, 2012.

Kanin, Garson. *Smash*. Viking, 1980.

Kazan, Elia. *Kazan on Directing.* Knopf, 2009.

Kelley, Kitty. *Elizabeth Taylor: The Last Star.* Simon & Schuster, 1981.

Kissel, Howard. *David Merrick: The Abominable Showman.* Applause, 1993.

Lahr, John. *Notes on a Cowardly Lion.* Knopf, 1969.

Lee, Douglas Bennett. *Stage for a Nation: The National Theatre, 150 Years.* University Press of America, 1985.

Leonard, William Torbert. *Broadway Bound.* Scarecrow, 1983.

———. *Once Was Enough.* Scarecrow, 1986.

Lewis, Robert. *Slings & Arrows.* Applause, 1984.

Little, Stuart W., and Arthur Cantor. *The Playmakers.* Norton, 1970.

Loggia, Marjorie and Glenn Young, eds. *The Collected Works of Harold Clurman.* Applause, 1984.

Loney, Glenn. *20th Century Theatre.* Facts on File, 1983.

Mandelbaum, Ken. *"A Chorus Line" and the Musicals of Michael Bennett.* St. Martin's Press, 1988.

———. *Not Since "Carrie."* St. Martin's Press, 1991.

Mann, William J. *Hello, Gorgeous: Becoming Barbra Streisand.* Houghton Mifflin, 2012.

Marsolais, Ken, with Rodger McFarlane and Tom Viola. *Broadway Day & Night.* Pocket Books, 1992.

Martin, Mary. *My Heart Belongs.* William Morrow, 1976.

McCullers, Carson. *"The Ballad of the Sad Café" and Other Stories.* Houghton Mifflin, 1951.

Mordden, Ethan. *Open a New Window.* Palgrave, 2001.

Morley, Sheridan. *A Talent to Amuse: A Biography of Noël Coward.* Little, Brown, 1969.

Murphy, Donn B., and Stephen Moore. *Helen Hayes: A Bio-Bibliography.* Greenwood, 1993.

New York Times Directory of the Theater. Introduction by Clive Barnes. Arno Press, 1973.

Newquist, Roy. *Showcase.* William Morrow, 1966.

Norton, Elliot. *Broadway Down East.* Boston Public Library Books, 1977.

O'Shea, Tessie. *Tessie O'Shea's Slimming Cookbook.* Cassell, 1974.

Ostrow, Stuart. *Present at the Creation, Leaping in the Dark, and Going Against the Grain.* Applause, 2005.

Plummer, Christopher. *In Spite of Myself.* Knopf, 2008.

Quirk, Lawrence J. *Paul Newman: A Life.* Taylor, 1997.

Redfield, William. *Letters from an Actor.* Viking, 1967.

Resnick, Muriel. *Any Wednesday.* Stein & Day, 1964.

———. *Son of Any Wednesday.* Stein & Day, 1965.

Rivadue, Barry. *Mary Martin: A Bio-Bibliography.* Greenwood, 1991.

Rose, Philip. *You Can't Do That on Broadway.* Limelight, 2004.

Sabinson, Harvey. *Darling, You Were Wonderful.* H. Regnery, 1977.

Sanders, Ronald. *The Lower East Side.* Dover, 2104.

Schanke, Robert A. *Shattered Applause.* Southern Illinois University Press, 1992.

Sebba, Anne. *Enid Bagnold.* Taplinger, 1986.

Seff, Richard. *Supporting Player.* Xlibris, 2007.

Sinfield, Alan. *Out on Stage.* Yale University Press, 1999.

Solomon, Alisa. *Wonder of Wonders.* Metropolitan, 2013.

Sondheim, Stephen. *Finishing the Hat.* Knopf, 2011.

Stephens, Frances. *Theatre World Annual, London, no. 12.* Barrie & Rockcliff, 1961.

Stevenson, Isabelle, ed. *The Tony Award.* Crown, 1984.

Stott, William, with Jane Stott. *On Broadway.* University of Texas Press, 1978.

Suskin, Steven. *A Must See!* Chronicle, 2004.

———. *Opening Nights on Broadway.* Schirmer, 1990.

———. *Second Act Trouble.* Applause, 2006.

Swayne, Steve. *How Sondheim Found His Sound.* University of Michigan Press, 2005.

Taubman, Howard. *The Making of the American Theatre.* Coward McCann, 1965.

Taylor, Theodore. *Jule: The Story of Composer Jule Styne.* Random House, 1979.

Tynan, Kenneth. *Tynan Right & Left.* Athaneum, 1968.

Viagas, Robert. *The Alchemy of Theatre.* Playbill/Applause, 2006.

Bibliography

Williams, Tennessee. *Notebooks*. Ed. Margaret Bradham Thornton. Yale University Press, 2006.
Young, B. A. *The Rattigan Version*. Atheneum, 1988.
Zadan, Craig. *Sondheim & Co*. Macmillan, 1974.
Zeigler, Joseph Wesley. *Regional Theatre: The Revolutionary Stage*. University of Minnesota Press, 1973.

Articles

"15 CBS Series Cast Negroes." *Variety*, May 2, 1968.
"All Show Biz Dims in Grief." *Variety*, Nov. 27, 1963.
Atkinson, Brooks. "S. N. Behrman, Author of 25 to 30 Plays, Faces an Old Theatrical Problem." *New York Times*, July 21, 1964.
Barnes, Clive. "They Cheered Their Beloved Peter Pan." *New York Post*, Oct. 21, 1985.
"Colleagues Recall Mary Martin as Musicals' Cockeyed Optimist." *New York Times*, Jan. 29, 1991.
"Distinguished Play Flops Distinguish Legit Season." *Variety*, Jan. 8, 1964.
Hamill, Pete. "Goodbye, Brooklyn; Hello, Fame." *Saturday Evening Post*, July 27, 1963.
"Hello, Carol!" *Theater Week*, Oct. 23, 1995.
Hewes, Henry. "Gilroy Was Here." *Saturday Review*, June 13, 1964.
Logan, Andy. "The Milk Train Stops at Tiffany's." *New Yorker*, March 16, 1963.
"Martin Saluted by Friends." *New York Times*, Oct. 21, 1982.
"Mary Martin: Perpetual Motion." *Look*, Aug. 30, 1963.
"Opening." *Washington Daily News*, May 5, 1952.
"TV's $40,000,000 JFK Coverage." *Variety*, Nov. 27, 1963.

Interviews

Ervin Drake, Josh Ellis, Jerry Herman, Hal Holbrook, Tom Jones, Lionel Larner, Marc Miller, Bruce Yeko

INDEX

*